the 100 best worldwide vacations to enrich your life

the 100 best worldwide vacations to enrich your life

PAM GROUT

NATIONAL GEOGRAPHIC

WASHINGTON, D.C.

Published by the National Geographic Society
1145 17th Street, N.W., Washington, DC 20036-4688

ISBN: 978-1-4262-0279-7

Library of Congress Cataloging-in-Publication Data available upon request.

Founded in 1888, the National Geographic Society is one of the largest nonprofit scientific and educational organizations in the world. It reaches more than 285 million people worldwide each month through its official journal, NATIONAL GEOGRAPHIC, and its four other magazines; the National Geographic Channel; television documentaries; radio programs; films; books; videos and DVDs; maps; and interactive media. National Geographic has funded more than 8,000 scientific research projects and supports an education program combating geographic illiteracy.

For more information, please call 1-800-NGS LINE (647-5463) or write to the following address:
National Geographic Society, 1145 17th Street N.W.,Washington, D.C. 20036-4688 U.S.A.

Visit us online at: www.nationalgeographic.com/books

Interior design by Peggy Archambault and Linda Johansson

Printed in the U.S.A.

contents

This book is for Jim,
whose infinite patience, strength, and steadfastness
prove that opposites do attract.

introduction

Travel is more than the seeing of sights; it is a change
that goes on, deep and permanent.
—Miriam Beard, American writer and traveler

Aldous Huxley once said that to travel is to discover that everyone is wrong about other countries. In this book, you'll discover that's a good thing. All your preconceived notions about other countries, other cultures, even your own abilities are nothing but a trap, a prison that keeps you stuck, revolving on the same old, tired axis.

With this book, we hope to shake things up a bit—your travel plans, your ideas, the very core of your existence. We've included 100 vacations around the globe, each with the potential to change your life. They're divided into four categories—vacations to work your creativity, your brain, your heart, and your potential. You'll find arts and crafts getaways, learning retreats, volunteer vacations, and wellness escapes. Take your pick.

Each of the 100 vacations is guaranteed to expand your possibilities which, of course, starts with the premise of what a vacation is meant to be. Instead of coming home from your next vacation with a suntan, why not return with a Malaysian kite that you made at the open-air workshop of an 70-year-old Muslim kitemaker, or with a snapshot of the wheelchair you assembled and the 10-year-old Cambodian land mine victim who is using it to get around? Instead of souvenirs, bring back memories of the Ugandan widow who invited you into her rural homestead or of the Tuareg who fed you bread baked under the Saharan sand.

Just know that each and every one of these vacations will grow your heart, stretch your soul, and make you realize that much of what you think you know is a very tiny piece of the greater puzzle.   —Pam Grout

CHAPTER

1

arts & crafts getaways

Art would be my shield and honesty my spear and to
hell with Jack and his close-set eyes.
—Maya Angelou

If you're like most people, you think of creativity as belonging to members of a private club, reserved like that corner table by the window for a select few. You believe it's passed out at birth to the Beethovens, the Matisses, and the Spielbergs of the world.

You, on the other hand (sigh!), are fated to be a consumer of creativity, decorating your foyer with *other* people's sculptures, spending your evenings watching *other* people's visions on a 26-inch TV screen. But the truth is that *all* of us are creative. All of us have the ability to think up new ideas, solve baffling problems, even produce art. This is why we sing in the shower, why we write jokes in the dirt on unwashed cars.

In this chapter, you'll find 23 vacations around the globe that will prove it to you once and for all that art is not a spectator sport. In fact, in many countries, art is a way of life, something that's impossible to separate from breathing. Kids in Senegal, for example, learn to drum and dance along with learning to walk.

In this country, where we learn to work from the time we're born, our job is to follow the rules, to rein in the imagination. But on vacation, you need a chance to wonder, to be surprised, to play. The vacations in this chapter not only offer time off from your everyday world but also will give you long, uninterrupted hours to finally write that screenplay, finish that quilt, or learn to tango.

Whether you're interested in pottery, painting, drama, photography, mosaics, or just writing a pithy Christmas letter, there's an international arts-and-crafts vacation in this chapter with your name on it.

learn to tango

BUENOS AIRES, ARGENTINA

*While I dance, I cannot judge, I cannot hate, I cannot separate myself
from life. I can only be joyful and whole. That is why I dance.*
—Hans Bos, dancer

1 Confucius said a nation's character is defined by its dancers. Certainly, Argentina—the inventor of the sassy, improvisational tango—would agree. Historically, the now world-famous tango was one of the first dances where partners were actually allowed to touch each other (only the Viennese waltz and the polka came earlier), and it's hard to separate Argentina's history from the brash dance that began in the disregarded periphery of the culture and gradually, over time, worked its way into polite society and indeed into the consciousness of the whole world.

The tango, in fact, was so popular in Argentina that after the 1955 coup which ousted Juan Perón, the new military government in a knee-jerk reaction not only imprisoned and blacklisted many tango artists but also imposed curfews, changed tango lyrics and titles, and banned meetings of more than three people. To the wealthy members of the new regime, large numbers of tango dancers seemed suspicious, an obvious cover for political agitation. After the 1983 fall of the military junta, a spectacular renaissance occurred, and today a tango fan can choose between up to three dozen *milongas* a day. And that's just in Buenos Aires.

Argentina Tango, a company that specializes in tango vacations to the city where it all began, offers 3-, 4-, 5-, 7-, 10-, and 14-day tango vacations that include daily lessons, a personal practice partner, and tours of Buenos Aires' best milongas. A milonga, in case you're new to the addictive dance, are places where tango is danced. At a milonga, sessions typically open with classes and a few demonstrations before the first *tanda*, a set of three to five dances in a row. The tandas are separated by a *cortina*, a musical break during which the floor is cleared and new partnerships are formed.

IT TAKES TWO . . .

Aspiring *milongueros*, as tango aficionados are known, might enjoy the following little-known facts about their dance of choice.

- The movie *Evita* was filmed in part at Confiteria Ideal, an old-fashioned Buenos Aires milonga where dances are held both afternoon and evening every day of the week.
- If you're under 30, you might prefer La Viruta, a hip, happening place in the cellar of the Armenian Community Center (Armenia 1366) where tango (and electrotango) mixes with salsa, rock, and cumbia.
- The first piece of music written and published in Argentina describing itself as a tango appeared in 1857. It was called "Toma Maté, Ché."
- Even though Argentinean politicians in the early 1900s condemned the tango, not wanting their new, prosperous nation associated with a "prostibularian" dance, it was popular enough that more than 100,000 copies of the tango "Yo Soy la Morocha" (I am the brunette) flew off the shelves in the first few months of 1906.
- By the early 1900s, the tango had spread overseas. In 1913, London's Waldorf Hotel staged weekly "tango teas" and a Grand Tango Ball held in Selfridges department store was declared the event of the season.
- In 1913, the tango also had a great influence on fashion. Women in Paris abandoned the corset in order to dance the sensual tango that was widely disapproved of in certain circles. Tulip skirts that opened at the front, making dancing easier, were sold along with tango shoes, tango stockings, tango hats, and tango dresses.
- In 1913 and 1914, a variety of how-to books came out to teach tango. *Secrets of Tango*, published in England under the name of an English author, was actually written by Juan Barrasa, an Argentinean whose parents thought he was studying engineering but who was actually teaching tango on the stage of the Queen's Theatre.

For the really serious student, Argentina Tango even offers a monthlong immersion course with 60 hours of lessons and 12 full hours with a personal instructor. All itineraries include a dinner and tango show, tango shoe shopping (yes, there are special shoes for tangoing), a city tour of Buenos Aires and its old dance halls, tips on milonga etiquette, and lists compiled daily with all of Buenos Aires' best milongas.

As Ann Francois, who learned to tango with Argentina Tango, says, "One cannot separate the tango from the great city of Buenos Aires. It is the breath that moves the air, the force that grows the trees. It is the beauty of the men and the sensuality of its women. The tango is the constant music of sincerity causing strangers to bare their humanity, to pledge their love in a glance of the moment. It is the thread that sews the city together."

Argentina Tango's teachers are among the nation's best, including Marcelo Varela and Analia Vega, who danced in the 1996 film *Evita*, as well as Julio Balmaceda and Corina de la Rosa, who have danced at Carnegie Hall and have been nominated for a Tony for their choreography of the successful Broadway production *Forever Tango*.

Prices for a tango vacation in Buenos Aires—hotel, breakfasts, a dinner and tango show, transfers, and all your lessons—range from $1,130 for a three-day vacation in a three-star hotel to $3,300 for a ten-day in a five-star hotel. If you really hit your groove, you can stay for a month, which costs up to $7,760.

HOW TO GET IN TOUCH

Argentina Tango, 1a Westleigh Road, Leicester, LE3 0HH, England, 44 718 701 5999, www.argentinatango.com.

fire pottery in a laotian village

All this of Pot and Potter—Tell me then,
Who is the Potter, pray, and who the Pot?
—Omar Khayyam, Persian poet

2 Each morning, you'll board a covered wooden longboat in the former Laotian royal capital of Luang Prabang that will take you down the Mekong River to the Ban Chan pottery village where you'll study coil/thrown pottery and learn to fire it in a wood-burning, underground, scorpion-shaped kiln. Organized by Denys James, an exhibiting studio artist from Canada who since 1996 has been leading ceramics-oriented travel excursions to Mexico, Turkey, Italy, and Thailand, this Laos excursion offers a one-of-a-kind opportunity to study with indigenous potters.

You'll stay in a historic hotel (no need for a key, as there are no thieves in this World Heritage site) in Luang Prabang, which today still has 33 temples and more than 500 monks (a pretty good ratio for a town of only 15,000). If you're an early riser, you can catch scores of the saffron-robed, barefoot monks filing out of their monasteries, bearing gold-topped wooden alms bowls. Camouflaged by palm trees and dense tropical foliage, tiny Luang Prabang sits on a peninsula at the junction of the Mekong and Khan Rivers.

Ban Chan, where you'll be working with resident potters, is a popular stop for Luang Prabang tourists, who come to watch pottery being made and to buy vases, flowerpots, figurines, and urns. Mention the village and local boatmen nod knowingly.

Although your daily excursion on the mighty river that cuts a swath through jungle-clad banks and limestone gorges is to the Ban Chan pottery village, you can, on your days off (every potter needs a break), take the same river to Ban Sang Haie, where moonshine whiskey is produced from rice; the entrancing village of Muan Ngoy, enclosed by lofty karst peaks; or the sacred Pak Ou Grottoes, which are filled with hundreds of gilded and wooden Buddha statues. The king of Laos used to visit the famous grottoes once a year, and on the Lao New Year, hundreds of pilgrims wend their way to the dramatic limestone cliffs in a candlelit procession.

When Luang Prabang was inscribed by UNESCO as a World Heritage site in December 1995, it was cited as the best-preserved traditional town in Southeast Asia, with temples dating back to the 16th century. In fact, the report called the isolated town, which had no contact with non-Asian countries until the French arrived in the mid-19th century, a kind of "outdoor museum."

Some of the don't-misses:

- The monastery of Wat Xieng Thong with its gardens of bougainvillea, frangipani, and hibiscus is a feast for the eyes and soul. When the sun sets, the dazzling gold-leaf Ramayana figures on one of the temples practically come to life, glowing in the diminishing light.
- All of the 30 *wats* or temples (there used to be twice that many) are treasure troves of mural painting, sculpture, and Buddhas made from all types of materials. And thanks to the World Heritage designation, they're being painstakingly restored along with 111 French-Laotian buildings.
- The Royal Palace houses Pra Ban, a 33-inch standing Buddha image estimated to be 90 percent gold.

On this 19-day itinerary, one of many that James has organized over the years, you will also get the chance to ride elephants, visit the Kuangsi waterfalls, hike to Hmong tribal villages, and visit Cambodia's Angkor Wat temples, the 13th-century Khmer temples near Siem Reap.

"I have blended my experiences as a ceramic artist, traveler, instructor, and lover of new things to develop this unique small art travel company," says organizer James. "I have always been excited when I find a Turkish, Mexican, or Thai potter using century-old methods and local materials to make vessels for daily use. On these trips, we explore below the surface of the tourist routes to experience local artisans at work."

The cost for the Laos pottery trip averages $3,895 and includes lodging, meals, local transportation, and the clay you'll fire in the kiln.

HOW TO GET IN TOUCH

Discovery Art Travel, 182 Welbury Drive, Saltspring Island, BC V8K 2L8, Canada, 250-537-4906, www.denysjames.com.

cane a chair or spin wool on an old english farm

SUDBURY, ENGLAND

Crafts make us feel rooted, give us a sense of belonging, and connect us with our history. Our ancestors used to create these crafts out of necessity, and now we do them for fun and to express ourselves.
—Phyllis George, actress, author, and former First Lady of Kentucky

3 Jane Austen would be proud.

If you're a fan of that British author whose collection of novels has kept Hollywood busy for decades, consider an arts-and-crafts holiday in the English countryside of Suffolk. Many visitors to England never get past London, but for a glimpse into Austen's world of 19th-century rural England, Assington Mill Farm, a 17th-century farm outside Sudbury, offers lessons in the very crafts that provided the picturesque backdrops for Emma and Harriet as they went about pining and scheming for Mr. Knightley, Phillip Elton, and Frank Churchill.

Lying in one of Suffolk's secret valleys, Assington Mill's 86 acres were purchased in 2003 by Bob Cowlin, a surveyor, and Anne Holden, a conservation officer, who were looking for a watermill that Cowlin could restore and use to mill grain. They found a mill, but the machinery had ceased to work back in 1868 when the squire "took the water for his own purposes" and the miller had to find a secondhand windmill.

Instead, the enterprising duo went to work restoring the ten outbuildings, establishing a private nature reserve, and offering classes in more than 40 traditional English crafts. They decided to focus on rural crafts such as gilding, spinning raw fleece, and cane-chair making that many lament have taken a big hit as family farms bite the proverbial dust and the bucolic English countryside gives way to development, roads, and airplane traffic.

Some of the classes available at Assington Mill are:

- **Book repair and restoration.** In this three-day course, you'll learn how to sew books, clean paper, and restore all your old family bibles, maps, and dilapidated books in the classic, traditional methods of bookbinding. Taught by a specialist in library conservation who has restored everything from priceless 16th-century volumes to much-loved children's books, this class is a must for bibliophiles.

- **Bushcraft.** Just in case you unexpectedly find yourself out in the woods, this one-day course teaches you how to light a fire, build a shelter, safely use a knife, and cook over an open fire. Be sure to bring your wellies!
- **Cane and rush chair seating.** Learn to repair your old chairs and stools with cane, sea grass, and rushes. Participants in this three-day workshop are requested to bring a wobble-free chair or stool that is already restored, cleaned, waxed, and painted. If your chair doesn't meet those requirements, consider enrolling in Assington Mill's furniture restoration class instead.
- **Storytelling.** In honor of Jane Austen (and all the other British storytellers from Chaucer to Carroll), consider the one-day storytelling workshop that takes place in Assington Mill's own storytelling hut, a Tolkienesque structure made with straw bales and plastered with clay—both harvested, of course, straight from the farm.
- **Dowsing.** Taught by a former airline pilot, this class on divining for water—a skill that can evidently be learned—shows not only how to find underground H_2O but also how to use the "dowsing skill," described as a response to unconscious or subliminal energies, to move beyond the confines of the other

---

D'OH!

When Twentieth Century Fox released *The Simpsons Movie* in England, the studio took some indecent liberties on the English countryside, creating a major cultural faux pas. The publicity team behind the 2007 movie hired British artist Peter Stuart to create a 180-foot painting of Homer Simpson right next to the Cerne Abbas Giant, a 17th-century British landmark in Dorset of a club-wielding pagan that's carved into the chalk under the turf.

Even though the giant Homer, holding a donut as large as his jockey shorts, was rendered in water-soluble, biodegradable paint intended to disappear after the first big rain, it did not sit well with the British public. The National Trust, which protects the Cerne Abbas site, restoring it every 25 years, took a lot of heat for allowing the American cartoon character to invade an area of scientific and historical importance.

---

five senses. You'll learn to develop these subtle dowsing skills, as well as how to estimate depth and volume flow and how to find archaeological artifacts such as henges, ceremonial trackways, and druidic temples.

- **And more.** Other classes include beekeeping, apple-cider making, hedge laying, hen keeping, plumbing for beginners, and one simply called "Badger," which, apparently, is a one-day indulgence in learning everything about the badger, including how to determine the difference between a rabbit hole and a badger wett, how to look for tracks, and tips on spotting these elusive creatures.

Prices vary depending on the class type, but one-day classes including lunch typically run £45 (about $90). Three-day workshops are £210 ($420). Lodging at Assington Mill in the timber-framed, thatch-roofed farmhouse where Cowlin and Holden live can be arranged for £25 ($50) per night. Camping is also possible at Assington Mill for £5 ($10) per night, with shower and toilet available.

HOW TO GET IN TOUCH

Assington Mill Farm, Sudbury, Suffolk, CO10 5LZ, England, 44 1 787 229 955, www.assingtonmill.com.

capture your vacation memories in sketchbooks

VIETNAM, TUSCANY, AND OTHER DESTINATIONS

*I pack the art stuff first and then weigh and see how
much I've got left for clothes.*
—Katherine Tyrrell, inveterate travel sketcher

4 Nowadays, travelers who want a visual record of their vacations pack a camera. But before 1900, when George Eastman first introduced the Brownie camera, travelers recorded their impressions of the places they visited in a notebook with ink, pencils, or watercolors. Think of Charles Darwin, who might not have come up with his theory of evolution if it weren't for the thousands of sketches he made of his trip to the Galápagos Islands.

The advantage, of course, is that sketchbook travelers really "see" the places they visit, and not just in a superficial, been-there, done-that kind of way. They are forced to look with different eyes. Let's take the famous lone cypress tree overlooking Pebble Beach near Carmel, California, as an example. Today's camera-toting tourists generally think, "Ooh, that's pretty," and proceed to snap a quick digital photo. But a travel sketcher would take the time to notice its trunk's subtle shading, its lengthening shadow, the yapping Pekingese that just ran circles around it.

"Taking a photo requires so little investment of one's attention," says Lewis B. Lehrman, a graphic artist and illustrator, professional watercolorist, and, for the past seven years, teacher of artistic journaling. "Artistic journaling slows your pace as you observe a scene for at least as long as it takes to sketch it."

Lehrman became passionate about artistic travel journaling after a trip to Budapest in 1977. While planning the trip with his wife, Lola, he serendipitously met a man who had just returned from Russia with a 6-by-9-inch sketchbook and a watercolor kit no bigger than a pack of cigarettes. "I had been planning to take along a French easel, watercolor paper, backing board, supplies, etc., knowing that the bulkiness of all this equipment, not to mention the four to six hours I'd have to block out to do a watercolor, would limit my efforts to just one or two paintings during the course of our two-week trip," Lehrman recalls.

By duplicating the setup of the Russian traveler, Lehrman was able to create hundreds of sketches. He documented train rides, dinners, sights, and other experiences, all of which he says still seem fresh to him 30 years later. That sketchbook was the first of 17 travel sketchbooks and the beginning of a career showing others how to capture on paper the memorable sights, events, and feelings of a journey.

Lehrman's travel journaling classes are usually offered in his hometown of Scottsdale, Arizona, but every year or so, he also offers an overseas class such as his 2007 "Journals & Journeys: The Traditions of the Travel Journal and the Exotic Beauty of Vietnam with Lewis Barrett Lehrman." On this 12-day workshop sponsored by the Scottsdale Artists School, travel sketchers explored

COLLECTIVE JOURNALING

In 2000, Brian Singer, a graphic designer from San Francisco who had long been fascinated with bathroom graffiti, bought 1,000 blank journals, assigned each a number, and stamped instructions inviting people to write, draw, paint, or otherwise fill up the pages. After participants had their say, they were asked to either leave the journal in a public place or pass it on to someone else. The idea was that each participant's narrative or drawing would add to the next, creating a quilt of poems, political rants, personal musings, advice, photos, sketches, and collages.

Singer has been able to track many of the journals' progress through e-mails and postings on the project's website, www.1000journals.com. So far the journals have traveled to 40 countries and to all 50 states. "Everyone has something to say," Singer believes.

Of the 1,000 journals, only one has made its way back to Singer so far. Number 526 traveled to 13 states, Ireland, and Brazil. "It came back in a velvet pouch—a sort of Crown Royal bag," Singer says. "I thought, 'That's cool—people are even accessorizing them.'"

the Vietnamese countryside, cruised Ha Long on a private junk, and sketched villages, markets, and the local people. He has led similar trips to Tuscany and Venice; check his website for upcoming trips.

In Lehrman's workshops, he teaches how to capture the essence of people, architecture, water, trees, and landscapes with spontaneous lines and color. But most importantly, he says, he teaches the "secret of transforming any boring, interminable wait—think airport, jury duty, auto being serviced, even a long car ride—into absorbing, pleasurable, creative time."

Lehrman's workshops vary in location and length of time. The 12-day Vietnam trip, including accommodations and all instruction, was $3,135.

HOW TO GET IN TOUCH

Lewis Barrett Lehrman, 9123 N. 115th Place, Scottsdale, AZ 85259, 877-471-8718 or 480-391-2640, www.lewisblehrman.com.

make a quilt in anne's land

PRINCE EDWARD ISLAND, CANADA

A quilt is a visible expression of the quiltmaker's soul.
—Edith Zakem, Prince Edward Island quilter

5 Prince Edward Island, the smallest and least populous of Canada's ten provinces, is world renowned for two things: Anne of Green Gables and its magnificent quilts. In fact, Lucy Maud Montgomery—the author whose eight books about the headstrong, red-headed orphan made PEI, as it's usually called, so famous—was a quilter herself. And many of the island's quilting shops sell quilts, quilt kits, and fabric with an Anne of Green Gables theme.

The early pioneer women of PEI who followed their husbands here from Scotland pieced together scraps of fabric in an effort to keep their families warm. They used recycled uniforms, school clothes, and even wedding dresses to create beautiful and practical quilts for the bed or for the shore. PEI's signature shore quilts, made from heavier fabric with layers tied with knotted string, were made by the wives of lobster fishermen for the bitterly cold winters.

The women of PEI didn't stop their quiltmaking after their families were equipped. Through the Women's Institute, a group these resourceful women started in 1911, PEI's quilt makers donated quilts to fire and flood victims, to orphanages, to the Prince County Hospital, and, in one community, to each new bride. During World War I, the group made 9,260 quilts for soldiers, refugees, and air-raid victims.

Today, the famous quilts from Prince Edward Island are exhibited around the world (Yokohama, Japan, for example, hosts an annual PEI Quilt Show), and people from far and wide come to PEI to learn about the gorgeous hand-stitched coverlets.

Contact Canada PEI, a company that specializes in home- and farm-stay vacations, organizes eight-day quilting holidays to the small farming villages and ocher cliff-lined shores that Montgomery depicted so alluringly in her Anne books. Although the trips are open to anyone, most of your classmates will probably be

MUSSEL MAN

Prince Edward Island is paradise for mussels, oysters, lobsters, clams, and scallops. In fact, if you've ever had a Malpeque, Colville, or Raspberry Point oyster—names commonly bandied about at upscale restaurants—the cold, clean waters of PEI are where it came from. "It's the Cognac of shellfish-growing regions," explains John Bil, who has won Canada's national oyster-shucking championship three times, the last in 2005 when he shucked 18 oysters in less than 90 seconds.

One of the best places to eat mussels is Flex Mussels in Charlottetown *(2 Lower Water Street, 902-569-0200, www.flexmussels.com)*. Chef Garner Quain, who even has a "musselcam" on his website (where you can watch a live mussel grow) offers an entire page of mussel dishes, using ingredients from brandy and chipotle peppers to duck and mango.

Japanese tourists, whose fascination with Anne (one study showed they were as gaga over Anne as they are over Godzilla) draws them to PEI in droves. Japanese couples have been known to plan civil wedding ceremonies in the same house where Montgomery married in 1911, and Japanese girls show up with dyed red hair, braided into pigtails, just like Anne's.

During the farm-stay holiday, you'll get three hours of quilting instruction daily, as well as walking tours of Charlottetown, PEI's charming seaside capital, cultural activities, and, of course, a full-day tour to Cavendish and a certain green-gabled, white farmhouse. If you come between late June and September, the tourist high season, you'll even get tickets to the *Anne of Green Gables* musical, the longest running show in Canada.

The price for the eight-day quilting holidays runs C$1,000 (about U.S.$975) and includes a private room with a family, three square meals a day, all quilting instruction, and tours.

HOW TO GET IN TOUCH

Contact Canada PEI, RR 2, Hunter River, New Glasgow, PEI C0A 1N0, Canada, 902-621-0086, www.eslhomestay.ca.

make a date with your muse

BELIZE, CHILE, AND FRANCE

I want you to foam at the mouth and wander into unknown fields.
—Natalie Goldberg, writing teacher

6 As much as you want to sit down, grab your pen or laptop, and start producing epic novels and award-winning screenplays, it's probably not going to happen. At first.

When first you commit to a life of writing, a lot of embarrassing and uncomfortable things are going to happen. It's nothing to be alarmed about. It's just that, as yet, you're unfocused. You have no idea what to write about. You're not hearing a single note from your muse. Yet you have this faint inkling, this tiny whisper, that suggests you might, just maybe, have something to say.

Let me assure you that you do. You do have something important to say, something the world needs to hear.

That conviction is sometimes enough to keep people going. Usually, though, it's not. The cold truth is that there are a lot of alligators in the pond. That's why writing workshops were invented. Not only do writing workshops provide able teachers, mentors, and inspiration, but you'll also meet fellow cheerleaders who will rah-rah you on as you beat back the alligators. It's something we all need.

Here are three places to find those pom-poms.

International Paris Writers Workshop. For a hundred years, aspiring writers have traveled to the City of Light, hoping that the atmosphere which inspired Henry James, Gertrude Stein, Ernest Hemingway, James Joyce, and many others would work its magic on them. Since 1988, the Paris Writers Workshop, France's oldest continuing creative writing workshop, has been offering three- and five-day programs by English writers from all over the world. In addition to workshops on everything from writing memoirs and screenplays to detective fiction and fantasy that will give you the chance to fine-tune your skills, there are also readings, walks around literary Paris, and informal gatherings à la salons of the early 1900s. Prices range from 300 euros ($441) for a three-afternoon workshop to 850 euros ($1,251) for a five-day workshop.

WICE, 20 boulevard du Montparnasse, 75015 Paris, France, 33 1 45 66 75 50, www.wice-paris.org.

Los Parronales Writing Retreat. Held twice a year in the heart of Chile's beautiful Central Valley amid 150 acres of vineyards and sweeping views of the Andes, these two-week writing workshops are facilitated by poet Susan Siddeley, a British transplant who now splits her time between Toronto and Chile, and such writers as Crysse Morrison and Ronna Bloom. The 14 days feature manuscript appraisals, one-on-one consultations, and morning and afternoon sessions in poetry and fiction. Four of the days are spent touring the Pablo Neruda museum, the Pacific Coast, and Santiago. The cost with lodging and meals is $100 to $120 a day.

YOU'RE IN GOOD COMPANY

In case you were thinking that great writers get up each morning and confidently sit down to pour out genius, here are some stories to tuck into your back pocket:

- Maya Angelou once admitted, "Every time I write a book, every time I face that yellow pad, the challenge is so great. Each time I think, 'Oh, they're going to find out now. I've run a game on everybody and they're going to find me out.'"
- Isabel Allende had to publish three novels before she felt comfortable enough to list "writer" rather than "housewife" as her occupation. "Writer" was such a big word, she explained.
- Pulitzer Prize–winning poet Anne Sexton was too scared to take her first poetry class, so a friend had to call and sign her up.
- After the president of Dartmouth College paid tribute to E. B. White for his "literary bravery," White made the comment, "He little knew."
- Gabriel Garcia Marquez declared, "All my life, I've been frightened at the moment I sit down to write."
- Anthony Burgess, author of *A Clockwork Orange* and dozens of other novels, constantly thought about giving up writing because of the debilitating fear that his work wasn't good enough.

Los Parronales, 473 Ontario Street, Toronto ON M4X 1M6, Canada, 416-968-0769, in Chile 56 2 207 3534, www.losparronales.blogspot.com.

Zoetrope Short Story Writers Workshop. Every year, *Zoetrope,* a literary magazine founded by filmmaker Francis Ford Coppola, holds a workshop for short-story writers. Guided by the magazine's editor and award-winning writers (in 2007, for example, Ben Fountain, winner of the 2007 Pen/Hemingway Award, led the charge), the workshop is held in Coppola's amazing lodge in the rain forest of Belize. The accommodations at the Blancaneaux Lodge, with its open-air, thatch-roofed cabanas on stilts filled with handcrafted furniture, are surpassed only by the food, much of which is grown in the rustic resort's 3-acre organic garden. The workshop, held for a week each summer, includes critiques, time to write, evening readings, and plenty of free time to ride horses, canoe through caves, and visit Caracol, the nearby exotic Mayan ruins. There's also a hot spring with a giant waterfall and a rain-forest medicine trail. The price for the seven-day workshop, including lodging, all meals, and workshops, ranges from $2,750 to $3,850, depending on the level of accommodation.

    Zoetrope All-Story, 916 Kearny Street, San Francisco, CA 94133, 415-788-7500, www.all-story.com.

jiggle, shimmy, and learn to "toss the belly"

GOKPINAR, TURKEY

> Beside the fire, as the wood burns black
> A laughing dancer in veils of light
> Whose dance transforms the darkness to gold.
> —Abu Abd Allah ben Abi-l-Khisal, *The Serpent of the Nile*

7 | Unless you have a really detailed map of Turkey, you probably won't find the tiny former nomadic village of Gokpinar. It's in the hills near the Aegean coast. At last count, it had a hundred residents, four cars, a dozen donkeys, one mosque, and one tiny teahouse.

Just up the hill from this remote village of carpet weavers and olive farmers is a dance studio/retreat center (officially called Gokpinar Music and Dance Center) that specializes in teaching the ancient Turkish art of *gobek atmak*. Translated into English, it literally means "to toss the belly," and in Turkey, the energetic, sensual dance we know as belly dancing is practiced by Turks of all classes and ages. Even men, known as *rakkas*, are known to perform the dance's sweeping turns, thrusting hip lifts, and floor undulations.

ALI BABA AND THE 40 T-SHIRT VENDORS

If you're looking for a belly-dancing costume, there are few better places to look than Istanbul's Grand Bazaar. One of the oldest shopping centers in the world (part of the building goes back to the ninth century), this grand spectacle of commerce has a whole street of nothing but goldsmiths, a courtyard filled with cobblers, a row of haberdashers, and as many stalls selling "I Love Istanbul" T-shirts as Ottoman antiques. There are 5,480 stalls spread over 65 covered streets. Needless to say, lots of them offer belly-dancing costumes.

Belly dancing is regularly featured on Turkish television and at nightclubs throughout the country, and a Turkish party, wedding, or even circumcision ceremony isn't considered complete without at least one belly dancer. Asena, Tanyelli, and Princess Banu, celebrity gobek dans, are as well known in the Turkish culture as Angelina Jolie and Julia Roberts are in ours.

At the Gokpinar Music and Dance Center, foreigners who come to this small village dance school spend their mornings learning about the expressive, playful dance and its Middle Eastern rhythms of *oud* and *ney*. On a stone terrace overlooking olive groves, pine woods, and lush gardens, they learn the belly dance's walk and posture, master the finger cymbals called *zil* and the wooden clappers called *calpara*, and find out how to make the most of the veils and other costume accessories. But most importantly, they experience Turkey away from the cities and prepackaged tours. Afternoons are free to lounge on a nearby beach, catch a ride on a *gulet* to the region's many islands and bays, or help the locals pick olives.

Gokpinar is located only 20 minutes from Bodrum, a charming Aegean town with whitewashed houses set among cascades of bougainvillea that has recently become the darling of the guided-tour set. The retreat center was opened in 1996 when Bulent Dogan, an accomplished Turkish drummer who studied tourism and hotel management at the university, decided to introduce foreigners to local culture. After serving for years as a tour guide, he opened the retreat center to show foreigners the other side, the noncommercialized side of his country.

Not only will you dance beside your new friends from the village, but you'll also share meals with them—soups cooked over the fire in clay pots along with such fresh produce as eggplants, plump tomatoes, parsley, lentils, rice, and, of course, olive oil sopped up with crusty bread. At the six-room retreat center, Dogan also offers classes in Turkish cooking and carpet weaving. Participants work with village weavers on their giant looms, ending their week of morning classes with a natural-dyed lamb's-wool carpet.

The price for the seven-day package, including all meals, shared accommodations, transfers, snacks, and lots of hot mint tea served in tulip-shaped glass cups, runs $975.

HOW TO GET IN TOUCH

Caravan Turkey, Mumcular, Bodrum, Turkey, 866-966-3166 or 90 2523 735750, www.caravanturkey.com.

study classic russian art at catherine the great's academy

ST. PETERSBURG, RUSSIA

> What can be more tragic than to feel the boundlessness of the surrounding beauty and to be able to see in it its underlying mystery . . . and yet to be aware of your own inability to express these large feelings?
> —Isaak Levitan, Russian landscape painter

8 | The St. Petersburg Academy of Arts was founded in 1757, 19 years before the United States came into being. Originally called the Academy of Three Noblest Arts, it was the brainchild of Count Ivan Shuvalov. Classes, open even to peasants as long as they had artistic promise, were held at his palace on Sadovaya Street until 1764 when Catherine the Great changed the name to the Imperial Academy of Arts and commissioned a new building that took two and a half decades to construct. Facing the Winter Palace across from St. Petersburg's famous Neva River, the art academy with many names and a neoclassic edifice even has 3,000-year-old sphinxes and griffins imported from Egypt.

In the early days, the prestigious academy sent its most notable painters abroad, encouraging them to study the art of France and Renaissance Italy. But nowadays, people come to the academy from abroad to study the sensitive and poetic art forms innovated by Russia. And as for those three noble arts—painting, sculpture, and architecture—they've been joined by classes in glass making, stone carving, weaving, mosaics, and making *matryoshkas*, the famous Russian nesting dolls.

ArtTours was started in 2002 by a group of St. Petersburg artists who were frustrated that visitors to the city, after visiting the Hermitage and the Russian Art Museum, were left wondering, "Where's the contemporary art and culture?" The company offers what it calls "master classes" in painting, iconography, sculpture, stained glass, jewelry, art restoration, and Russian theater and ballet. It also offers a sprinkling of two-hour workshops, including one in painting the famous Russian Easter eggs.

YOU'RE IN GOOD COMPANY WHILE YOU'RE THERE

St. Petersburg, created by Peter the Great in 1703 to be his "window on Europe," is often called one big open-air museum. It also happens to have 140 museums of the sort that have walls and ceilings, along with 100 theaters and a reputation as the cultural soul of modern-day Russia. While it's impossible to see everything, here are a couple of artistic shrines for starters:

- **Church of the Savior on the Spilled Blood.** The blood in question belonged to Alexander II, who was mortally wounded on this site on March 13, 1881. The reason artists, rather than nurses, should show up is because it contains more than 25,000 square feet of intricately designed mosaics—more than any other church in the world—designed by the most celebrated artists of the day, including Viktor Vasnetsov, Mikhail Nesterov, and Mikhail Vrubel.
- **SS Peter and Paul Fortress.** The oldest building in St. Petersburg (1703), this ancient fortress not only has the burial vault for Peter and other Russian tsars but also served as the political prison for such literary luminaries as Dostoevsky and Gorky. Peter's own rebellious son Alexei even served time at the high-security jail.

ArtTours also publishes art catalogs, conducts art exhibits, and maintains a database of contemporary St. Petersburg artists, refuting the rumor that new art movements were forbidden during Soviet times. And even though ArtTours is actively working to promote contemporary art, it would never dream of forgetting the rich tradition from which these artists hail. Most of the master classes are taught by professors at the academy and take place either at studios inside the opulent school, at artists' private workshops, or at nearby Peterhof in a former nobleman's mansion.

The master classes are custom designed and can run anywhere from five days to three months. Master classes start at 10 euros ($15) an hour. The price for the two-hour workshops ranges from 5 euros (about $7.50) for pictorial art to 30 euros ($45) for jewelry making. Accommodations and meals are extra, but ArtTours can help arrange a hotel or B&B, as well as arrange art-shopping tours, portrait or landscape commissions, and legal documents for transferring artworks to other countries. They'll also help you commission a famous Fabergé-inspired artist to create a memorable piece of jewelry.

HOW TO GET IN TOUCH

ArtTours, 7 Mytninskaya Street, St. Petersburg 191144, Russia, 7 812 320 1072, www.art-tours.org.

whip up a mole with a celebrity chef

CULINARY HOT SPOTS WORLDWIDE

I don't like gourmet cooking or "this" cooking or "that" cooking.
I like "good cooking."
—James Beard, American chef and food writer

9 The story of how one eats is the story of how one lives. In fact, it's impossible to fully understand a culture or a place without understanding its cuisine. And that could explain why cooking vacations today are hotter than Paula Deen's deep-fat fryer.

It's not just foodies imbibing, either. Participants in gastronomic getaways include everyone from professional chefs looking to master a few new parlor tricks to newbies trying to figure out which end of the knife to use, not to mention a lot of folks who simply enjoy the soul-satisfying experience of creating a meal together.

Options for cooking vacations are diverse and abundant. You can choose your gastronomic getaway by country, by cuisine, by favorite celebrity chef, even by ingredient. Prices range from $18 for a half-day class in Vietnamese cuisine in Vietnam itself (Red Bridge Restaurant and Cooking School, 84 510 933222, www.visithoian.com), where you'll take a boat to a busy market to buy ingredients

TURN UP THE HEAT

There's more than one room in the house to spice up your relationship. According to a survey by Sears, Roebuck and Co., couples who cook together are happier than those who go their separate ways in the kitchen. Eighty-three percent of couples who cook together rate their relationship as excellent, as opposed to 26 percent for those who don't. As for their sex lives, 58 percent of the couples who "start" in the kitchen have a satisfying sex life, compared to 30 percent for the others.

for such dishes as crispy *hoi an* pancakes with shrimp, herbs, and peanut sauce, to as much as $49,500 for a two-week private jet "Cuisine and Culture Journey" with food critic Gael Greene and author Simon Winchester (646-415-8092, www.remotelands.com). Most of the weekend to weeklong trips fall somewhere in between.

To find a cooking vacation that's right for you, google "cooking vacations" along with other keywords of interest—say, "Patricia Wells" or "Jordan" or "dim sum." In the meantime, here are a few tasty cooking vacations to nibble on:

Italian Cooking Vacations. In Italy, they say, "Non è sano mangiare da solo"— "It's not healthy to eat alone." Lauren Scuncio Birmingham, a fifth-generation American of Italian descent who offers weeklong cooking vacations to picturesque Italian villas, farmhouses, and palazzos, says that, in Italy, cooking is a way to show love. The kitchen is the center of conversation, laughter, fun, and affection. During a delicious week in Tuscany, Sicily, Rome, Umbria, or Campania, where generations of Birmingham's family lived near the Amalfi Coast, you'll measure, knead, cook, and eat, as well as visit pastry makers, fish markets, wine cellars, butchers, and Giuseppe, a talkative cheese farmer from Umbria who'll likely invite you into his cottage to break bread. Depending on the location, you might pick lemons for a granita, a yummy Italian slush, or hunt exotic white truffles. So say *Arrivederci* to Domino's pizza and learn true Italian cooking in its place of origin. Historical notes are given for each recipe, many that are five generations old, handed down from Birmingham's great-grandmother Lucia. Prices for a week's vacation vary considerably, but average around $2,000.

Cooking Vacations International, 304 Newbury Street, Suite 318, Boston, MA 02115, 800-916-1152 or 617-247-4112, www.cooking-vacations.com.

La Villa Bonita School of Mexican Cuisine. Offering four-day and weeklong classes in nouvelle and traditional Mexican dishes, this school offers daily hands-on cooking classes, as well as culinary and cultural field trips. Classes, often booked six months ahead, are taught by Ana Garcia, a famous Mexican chef whose great-grandmother, a well-known butcher revered for her chorizo and longamiza sausage, ran a stall in Cuernavaca's busy *mercado*. She supported four kids while Garcia's great-grandfather was out fighting the Mexican Revolution with Emiliano Zapata.

"In Mexico, food is not just about making a meal. It's about being together in the kitchen, creating an experience together with family and friends," Garcia says.

"And what Americans think of as Mexican food is very limited. We have culinary influences from all over the world. But unfortunately most Mexicans just give the Americans what they've come to expect. They'd rather do that than take the time to educate them."

Not Garcia. Using fresh ingredients picked up in the market each morning, she educates her eager students about Mexican chiles, mole sauces, herbs, and spices. She shows them how to season a *molcajete*, a traditional grinding bowl made from lava rock that's used to crush jalapeños, tomatoes, and garlic into authentic salsas. She provides samples of *mamey*, *zapote negro*, *guanabana*, and other popular Mexican fruits that Taco Bell has so far failed to include on its menu.

Limited to only six students at a time, Garcia's classes are intimate, with students spending family time with Garcia, her husband, and their children. But book now. The vivacious chef is about to star in a new PBS cooking show called *My Mexico with Chef Ana Garcia*, and reservations are going to be even harder to come by. Four-day classes start at $1,150 and weeklong sessions run $1,550 for double occupancy.

La Villa Bonita School of Mexican Cuisine, Netzahualcoyotl 33, Col. Centro, Cuernavaca, Morelos, Mexico 62000, 800-505-3084, www.lavillabonita.com.

Middle East Cuisine. The rose-red city of Petra, Jordan, probably doesn't spring to mind as a culinary hotbed. However, the spot where Moses was allegedly last seen has an epic cuisine—fragrant rices with almonds, mezzes, hummus, falafel, baba ghanouj. Although Petra Kitchen, a cooking school run by converted Texan Wendy Botham, is actually just outside the deserted city, it mixes lessons on ancient Jordanian cuisine with tours of Wadi Musa, soaks in the Dead Sea, and produce-gathering trips to orchards, farms, and local *souqs*. You'll stay at Taybet Zamaan, a four-star hotel converted from an 18th-century Bedouin village. You'll learn to make *maglouba*, a layered dish of rice, vegetables, and chicken, as well as *mansaf*, an entree made with goat and reserved for special occasions. The eight-day trip includes seven nights' accommodations, four cooking sessions complete with dinner, local excursions, and all transfers and runs £799 ($1,600), double occupancy. It's hosted by Holiday on the Menu, a British cooking school, which also plans cooking holidays to Morocco, India, Australia, Vietnam, and other exotic locales.

Holiday on the Menu, 68–70 North End Road, West Kensington, London, W14 9EP, England, 44 8708 998 844, www.holidayonthemenu.com.

make *waus* and other malaysian crafts

KAMPUNG BANGGOL, KELANTAN, MALAYSIA

Throw your dreams into space like a kite, and you do not know what it
will bring back, a new life, a new friend, a new love, a new country.
—Anaïs Nin, French author

10 Even though Kelantan lies in the northeast corner of Malaysia, right near the Thailand border, this Islamic state with its 60 miles of undeveloped coastline is the very heart and soul of the country's rich art-and-crafts heritage. In Kota Bharu, the capital of Kelantan, you can visit Balai Getam Guri, a handicraft museum that showcases Kelantanese textiles, basketry, embroidery, batik printing, and silversmithing, and see regular demonstrations of *silat* (a combination martial art and folk dance), *wayang kulit* (puppetry), *gasing* (top spinning), and *wau* (kite flying).

But since art shouldn't be a spectator sport, we recommend heading down Jalan PCB, a road leading from Kota Bharu's Chinatown (one of the few places to get a beer, since the city is Islamic and frowns on that sort of thing)

GONE FISHIN'

Few tourists head as far north as Kelantan, which is a shame since it's the perfect spot for seeing Malaysia as it was before foreign influence. But there's one class of visitor who regularly shows up: treasure hunters. Gunung Stong, one of Kelantan's highest mountains, has a cave that reputedly bears a hidden treasure. Called Gua Ikan (Fish Cave, named for a fish-shaped rock near the entrance), this cavern attracts booty seekers from around the world who are looking for a cache of gold allegedly left by the Japanese Imperial Army during its World War II occupation.

LAND OF LIGHTNING

Even though Kelantan, which means the "land of lightning," is one of the strictest Muslim states in Malaysia, it prides itself on tolerance. When members of Kota Bharu's Thai community asked to build an extremely large Buddha statue, a permit was given without objection. Although alcohol is officially illegal, Harry Mulder, the proprietor of Pasir Belanda, with a wink and a nod, knows plenty of places to find it. And *khalwat*, the Islamic rule on proximity between males and females, applies only to Muslims. Still, Islamic principles are observed throughout the region, and Kota Bharu, which in 2005 officially declared itself The Islamic City, has Malaysia's oldest mosque and supermarkets with separate checkout counters for males and females.

to Kampung Banggol, a quaint village where the *penghulu* (village headman) not only will greet you with the drums and gongs of gamelan music but also will make sure you get some hands-on experience of your own. A quick wander around the *kampung* (village) will reveal a long string of cottage industries, with craftsmen and craftswomen making moon kites, painting batik, building boats, and weaving a decorative gold-threaded cloth known as *songket*. Here, fishermen throw nets to catch fish, and monkeys pick coconuts for their owners.

Since many penghulus don't speak English, your best bet is to book a room at Pasir Belanda, a village hostelry—five cabins on stilts—that's run by a Dutch couple who abandoned their country five years ago to open this rustic haven in Malaysia's lush tropical jungle. Harry and Annemieke Mulder, who speak fluent English, will happily set you up with lessons in kitemaking, batik painting, or Malay cooking. Even just gazing around your chalet will offer insight into the rich tradition of Malay woodcarving, as the beams, balustrades, doors, and stilts of your traditionally built Malay home-away-from-home show off the work of Malaysian woodcarvers.

Pasir Belanda is a short 15 minutes from Kota Bharu and is perfect for explorations on foot, bicycle, horse, or *prau*, the traditional Malay boat. Plus, it's only five minutes from Puntai Cahaya Bulan (Moonlight Beach, or PCB, as the locals call it), a famous coconut-palm-fringed beach on the South China Sea. PCB, in keeping with Muslim sensibilities, was recently renamed from Pantai Cinta Berahi (Beach of Passionate Love), the name it acquired during World War II from a lovelorn British soldier.

As for the wau factor, this area has three well-known kitemakers: 70-something Ismail bin Jusoh, who started making kites when he was 12; Sapie Yusof, who's so devoted to his kitemaking that he might not hear you approaching his doorstep; and Yasok bin Umat, who takes kitemaking apprentices from around the world and has traveled to kite festivals in Europe. If you study under bin Umat, whose house is a bit hard to find down a tiny dirt lane, you'll be serenaded by a caged black cabao, a mynah-like bird that chirps, buzzes, croons, and meows like a cat.

Malaysia's kites are different from those in other parts of the world. They are made from intricately cut paper panels of many colors that are pasted to a translucent, single-color tissue. You'll make your frame from *buluh duri* (thorny bamboo) that has been dried for a week before being split and trimmed. Although Malaysian kites, which are displayed in yearly kite festivals, are often fashioned in the shape of fish, caterpillars, and birds, the traditional moon kite is still the most popular.

Kite-making workshops are 25 ringgits ($7). Rooms range from 149 ringgits ($45) to 199 ringgits ($60) per night.

HOW TO GET IN TOUCH
Pasir Belanda, Kampung Banggol, Jalan PCB, 15350 Kota Bharu, Kelantan, Malaysia, 60 9 747 7046, www.kampungstay.com.

join a pottery brigade

NICARAGUA

*We're a culture of spectators, and this is not about being a spectator.
This is about doing, making things happen, finishing something.*
—Mark Hansen, founder of the North House Folk School

11 Paul Soldner, a famous ceramicist who visited Nicaragua's pottery villages in the early 1990s, said as much could be learned about pottery in a two-week Potters for Peace (PFP) brigade as in a four-year university education. That's because you visit remote Nicaraguan cooperatives where women have been digging clay, mixing it with sand and water, and forming it into pots, bowls, and *comales* (saucers for cooking tortillas) for thousands of years.

And while they may not have studied with the likes of Soldner and other leading university ceramics teachers, these poor *campesinas* have figured out how to make kilns out of little more than bricks, mud, and sticks, how to use river stones to smooth and glaze their bowls, and how to turn the earth around them into things they can use every day.

PFP, a group of international artists that offers support, solidarity, and friendship to developing-world potters, organizes a two-week brigade to Nicaragua every January. Participants fly into the capital Managua and from there travel to studios and cooperatives all over the country, such as one that makes an internationally recognized ceramic water filter. In 1998, after Hurricane Mitch devastated much of Nicaragua and left the country sorely in need of potable water, PFP volunteers taught the Nicaraguan potters how to press these innovative water filters, which are able to eliminate 99 percent of waterborne bacteria. Since that time, the Nicaraguan cooperative has made and distributed tens of thousands of these inexpensive filters through such organizations as the Red Cross, UNICEF, and Doctors without Borders, and PFP has gone on to train potters in many other countries how to make the low-tech, low-cost filters (see sidebar p. 39).

SAFE WATER FOR ALL

It has been more than 150 years since John Snow first figured out that a contaminated water pump was the culprit for a cholera outbreak in London. Yet today, two million people (most of them kids under age 5) still die every year from water-related illness. Eighty percent of all disease in the developing world can be traced back to inadequate water and sanitation. Needless to say, Potters for Peace and its ceramic water filter projects will go a long way toward helping the United Nations meet its 2015 goal of reducing by 50 percent the number of people unable to reach or afford safe drinking water.

This PFP project, which has taken volunteers to Cambodia, Bangladesh, Ghana, El Salvador, the Darfur region of Sudan, Myanmar, and many other places, kills two birds with one stone: It meets rural and marginalized communities' urgent need for safe water, while at the same time providing employment for local potters.

PFP also helps Nicaraguan potters find markets for their work, including a 1998 order by Pier 1 stores for 18,000 bowls.

Potters for Peace was started in 1986 when a group of ceramicists affiliated with the Quixote Center in Washington, DC (Quixote's mission was to match U.S. military aid to the Nicaraguan contras dollar-for-dollar with humanitarian aid) traveled to Nicaragua, befriended a women's pottery cooperative, planned a fundraiser, and vowed to return every year.

The annual Nicaragua brigade is open to anyone interested in pottery. Although the villages and studios vary from year to year, you are guaranteed to visit and work with a wide variety of potters, learn firsthand about their ceramic traditions, and see how they confront the realities of creating and marketing in the developing world. PFP brigades always include a Nicaraguan potter as travel companion—a learning experience for him or her as much as for you.

You might visit Ducuale Grande Women's Pottery Cooperative in Esteli; the Guitierrez sisters, who make ceramic piggy banks; or El Bonete, a small, remote village where they make clay jewelry. Each trip includes a stop in San Juan de Oriente, the famous pottery village of mainly Nahuatl

Indians who settled along the Pacific Coast of Nicaragua 5,000 years ago. When Spanish colonizers first arrived, they called this remote and still undeveloped village the "town of the *platos* (dishes)."

If you don't speak Spanish, that's okay—you'll be provided with translation. Or get a jump on your *"¿Comó estás?"* and *"¿Como se llamas?"* by arriving early and attending a Spanish language school. Several schools offer weekly sessions of intensive study, from beginning to advanced; to top it off, you stay with a Nicaraguan family.

The cost for the two-week brigade, including lodging, all meals, transportation, and snacks, is $1,100. The language tuition is extra.

HOW TO GET IN TOUCH

Potters for Peace, P.O. Box 1043, Bisbee, AZ 85603, 520-249-8093, pottersforpeace.org.

make goods from the woods

INSJÖN, SWEDEN

*It's very common for people to separate the things they do from the
things they need. It's very uncommon that people take a raw material to
make a thing, and then use it.*
—Jögge Sundqvist, Swedish woodworker

12 Admittedly, you do not have to travel all the way to Sweden to learn how to fashion spoons, bowls, and furniture from the branches in your backyard. In fact, you don't even have to go to Sweden to study with Jögge Sundqvist, Sweden's premier wood-carver, who brought wood turning and carving back into vogue. Sundqvist gives regular workshops right here in North America at such spots as the Folk Art Center in Asheville, North Carolina; the Furniture Society's annual convention; and Country Workshops, a small crafts school in Madison County, North Carolina, that even sells do-it-yourself DVDs of Sundqvist's carving techniques.

But if you really want to experience the renaissance of Swedish woodworking (along with Sweden's other heritage crafts), plan a trip to Sätergläntan College of Handicrafts, which offers short courses (up to 11 days) with Sundqvist and other Swedish craftsmen, as well as one- and two-year programs in carpentry, weaving, blacksmithing, and sewing.

HORSE OF A DIFFERENT COLOR

Nothing represents Sweden more than the gaily painted Dala horse, first made by Dalarna's furniture makers and clockmakers, who whittled leftover pieces into toys for their youngsters. By the late 1700s, however, a cottage industry sprang up after these local artisans bartered the red-orange tailless horses with the intricately painted saddles for bowls of soup. Most Dalas are carved from pine, dried for three to four weeks, and then painted, often with brushes employing two colors of paint. In Nusnas, where more than 250,000 Dalas of all sizes are individually carved and painted each year, you can have your name painted on one.

The school, owned by the Swedish Handicrafts Organization, is beautifully situated on the hillside of Knippboberget, high above the village of Insjön in Dalarna, the heart of Sweden's age-old crafts traditions. During the 18th and 19th centuries, craftspeople from Dalarna trekked throughout the Swedish countryside finding markets for their chip baskets, weaver's reeds, carved wooden horses, handmade bobbin lace, and brooches made of human hair. With its centuries-old traditions, colorful costumes, midsummer festivals, and rolling landscape dotted with red-painted houses, pristine lakes, and rich forests, Dalarna represents Sweden at its quintessential best.

As for Sundqvist, he learned wood carving at the knee of his father, world-renowned carver Wille Sundqvist, when he was all of four. In his classes, the younger Sundqvist teaches traditional Scandinavian carving techniques that date back to the 17th century. Called Slöjd, Sundqvist's philosophy proclaims that woodworking, in addition to merely creating furniture, also builds character, industriousness, and intelligence.

In Sundqvist's classes, you'll learn about such hand tools as axes, adzes, and gouges. You'll learn how to gather materials, green and straight from the forests, about the importance of your medium's color and texture, and how to carve your family mark (and if you don't have one, you'll learn how to create one) into your signature pieces. From Sätergläntan, you'll also take study trips to crafters' homes, village halls, museums, and a Fäbod, a traditional mountain dairy farm.

Sätergläntan meals, made fresh daily from locally grown food, are served—needless to say—in beautiful handcrafted bowls and are eaten with equally beautiful wooden spoons made by the area's craftspeople.

Although instruction is typically offered in Swedish, all instructors speak fluent English and are happy to provide English notes.

Price for the courses range from 1,900 kronor (about $300) for a five-day course to 2,600 kronor ($410) for two weeks. Bed and board ranges from 2,800 kronor ($440) for a five-day double room to 4,750 kronor ($729) for a two-week double; there's a supplementary fee for singles.

HOW TO GET IN TOUCH

Sätergläntan College of Handicrafts, Knippbodarna 119, 793 41 Insjön, Sweden, 46 247 410 45, www.saterglantan.se.

strut your stuff at rio's carnaval

RIO DE JANEIRO, BRAZIL

The United States is all work. People don't sing, people don't dance,
and people don't play an instrument. And it's sad, really,
because that's part of the human dance.
—David de Hilster, whose International Samba School became the first
non-Brazilian school allowed to play for the Rio Carnaval

13 Don't let the name fool you. A samba school is not an educational institution, but rather a social group that knows how to throw one heck of a party. In fact, Rio de Janeiro's 51 samba schools spend the whole year preparing for the four-day party we know as Mardi Gras or Carnaval. They spend an average of $500,000 (the top schools twice that much) making costumes and floats and rehearsing for their part in a 65- to 80-minute performance that involves up to 5,000 people parading through the 85,000-seat Sambódromo.

Although a few of Rio's samba schools have banned foreigners from participating—claiming that they don't know enough Portuguese to learn the songs and will ruin a whole year's work, not to mention the schools' chances of staying in the top 14 that get to perform in the big two-day parade—other samba schools are more than happy to take out-of-towners' money in exchange for participating in everything from costume assembling to drumming to shaking their rumps in the parade. "We spread the foreigners around the wings so they aren't noticed by the judges," said Jean Claudio of the Vila Isabel school.

For the right price, you can choose from among a wide variety of elaborate costumes (they're called *fantasias*) made with everything from ostrich and peacock feathers to sequins and glitter, although the best costume spots (a particular place in the lineup), some of which take cranes to get into, are reserved for locals who have been attending weekly samba practice since September.

If you show up a week or two early for the pre-Lenten festivities (and samba schools encourage that), you can visit their *barracãos* (workshops), help with last-minute costume making, and practice with your *ala* or section, whose members will have similar costumes to yours.

Sambista wannabes can use the Internet to preorder costumes (the 13 premier-league schools each have their own website with colored photos of the costumes for each section), liaise with section leaders, and get the music and lyrics to practice on your own. By Christmas, the theme for each school has been chosen, the music written, costumes designed, dances choreographed, and sambas recorded and available at music stores (or through the Postal Service).

Five-night Carnaval packages with breakfast start at $400.

Below is contact information for several samba schools in Rio. Check out their websites or give them a call to see if they're taking outsiders.

- *Beija-Flor,* Pracinha Wallace Paes Leme, 1.025, Nilópolis, 55 21 2791 2866, www.beija-flor.com.br
- *Caprichosos de Plares,* Rua Faleiros, 1, Pilares, 55 21 2592 5620
- *Grande Rio,* Rua Almirante Barroso, 5, Duque de Caxias, 55 21 2771 2331, www.granderio.org.br
- *Imperatriz Leopoldinense,* Rua Professor Lacê, 235, Ramos, 55 21 2560 8037, www.imperatrizleopoldinense.com.br
- *Imperio Serrano,* Avenida Ministro Edgard Romero, 114, Madureira, 55 21 2489 8722, www.imperioserrano.com.br
- *Mangueira,* Rua Visconde de Niterói, 1.072, Mangueira, 55 21 3872 6786, www.mangueira.com.br
- *Mocidade,* Rua Coronel Tamarindo, 38, Padre Miguel, 55 21 3332 5823, www.mocidadeindependente.com.br
- *Portela,* Rua Clara Nunes, 81, Madureira, 55 21 2489 6440, www.portelaweb.com.br
- *Porto da Pedra,* Rua João Silva, 84, Porto da Pedra, São Gonçalo, 55 21 2605 2984, www.gresuportodapedra.com.br
- *Rocinha,* Rua Bertha Lutz N. 80, São Conrado, 55 21 3205 3303, www.academicosdarocinha.com.br
- *Salgueiro,* Rua Silva Teles, 104, Andarai, 55 21 2288 3065, www.salgueiro.com.br
- *Unidos da Tijuca,* Rua Rivadávia Correia 60, barracão 12, Cidade do Samba, 55 21 2516 2749, www.unidosdatijuca.com.br
- *Unidos de Vila Isabel,* Avenida 28 de Setembro, 382, Vila Isabel, 55 21 3181 4869, www.unidosdevilaisabel.com.br
- *Unidos do Viradouro,* Avenida do Contorno, 16, Barreto, Niterói, 55 21 2628 7840, www.unidosdoviradouro.com.br.

Or you can contact the Blumar Travel Agency (55 21 3875 9300, www.blumar.com.br), which offers Carnaval packages complete with fantasies.

learn the art of herbology

ASHHURST, NEW ZEALAND, AND TASMANIA, AUSTRALIA

Let thy kitchen be thy apothecary; and,
Let foods be your medicine.
—Hippocrates, the father of medicine

14 A recent Harvard study found that some 38 million Americans collectively spend $4.2 billion on herbal medicine each year. And that doesn't include the folks who unconsciously treat themselves with ginger (soothes upset stomach), garlic (controls cholesterol and reduces the risk of certain cancers), and other "medicinal foods" that show up in common, everyday recipes.

Medicinal herbs—the growing of them and the creating of tinctures and creams—define an art that can be studied and used by nonmedical personnel. Here are two great places to further your education in nature's pharmacy:

The Herb Farm. With 14 themed gardens, a natural foods café, and a retail shop that sells its many homegrown and produced creams, tinctures, and oils, The Herb Farm outside Ashhurst, New Zealand, offers workshops in herbal healing, aromatherapy, and natural skin care. You can even create your own all-natural healing creams to take with you. Using herbs plucked from the farm's own raised beds, you'll learn about Gaia, the philosophy that says the Earth participates in its own healing. You'll learn about the healing properties of plants, how essential oils are extracted from plants, and how these extracts are used to make various products. The Herb Farm's rural tranquility was Lynn Kirkland's answer to the strong desire she had to raise her children, Sarah and Craig, in as natural an environment as possible. In 1990, she completed an herbal diploma and, after demand grew so large for her herbal extract products, she opened the farm to the public. Sarah, who is now in her mid-20s, returned home after working overseas as an international fashion model to join the business. Workshops are NZ$17.50 (about U.S.$13.50).

The Herb Farm, Grove Road, RD10, Ashhurst, Manawatu, New Zealand, 64 6 326 8633, www.herbfarm.co.nz.

Pindari Herb Farm. Offering one- to five-day workshops in medicinal herbs and self-sufficiency, this hilltop farm in the rugged bush near Longford, Tasmania, was started by Ken Atherton, a third-generation pharmacist who began compounding and dispensing herbal and homeopathic medicine in his storefront pharmacy before moving to the farm to grow and handcraft his own herbal medicines, around a hundred at last count. He and his wife, Giovi Di Matteo, and their two children have created a comprehensive medicinal dispensary of both skin-care products and herbal remedies for common ailments. In the live-in workshops, you'll learn to identify, grow, process, procure, and use medicinal herbs. After 15 years of hard work, Ken and Giovi have created their own solar-, wind-, and steam-power production, as well as the extensive organic vegetable and medicinal herb gardens. The five-day retreat, which includes six nights lodging at the farm, all meals, and materials, is A$720 (about U.S.$640). One-day workshops are also offered at A$40 to $50 (U.S.$35–$45).

Pindari Herb Farm, 200 Norwich Drive, Longford, Tasmania, 7301 Australia, 61 3 6391 1799, pindariherbfarm.com.

BOTANICAL MEDICINE CHEST

Below are some of the more well-known herbal medicines. *Note to reader:* This sidebar was not paid for by a pharmaceutical giant.

- **Echinacea:** Also called the coneflower, this plant helps fight colds.
- **Elderberry:** Hippocrates prescribed elderberries to his patients, and it seemed to speed recovery from common flus.
- **Garlic:** Tests have indicated garlic's effectiveness at lowering cholesterol.
- **Ginkgo biloba:** Often taken for clearer thinking and memory improvement, studies indicate it may ward off Alzheimer's disease and other forms of dementia.
- **St. John's wort:** Widely used in Europe to treat depression. Clinical trials have shown it to be as effective as Prozac, Zoloft, and other commonly prescribed antidepressants.
- **Saw palmetto:** Grown in the Everglades and used by the Seminole Indians as food, this "medicine" treats benign prostatic hyperplasia, which makes it difficult to empty the bladder.
- **Valerian root:** Used as a perfume in the 16th century, this plant is used to treat (pardon the yawning) insomnia.

paint virgin island landscapes

ST. THOMAS

It's on the strength of observation and reflection that one finds a way.
—Claude Monet, French Impressionist painter

15 | The 55 landscape artists who bucked the system in France back in 1874 became known as the Impressionists. Maria Franco calls her troupe of itinerant landscape painters the "Painting Gypsies." Like their more famous counterparts, Franco's group sets up their easels beside the sea, in botanical gardens, and around anything that makes their hearts beat faster.

"You have to paint what you love," Franco says. "Otherwise, it's just an exercise. When you paint a mango tree for the first time, you come to understand it for the first time. You learn how it grows, how it blossoms. You discover life through painting it."

Whether your subject of choice is Dronnigens Gade, a busy street in Charlotte Amalie, Magens Bay on the rugged north shore, or a windsurfer near Pettyklip Point, you'll have the whole afternoon to see it, understand it, and put it on canvas.

Franco says that the Painting Gypsies, a company that basically organizes "plein air painting parties" for travelers, is the fulfillment of a lifelong dream. After her kids were grown, she returned to painting, something she had studied at Andover, the University of New Hampshire, and the Universidad Menedez Pelayo in Santander, Spain. She also began taking workshops at the Parsons School of Design, the Art Students League, and the Metropolitan Museum of Art. At an outdoor painting workshop in New York's Central Park, she met two comrades, renegades like herself, who became her partners in the Painting Gypsies. In their search for the perfect light and air, Franco and her fellow gypsies paint in Spain and India, as well as in St. Thomas in the U.S. Virgin Islands.

The workshops, which are open to anyone with an interest in plein air painting, work like this: You begin the day at a designated location, say, a historic banana plantation that happens to have acres and acres of wild orchids. While munching on pastries and sipping coffee, a professional painter-instructor offers inspiration, does

GOING BANANAS

Although Franco didn't mention whether any of the Painting Gypsies have re-produced a St. Thomas banana daiquiri, we do know this: More than six million of the frothy drinks have been served at Mountain Top, the rustic restaurant that supposedly invented them back in 1949. The daiquiri—the non-banana version—originated in Santiago, Cuba, at a bar named Venus. According to the story, an American mining engineer named Jennings Cox came up with the drink after accidentally running out of gin. He named it a daiquiri after a nearby beach and iron mine. Ernest Hemingway and John F. Kennedy both counted the Cuban daiquiri among their favorite drinks. At Mountain Top, a favorite of St. Thomas tourists mainly because of its striking views of Magens Bay and its teal-green seas, the popular drink was adapted to include bananas.

---

a demonstration, and gives tips. Then, after lunch—or sometimes before, if the light so lures—participants head to a picturesque spot of their choice to set up their easels and begin painting. When the light begins to fade, everyone returns to a designated meeting spot for a wine-and-cheese-fueled critique, but, as Franco is quick to point out, "There's no such thing as good and bad. We don't use those words."

"Painting like this [in a group] is a chance to 'try on a new outfit,' an opportunity to toss aside social conventions," Franco explains. "It works the same way group therapy works. It allows you to take some chances, to be brave, to expose yourself, to bring out what's buried deep within."

The price for the five-day St. Thomas package that comprises lodging, breakfasts, lunches, transportation to and from various plein air locations, all instruction, and a wine-and-cheese reception is $1,995.

HOW TO GET IN TOUCH

Painting Gypsies, 6 Fieldstone Court, Oakland, NJ 07436, 201-651-1275, www.paintinggypsies.com.

ignite your imagination

CRETE

> Critical judgment—the part of our brain that says, "Yes! No! It's not good enough."—should stay at home, locked in a closet.
> —Shelley Berc, playwright, novelist, and
> cofounder of Creativity Workshop

16 You may not come home from this eight-day workshop on the Greek island of Crete with a suitcase of paintings or a briefcase full of poems. But you will come back with a heart full of artistic passion, completely convinced that creativity and imagination—yours and everyone else's—is the answer to just about any question the world could pose. Plus, you'll have the tools to enable you to fill a whole cargo hold's worth of luggage with paintings, poems, drawings, and essays.

Playwright Shelley Berc and her husband, Alejandro Fogel, a painter and multimedia artist, launched the Creativity Workshop in 1993 to help artists and anyone else interested in the creative process to get "out of their own way." They became convinced, after many years in a university setting, that creativity often gets squelched by one's own judgments and by a culture that has turned it into a commodity.

CREATIVITY TEST
(excerpted from *Art & Soul* by Pam Grout)

There's the SAT to see if you're bright enough to get into college, the LSAT to see if you can make it in law school, the MCAT, which opens doors to med school. But here, being offered for absolutely no charge, is the very best test I know for measuring creativity in human beings.

Get out your pencil.

Pam Grout's Test of Creativity
1. Are you breathing? *Yes*_____ *No*_____
Check your score here. If you answered yes to the above question, you're highly creative.

"Creativity, like so much else in our world, has been co-opted into consumerism, and its worth calculated by how much money it generates," Berc says. "We live in a culture that doesn't encourage adults to be creative unless it looks like they are going to make money at it. But without imagination, we would not have any great scientists, thinkers, or artists."

The aim of their workshops is not to find the next da Vinci or an up-and-coming Proust. Rather, they hope to deepen the sensibilities of the 8 to 12 lucky individuals who enroll in them. Instead of focusing on any one art form, participants in the Creativity Workshop do it all—they write, they draw, they tell stories, and, most importantly, they learn to play, play, play. "If creativity is any one thing, it is play," Berc says. "For a child, life is just one big erector set to be snapped together and pulled apart in a thousand different ways. But as adults, we often lose that flexibility and put away our toys as we acquire jobs, kids, and mortgages."

Berc and Fogel believe creativity is encoded into every human's DNA and that, even though adults become less flexible as they age, that sense of wonder and reckless imagination can be regained. In fact, by focusing on imagination rather than on creating a product per se, creativity becomes a way to view and appreciate life.

The pair know what they're talking about. Berc, a 16-year veteran of the Iowa Writers Workshop, has written novels and plays that have been performed by such celebrities as Stanley Tucci, Patrick Stewart, and Tony Shalhoub. Fogel, whose award-winning work can be seen in museums and public and private collections across the globe, is not only a painter but also an expert in cultural myths and legends.

In their workshops held annually in Crete (and also in other European hot spots such as Paris, Florence, and Dublin and in New York), they lead exercises in free-form writing and drawing, associative thinking, mapmaking, sense perception, and other techniques that help people access and develop their innate creative nature. During the eight days, you'll spend three and a half hours per day with Berc and Fogel. The rest of the time is free to sit on a beach, nap, or explore the island that many consider to be Greece's finest.

The workshop, including daily creativity sessions and lodging in the gorgeous seaside town of Hania, run from $1,985 to $2,495, depending on the level of accommodation.

HOW TO GET IN TOUCH

Creativity Workshop, 245 E. 40th Street, Suite 25H, New York, NY 10016, 212-922-1555, www.creativityworkshop.com.

PCFE FILM SCHOOL

make films in prague

PRAGUE, CZECH REPUBLIC

Filmmaking is a chance to live many lifetimes.
—Robert Altman, director

17 If you fancy being the next Sofia Coppola, consider a quickie course in filmmaking at PCFE Film School in Prague.

Prague, of course, has been at the forefront of filmmaking for more than a hundred years—think Milos Forman, Jiri Menzel, Jaromir Sofr, Jan Sverak. Even during its 40-year communist hijacking, Prague filmmaking, albeit censored and financially controlled by the state, managed to keep its elbows shoving and pushing. And if you've been to the movies at all in the past few years, you know that Prague played a starring role in such blockbuster hits as *Mission Impossible, The Bourne Identity,* and *The Chronicles of Narnia,* to name just a few.

PCFE offers a yearlong filmmaking program that won it a spot on *Premier* magazine's list of the world's top film schools. The monthlong summer workshops, open to anyone from rank beginner on up, provide the perfect excuse to combine a vacation in one of Europe's most stunning cities with that dormant desire to create your own cinematic masterpiece. You're guaranteed to leave with a finished film (unless, of course, you get too caught up in Prague's rich Bohemian nightlife and miss your early morning editing class).

During your four weeks in Prague, you'll receive hands-on instruction in all the fundamentals of filmmaking, concentrating on the biggies such as screenwriting, directing, editing, and cinematography. You'll have access to state-of-the art equipment, editing suites, sound studios, and top teachers, including Oscar and Cannes award-winning directors and professors from Prague's National Film Academy.

Despite being based near the banks of the fairy-tale Vltava River, the courses are taught in English, so no need to learn the Czech for "Cut!" or "Get that dolly

BARRANDOV FILM STUDIOS

Remember Vaclav Havel, the renowned playwright and author who led the popular opposition during the famous Velvet Revolution and became the first Czech president? His father, also named Vaclav Havel, had started a movie studio that put this Eastern European capital on the filmmakers' map. His Barrandov Studios, founded in the early 1930s, survived the takeover by Nazi Germany, four decades of communism, and the eventual privatization and is now known as the "Hollywood of Eastern Europe." It's one of the largest and oldest studios in all of Europe.

Even under communist rule, the studio, with its 260,000 costumes, hairpieces, and accessories, managed to produce Oscar winners. The gleam of Milos Forman's eight gold-plated Oscars for *Amadeus,* produced at Barrandov five years before the Velvet Revolution, brought the then 50-year-old studio back into the spotlight. That movie was followed by Barbra Streisand's *Yentl, Les Misérables, The League of Extraordinary Gentleman,* Bruce Willis's *Hart's War,* and more than 2,500 Czech and international films.

---

grip over here now!" You will be provided with a local Czech-speaking production assistant to help in sticky situations, as well as a database of professional actors who will gladly appear in your film.

Only 12 students are admitted per summer session. They are split into crews of three or four doing camera, editing, and sound work. The workshop concludes with a screening of your film (along with the films of your classmates) at a local cinema that's open to your admiring public.

Prague, with its cobblestone streets, medieval squares, and lively artistic subculture, provides a naturally photogenic backdrop. And compared to Western capitals, its pubs, cafés, clubs, and coffeehouses are two to three times less costly. While the summer course doesn't come cheap, it's a veritable bargain compared to its counterparts in New York, L.A., or London.

Tuition for the four-week workshop is 2,460 euros ($3,700). Accommodations are not included.

HOW TO GET IN TOUCH
PCFE Film School, Pstrossova 19, Prague 1, 110 00, Czech Republic, 420 25753 4013, www.filmstudies.cz.

explore batik and other traditional balinese arts

UBUD, BALI

Bali taught me how to be gentle again—both to myself and others.
—Jean Ingram, owner of Ubud's Threads of Life

18 Ubud, Bali, is a great hang for creative types. Whether your art is dance, song, writing, painting, sculpture, or something in-between, this little town in the heart of Bali, amid terraced rice paddies and lush mountains, radiates enough creative energy to sustain them all. In fact, even nonartists show up and suddenly find themselves grabbing batik paintbrushes; penning long, sloppy odes to travel; or swaying to gamelan music, Bali's haunting syncopation of gongs, drums, and flutes.

Ubud's reputation as the SoHo of Bali began in the 18th century when Dewa Agung Anom, head of the Sukawati royal household, invited musicians, dancers, puppeteers, and sculptors from all over the island to live and practice their craft in his court. His descendant, Cokorda Gede Agung Sukawati, who came onto the scene in the 20th century, even went so far as to invite foreign artists to share the Ubud palace.

Needless to say, Ubud is a great place to take workshops in the many Balinese arts. Near-daily classes in batik fabric painting, perhaps the most internationally

MONKEY BUSINESS

Running through Ubud is a street called Monkey Forest Road, and that's not just some crazy name. It leads to Ubud's Sacred Monkey Forest, a small nature preserve on the outskirts of town. Besides the hundreds of Balinese long-tailed macaques that get a kick out of swiping sunglasses, hats, bags, and any other items not sturdily attached, the forest has Hindu temples, stone sculptures, walking paths, and a sacred spring complete with swimming koi.

famous of the Balinese arts, are offered in the workshops of such local batik artists as Ketut Sujana and Nyoman Suradnya.

Not only will you learn about the rich history of Javanese batik, but you'll also learn how to stretch the fabric on a frame, make designs with paraffin and beeswax, and apply dye using a canting needle, a paintbrush, stamps, and a variety of other hand tools. By day's end, you'll have created your own handmade piece of batik art.

Balinese batik artists consider the process of creating the wax paintings "meditation in action." They claim that applying wax and dye is a potent method of centering the mind and liberating the heart. Sujana says batik helps "discover in physical form the images we carry in our heart" and, to make the point, Suradnya named his studio "Nirvana."

Threads of Life, a company/studio/art center started by Westerners Jean and William Ingram to preserve and sustain the indigenous textile arts, offers a variety of classes in what they call "textile appreciation" and natural-dye batiks. In their daylong class in indigo dyeing and batik, you'll explore natural indigo dyeing and hand-weaving and learn how raw cotton becomes handspun thread.

In Ubud, you can also take workshops in ceramics, drawing, silversmithing, a cappella singing, cooking, and writing. The Pondok Pekak Library and Learning Center, a comfortable oasis with more than 10,000 books, also offers classes in Balinese dance and music.

With so many amazing art options, it was inevitable that somebody would eventually come along and make the classes easy to access. Enter Meghan Pappenheim, a former New Yorker who married a Balinese furniture designer, opened a yoga studio, and, after the 2002 terrorist bombing on the island, became a one-woman promotion committee for everything holistic and artistic. Known around town as the "Bali Spirit Chick," she started a website that lists Ubud's many art workshops, as well as hotels, island ceremonies and events, healthy restaurants (her Kafe is a great organic option), spas, nonprofits, and nearby tours.

Prices for the Bali workshops start at $35.

HOW TO GET IN TOUCH

Bali Spirit, J1 Hanoman #44B, Padang Tegal, Ubud, Bali, Indonesia, 62 361 970 992, www.balispirit.com.

shoot a tiger
(with a camera, of course)

INDIA

Look at it this way: Even if you don't get a great shot, you've just spent a
day in nature's arms.... Beats the hell out of a day in the office,
doesn't it? Enjoy what the wild gives you.
—Vandit Kalia, founder of Photo Safari India

19 Vandit Kalia, an avid wildlife photographer who
leads photo safaris throughout India, says no
matter how many times he has been privileged to see a tiger,
the excitement never fades. "Mere words are inadequate in
describing the emotions stirred by seeing a tiger in the wild.
No other animal that I can think of arouses the same feelings
of admiration, awe, respect, and excitement," he says, even
though he does occasionally pull himself away from the 450-pound beasts
(100 pounds bigger than lions) to track other Indian wildlife. The best part: He'll
take you to remote places that a jeep driver can't access, and stalk the elusive cats
with every intention of getting a shot you'd be proud to frame

Now *that's* a vacation!

Myriad organizations in myriad countries offer photography vacations.
Here we highlight two on the subcontinent of India, whose brilliant colors,
exotic architecture, and the chance to spot a wild tiger will excite even the
most jaded shutterbug.

In search of tigers. Kalia takes photographers on weeklong tiger treks. He doesn't
guarantee that you'll get a viewfinder on one of Bandhavgarh Park's 35 tigers, but
if anyone can do it, he can.

Patience plays a big part. "I can happily watch a sleeping tiger for hours,"
he says. "Having a passion for wildlife observation makes the hours of waiting a

INDIA'S MENAGERIE

On your tiger hunt, you'll hear this question a lot: *"Dikha?"* It's Bengali for "Did you see one?"

On Kalia's trips, the answer thankfully is often *"Ji,"* yes. But you can also answer ji to the question of whether or not you saw any pandas, gaurs, nilgais, Asiatic elephants, one-horned rhinos, hyenas, bears, black buck, leopards (including snow and cloudy leopards), Tibetan wild asses, bharals (Himalayan blue sheep), barasinghas, monkeys, wild dogs, foxes, or more than 1,200 species of birds.

And if you add on a couple of days at Kalia's Island Vinnie's Dive Center and Beach Cabanas in the Andaman Islands, you can also answer ji to whether or not you saw swimming elephants; Vinnie's (that's Kalia's name in the islands) dogs, Obi-wan and Obi-two; and Dogfood, his cat. Don't ask.

---

reward, rather than a chore."

You also need to be willing to get up at the crack of dawn. Kalia's tours make use of what photographers call the "golden hours"—early morning and late afternoon when the rich sunlight colors add to the photogenic mix.

Another factor is having insider's knowledge. Kalia, for example, knows exactly where the tigers are likely to be in any given month, the best spot to view sunrise over Kanchendzonga, where to see one of the four pairs of India's black-necked cranes, and how to get away from the tourist traps in Rajasthan.

Although Photo Safari India offers group trips (the 15-day "Wildlife Explorer," "Birds and Beasts," "Best of Ladakh," and "Pushkar Camel Fair" are recent offerings, as well as the "Tiger Trails Tour"), Kalia is also happy to custom-design a trip for, say, a single photographer who is looking for a particular orchid or who wants to shoot a one-horned rhino at Kaziranga during the full moon. New destinations are always in the works as well; trips to Chilka Lake (one of India's best places to photograph waterbirds) and some of South India's fabulous national parks, for example, are on the drawing board.

Kalia was a self-described "corporate drone," working as a telecom manager, until in 2000 he reached what he calls "a very early midlife crisis." He was 28. He took a yearlong sabbatical, discovered photography, took up diving, and eventually opened his own dive operation in India's Andaman Islands. He has a thing about finding World War II shipwrecks. But in 2002, his own call of the wild urged him to start leading others on photo safaris through India's forests, mountains, and trails.

In addition to the seven-day tiger trek, Kalia leads photo safaris to the Himalaya (Ladakh and Zanskar), Rajasthan and the Thar Desert, Goa, and, of course, the Andamans for underwater photo safaris. He also gives four-day introductory courses for those just getting started in wildlife photography. Kalia has a full range of camera gear, access to regularly updated laptops loaded with the latest photo-processing software, spare tripods and heads, emergency storage, and everything a photographer could ever need to get Kodak moments from the awe-inspiring, orange-and-black-striped cat.

As Kalia says, "The best photography comes about when you connect emotionally with your subject, and we try to provide that emotional connection."

The "Tiger Trails Safari" runs $1,750 and includes accommodations in upscale hotels and lodges, meals, game viewing, and local transfers.

Photo Safari India, FE 220, Sector 3, Near Tank #12, Kolkata 700106, India, 91 993 208 2204, www.photosafariindia.com.

Expert advice in Rajasthan. Dazzling desert cities, intriguing people, and brilliant colors have long lured award-winning National Geographic photographer Nevada Wier to northern India. In fact, she's currently living there, working on a book about the Ladakh region. Now you can join her on a once-in-a-lifetime photography expedition to Delhi and Rajasthan. Shooting alongside an expert, you'll capture images of frenetic markets, fortresses, and magical palaces with your camera. Highlights of this National Geographic Expedition include the colorful Pushkar Festival, where the fabled bartering of camels is complemented by music, swirling dancers, and religious rituals; and the desert villages of Jamba, home of the Bishnoi tribe, whose brightly clad women and painted adobe stand out vividly against the desert hues. The 13-day trip costs $7,685 per person, double occupancy.

National Geographic Expeditions, 1145 17th Street, N.W., Washington, D.C. 20036, 888-966-8687, www.nationalgeographicexpeditions.com.

paint wild south africa

JEFFREYS BAY, SOUTH AFRICA

My "office" is wherever I decide to set up to paint, and everything under
the sun and moon is fair game.
—Kenn Backhaus, plein air painter

20 If you're a surfer, J-Bay—as Jeffreys Bay, South Africa, is known in the world of riptides and sea curls—is probably on your lust list. You know, that list of wish-I-coulds that dominate those last thoughts before drifting off each night. J-Bay's giant 8- to 12-foot supertubes are widely acknowledged as among the top waves on the planet, and the annual Billabong Pro competition draws surfers from practically every country in the world.

But if you're a painter, especially a painter who likes to set up an easel outside, this town in the Eastern Cape province of South Africa might not have yet made it onto your radar. Big mistake. Not only is the climate in this former hippie town near perfect, but the list of landscape subjects would drop the average plein air fan to his paint-splattered knees. Beaches. Check. Mountains. Check. Forests. Check. Nature and game reserves with lots of exciting wildlife. Check, check, check.

Imagine setting up your easel at the Shamwari Game Reserve, where gnu, gazelles, and white rhinos play. Or along South Africa's wild coastline backed by a spectacular subtropical rain forest. Or on the rare *fynbos* belt that boasts more than 8,500 different plant species, 5,000 of which occur nowhere else. Just painting the king protea, South Africa's national flower, could keep you busy for a lifetime.

To make things even better, there's a peaceful B&B on a hundred-year-old farm only a few minutes outside J-Bay that's run by a Dutch landscape rtist who long ago mastered that all-important kindergarten lesson about sharing. Adelheid Peltenburg, who owns Artist's Paradise Bed and Breakfast, offers unlimited use of her paints, brushes, and studio, a former horse stable that she converted soon after buying the place. She even has a small on-site art supply store. And for those not confident enough in

SOUTH AFRICA'S FIRST ARTISTS ROCK ON

The southwest coast of South Africa was originally inhabited by the nomadic San people. They joined with the Khoi-Khoin tribes and eventually became known as the Khoi-San. These peace-loving people walked the coastline of South Africa, living off the sea and never claiming ownership of any land. They became known as the Strandlopers (Beachwalkers) and were eventually driven farther and farther ashore once Vasco da Gama, the Portuguese explorer, landed and began exploiting the land and the people. Today only small pockets of Khoi-San remain, scattered among the sands and deserts of the arid Skeleton Coast.

But the Khoi-San did leave their mark behind in thousands of cave paintings and etched rock art. There are 15,000 known San rock-art sites in South Africa, perhaps as many as 50,000 in southern Africa. The art was not painted to decorate the walls of a rock shelter, but as part of a powerful ritual to contact the spirit world.

their painting skills to dive right into the region's optimal light and atmosphere, Peltenburg brings in a fellow landscape painting teacher to dispense drawing and painting lessons.

Regular workshops are offered in acrylics, aquarelle, and, of course, plein air in the area's Baviaanskloof (Valley of the Baboons) Wilderness, Langkloof and Gamtoos Valleys, and Seekoei River and Noorsekloof Nature Reserves. Not that you'd need to go very far for captivating subjects. Right on the 120-acre cattle farm, you can find wandering bushbuck, red duikers, Cape grey buck, velvet monkeys, and lynx. Oh, yes, and Domino, Peltenburg's friendly Dalmatian.

The plein air workshops can be arranged for anywhere from one to two weeks, with costs ranging from $620 to $1,400 and including a welcome buffet, a bon voyage party, and reserve entrance fees.

HOW TO GET IN TOUCH

Artist's Paradise, Box 1025, Kabeljous River, Jeffreys Bay, EC 6330, South Africa, 27 42 2932108, www.artists-paradise.co.za.

design your own wardrobe

PRATO, ITALY

Fashion is not just in dresses. It is in the sky, in the street. Fashion has to do with ideas, the way we live, what is happening.
—Coco Chanel, legendary French fashion designer

21 Most of the year, Fashion Art Italy, a small design firm run by Serena Fumanti and her team of gutsy young designers, is busy creating bags for Stella McCartney, fabrics for Giorgio Armani, or ecologically friendly furs for Lanificio Guasti. One year, they even designed the evening gowns for the Miss Italy competition.

But each summer for three weeks, these revolutionaries on the art and fashion scene throw open the doors to their inner sanctum, offering lessons to would-be fashionistas. They willingly give introductions to the history of costume, the Italian fashion system, the latest textile technology, and pattern draping and drafting.

But don't expect to sit through a lot of lectures. Rather, Fumanti and her hip design team have re-created an artisan/apprentice-style approach to learning, similar to that of the Middle Ages when Prato, their ancient walled home, first surged into prominence as a textile hub.

You'll get one-on-one instruction passed down personally, as Fumanti likes to say, "from artisan to apprentice." That way, she says, "we can be far more flexible and adapt our inside knowledge to each student's individual qualities and skills."

"But working this way," she advises, "students do need to apply their own motivation." In the three-week workshop, students will have the chance to develop a portfolio, whet their personal creativity, discover new fashion trends, and learn about traditional Tuscan art methods.

Surrounded by the Val di Bisenzio mountains and the Montalbano hills, Prato, just a 25-minute train ride from Florence, has long been Italy's textile-making capital. Even its old city wall, 49 feet tall and topped with battlements, cinches the city's marble cathedral, baroque churches, and palaces like a belt. Long on innovation, one of Prato's top textile design firms recently came up with what it calls "smart fabric," a unique system of cabling fiber optics straight into the weave.

When you're not focusing on fashion (classes are held each morning), you can partake of Prato's tremendous wealth of art and architectural jewels, from priceless frescoes by Filippo Lippi and Agnolo Gaddi to the Chapel of the Sacro Cingolo. And you'll certainly want to stop by the famous Textile Museum (Museo del Tessuto), where classic Dior gowns are displayed along with contemporary works and ancient religious garments. Opened in 1975 thanks to the generous bequest of more than 600 pieces from noted collector Loriano Bertini, the museum now has more than 6,000 items dating from as early as the fifth century, including machinery and equipment used to process and dye textiles (Via S. Chiara, 24, Prato (PO) Florence 59100, 39 574 611503, www.museodeltessuto.it).

Fashion Art Italy's three-week course runs 1,500 euros (about $2,230) and includes lodging at a local hostel and one field trip. Meals (both lunch and dinner) can be purchased each day at the hostel for 7.50 euros (about $11).

HOW TO GET IN TOUCH

Fashion Art Italy, Via Guizzelmi, 6, Prato (PO) Florence 59100, Italy, 39 340 460 9034, www.fashionart.it.

JUST SAY SLOW

The Slow Food movement, which started in Italy in 1986 when Italian food writer Carlo Petrini organized a demonstration protesting Rome's new McDonald's, thrives in Tuscany. Prato, a typical Tuscan country town, is a huge proponent of "slow food" and its call for the need for superlative cuisine, locally sourced ingredients, the humane rearing of animals, and the preservation of traditional foodstuffs. The need for conviviality and pleasure in the buying and eating of food is also emphasized—all the things being lost in a fast-living, modern industrialized society.

Prato's most renowned traditional food is *biscotti di Prato* or *cantucci*, a cookie first exhibited at the 1867 World Exhibition in Paris. Confectioner Antonio Mattei won an award at the exhibition for these Tuscan cookies made from flour, sugar, eggs, and almonds or pine nuts. Cantucci, now available worldwide, are traditionally served with Vin Santo, in which the rustic biscuits are dipped.

---

master tribal drumming

YOFF, SENEGAL

The world without griot would be as dull as rice without sauce.
—Senegali proverb

22 Pape Mbaye, your teacher for this infectious African drumming workshop in the seaside village of Yoff, Senegal, is what the Senegalese call a "griot." That means he's the village storyteller, the guardian of Senegal's oral and music traditions, a lineage that traces its roots back 800 years. For two and a half decades, Mbaye was not only the keeper of the history, the legends, and the music for this fishing village 20 minutes or so from Dakar but also its head drummer.

Not that anybody can *keep* the music. It flows out of African tradition like water from an American faucet. It's pure, it's sweet, and it's always there.

Mbaye, who has drummed alongside B. B. King, Miles Davis, and even Ringo Starr, moved to Sydney, Australia, in 1999. He returns to his native Senegal every summer to lead two- and four-week drumming and dancing workshops that are as much about Senegalese culture as they are about learning an instrument.

Along with his large extended family, who serve as co-teachers, guides, cooks, and playmates, Mbaye gives lessons in *tama* (talking drums), *djembe* (a common West African drum), and *sabar* (a smaller drum unique to Senegal). In addition to teaching you how to play each of these drums, Mbaye will show you how to make them out of gourds, goatskin, and logs of teak and other indigenous woods. You'll also get the chance to play the kora (an African harp) and *balafon* (a wooden xylophone).

You'll stay in Le Toucan, an eight-bedroom, four-story, one-star hotel that's clean, secure, and only a short walk from the beach. You'll feast on such Senegalese dishes as *tieboudienne,* a light fish stew with rice, chicken *au yassa, maffe,* and boiled peanuts. You'll be a full participant in village life, invited to village weddings, tea ceremonies (see sidebar p. 64), and perhaps a *ndeup,* an exotic healing ritual (normally not open to Westerners) where sabars are used to excite, heckle, praise, and exorcise demons.

Your weekday curriculum includes two hours of drumming, an hour of singing, and two hours of dancing, taught open-air on the hotel rooftop. There

SLOW TEA

Most people associate elaborate tea ceremonies with Japan. But in Senegal, tea is prepared and presented in a ceremony, known by the Wolof word *attaya* or *ataaya*, that can easily take all afternoon. The green tea, usually "gunpowder tea," so called because it's rolled into hard pellets, is brewed with mint on charcoal braziers and then poured, holding the teapot at least 12 inches above the table, into small shot glasses. Each serving, usually comprising three rounds but sometimes up to seven, comes in slow succession, getting sweeter and sweeter with each go-round. The first round is strong and bitter, like death; the second gentle, like life; and the third sweet, like love.

will also be lots of free time to visit the beach or participate in village activities.

There's an after-hours curriculum, as well: pilgrimages to the clubs of Dakar, many of which don't get under way until after midnight, headlined by such Senegalese stars as Youssou N'Dour, Baaba Maal, and Toure Kunda, whose *mbalax*, an infectious fusion of tama, sabar, and electric guitar, is famous from West Africa to Paris.

On weekends, Mbaye and his family and friends will show you the sights, proving there's never a reason to be alone in Senegal. Some of the things your new high-spirited friends might show you are Lac Rose, an all-pink salt lake; Île de Gorée, an island with historical ties to the old slave trade; Soumbedienne, the fishermen's pier; and, of course, vibrant Dakar, with its open-air markets, cafés, and art galleries.

The people of Senegal take great pride in what they call *teranga* (hospitality), and you'll quickly learn that *"Nanga def?"* means "How are you?" because you'll hear that Wolof (the local language) greeting dozens of times a day. And even though you're probably light-years behind even the youngest drummers who pound out rhythms on old butter and ice-cream tubs, you and your budding music will be treated with great respect and acceptance. As Mbaye likes to say, "If you are even a little OK, that's great, because you're not African." The goal for each student perhaps is to become "just a little bit African."

The four-week workshop offered each July is priced at $1,400, or you can opt for two weeks at $900. Both include lodging and all meals, drum lessons, dance lessons, lessons in drum repair and tuning, participation in village activities, and a detailed booklet with basic words and phrases in Wolof.

HOW TO GET IN TOUCH

Drum Africa, 37 Wells Street, Newtown, NSW, 2042, Australia, 221 411 718 050, www.drummingafrica.com.

fiddle with a scottish legend

ISLE OF SKYE, SCOTLAND

Hale be your heart
Hale be your fiddle
Lang may your elbuck junk and diddle
—Robert Burns, Scotland's national poet

23 If you saw the movie *Titanic* (and who didn't?), you've heard Alasdair Fraser. The famous Scottish fiddler's solo on the movie soundtrack is just one of many venues in which you could have caught his dizzying tunes over the past few years. He has also played for *Braveheart, Last of the Mohicans,* National Public Radio, and *CBS Sunday Morning,* and in 1999, when the Kennedy Center honored Sean Connery, this fellow Scot performed a moving solo tribute.

Every year, this fiddle maestro offers anyone interested in traditional Scottish music the chance to learn and play along. Since 1983, Fraser has offered a weeklong fiddle camp, the Valley of the Moon Scottish Fiddling School, at rustic Camp Campbell in the Santa Cruz Mountains in California. Here participants of all ages can not only choose between a list of daily fiddle workshops but also learn Scottish dance, piano, guitar, cello, and percussion. The camp concludes Saturday night with a big concert at the Santa Cruz Civic Center.

Three years after Fraser started Valley of the Moon, he began sharing Scottish fiddling skills at Sabhal Mòr Ostaig, a Gaelic college on the Isle of Skye in Scotland. This weeklong course, which Fraser offers each August—when Sleat, where the college is located, is particularly inviting—is geared for fiddlers who already have a rudimentary foundation in Scottish fiddling.

Scottish fiddling (which is quite different from other forms of Celtic fiddling, thank you very much) has had a renaissance in the past couple decades, partly due to Scotland finally getting its own parliament and partly due to Fraser himself, a petroleum engineer until he began "following the fiddle," as he describes it. Fraser had nine CDs out at last count, from intimate solo albums to energetic Celtic fusion with his band Skyedance.

For three centuries Scotland was occupied by England, and as people under domination tend to do, the Scots often disavowed their own culture. Many of their songs had been spirited away to Nova Scotia to protect them from roving Presbyterian preachers who hunted down sheet music and stray fiddles to kindle their fires.

"By asking questions," he says, "I gradually became aware of this incredible…what I call a 'dark blanket' that was lying over the country. And with my music, I did my little bit to pierce some holes in the blanket and let some light in. The thing about these tunes is they are very resilient. They can reinvent themselves and stay appropriate, you know. They can make people dance when they weren't expecting to and also be there for you when you're trying to express some kind of solace."

Traditional Scottish music is typically learned by ear, so don't expect lots of handouts. What you can expect is lessons

ISLE OF SKYE

Before 1995, the only way to get to the Isle of Skye, the second largest Scottish island, was by ferry. Fiercely independent locals liked it that way. It allowed them to maintain their culture, get away with speaking Gaelic, and not be swayed by the homogenization of the rest of the world. Or for that matter, the rest of Scotland.

After the Skye Bridge was opened, linking Skye and its tiny villages, jagged Cuillin ridge, and one-lane roads to the rest of Scotland, locals organized a boycott. They were vehemently opposed to the excessive tolls (£5.70 each way) and they made sure everybody knew it. Finally, after nearly ten years of pressure, the locals won. The Scottish government bought the bridge and removed the tolls.

Today, tourists flock to the misty island for its dramatic scenery, hiking, castles, and, of course, ancient traditions. On the shores of Loch na Dal, near Sabhal Mòr Ostaig, is a circa-1680 manor house run by Lady Claire Macdonald, wife of Godfrey Macdonald, high chief of Clan Donald. As the author of 17 cookbooks and the host of a British cooking show, Lady Macdonald offers cooking classes at the classy ten-room Kinloch Lodge for £435 to £585 ($870–$1,170) per person. *Kinloch Lodge, Sleat, Isle of Skye, IV43 8QY T, Scotland, 44 1471 833 333, www.claire-macdonald.com.*

on bowing, Scottish ornament and rhythmic drive, collaboration with lots of other musicians, informal nightly playing sessions, and a great history lesson on the rich, lyrical heart of Scottish music. Each workshop also includes a ceilidh (pronounced KAY-lee), a traditional Celtic party with dancing, lots of lively cheerful music, and the same energy that caused *Titanic's* Rose to fall in love with Jack.

The Isle of Skye workshop runs £190 ($380), with accommodations available at the college for £174 ($350). Meals are extra. The annual seven-day Valley of the Moon camp (also usually held in August) in California includes lodging, food, and all instruction for $775.

HOW TO GET IN TOUCH

Sabhal Mòr Ostaig, Sleat, Isle of Skye, IV44 8RQ, Scotland, 44 1471 888 000, www.smo.uhi.ac.uk/en/cursaichean/cg/cursaichean.php, or **Valley of the Moon Scottish Fiddling School,** 1281 Fifth Avenue, San Francisco, CA 94122, 415-566-4355, www.valleyofthemoon.org.

CHAPTER

2

volunteer vacations

*We are all visitors on this planet. During this period we must try
to do something good, something useful with our lives.*
—Dalai Lama

Who, when you really think about it, longs to do unimportant and uninteresting things? Yet look how we spend our time. Look at the headlines in the magazines we read. Look at the TV shows we're addicted to.

Despite what Madison Avenue tells you, you don't really care which perfume you're wearing or whether or not you have a Texas-size house. You care about what happens to the world's children. To the rain forests and the coral reefs. To the big, beautiful dream of freedom, equality, and justice for all. You care about your soul, about God, and about making the world a more beautiful place.

That's what this chapter is all about: the big, beautiful dream. The dream we all have, to know ourselves, to understand the world, and to contribute to the greater good.

If we stay in the restrictive ruts we're in now, we will never solve the world's problems. And there are lots of problems that need solving, a lot of big things that need doing. We can no longer sit back, flip through channels with our remotes, and say, "Tut, tut! What a shame!" We must act. We must grow out of our wimpy, apathetic lives and take action—any kind of action.

As long as there is prejudice, environmental destruction, people in need, there is something to do. We don't have the right or the luxury to be small. The answer to your problems and the world's problems are one and the same. And that answer is you. Us. Now.

maintain trails on kilimanjaro

MOUNT KILIMANJARO, TANZANIA

Like the rest of Africa, Tanzania is a developing country.
Those who require uninterrupted electricity, daily hot showers,...and
wireless Internet access may find a weekend at home with the
Discovery Channel more to their liking.
—Diane Carman, climber of Kilimanjaro with
Adventures within Reach

24 Anybody who has ever climbed Mount Kilimanjaro knows at least one Swahili word: *pole.* It means "go slowly." Guides repeat it over and over again, hoping to convince climbers of the importance of taking their time, letting their bodies acclimate as they make their way up the dormant volcano that dominates the plains of northeastern Tanzania.

Because it requires no specialized training, ropes, or ice picks to get to the top, this mountain that Ernest Hemingway described as "wide as all the world, great, high, and unbelievably white in the sun" is known as Everyman's Everest. Anybody in moderately decent shape can scale it. But that's not to say it's risk free. Every year, a hiker or two dies from acute mountain sickness caused by lack of oxygen. Others go temporarily blind or loco, not even remembering that they beat the 19,341-foot monster.

Done right, the Machame Route, one of six paths to the summit of Africa's highest mountain, takes six days. On Adventures within Reach's volunteer vacation to Tanzania, you'll definitely "pole-pole," because you'll be taking eight days on the climb, while helping the Mount Kilimanjaro Porter's Society clean up the trails.

Robin Paschall, owner of Adventures within Reach, will never forget her first summiting of the snowcapped giant. "Here we were at 16,000 feet and there was all this trash," she says. "We gathered it up and tried to burn it, but it was moist, and there wasn't enough oxygen. We did what we could, but we knew that another strong wind would soon come along and the trash would be right back where it started."

So now the trekking and safari company from Boulder, Colorado (they also offer what they call "dream adventures" to the Himalaya, Peru, and the Galápagos Islands) organizes volunteers to maintain the trails.

On this yearly volunteer vacation, which also includes seven days helping out at the Shalom Orphanage in Karatu, you will, of course, have the chance to summit the famous white-topped mountain (although some on this volunteer vacation opt not to take the full-moon, midnight journey to the top), and you will also go on safari. But most of your time will be spent bettering the lives and the environment of the Tanzanian people.

Paschall inadvertently discovered the Shalom Orphanage, an out-of-the-way home and school in desperate need of funding, while on safari herself. "All these darling kids came out and waved," she says. "It's one thing knowing foreign tourism dollars provide jobs, but we believe travelers and especially tour operators have an additional responsibility to address the overwhelming needs of the countries we visit." Shalom, located in the village of Karatu between Lake Manyara and the Ngorongoro Conservation Area, has 33 kids between the ages of 1 and 8.

"Invariably, our travelers would come back from their trips and want to send things over to help out the porters or help the kids at the orphanage. As much

THE GREATER GOODS

Adventures within Reach also offers a volunteer trip to poor, remote villages in Nepal. Working with the Butterfly Project, this Free-a-Child volunteer vacation aims to prevent sex trafficking. Every year, up to 10,000 Nepalese children between the ages of 8 and 16 are tricked, bought, or kidnapped to work in the brothels of India.

Because these kids live in dire poverty and have little or no education, Free-a-Child works not only to inform families in highly trafficked areas about the problem but also to provide training in such income-producing businesses as goat and buffalo farming, ginger and mushroom cultivation, tailoring, and paper crafts. This 13-day trip, including cultural tours in Kathmandu and a visit to the Chitwan Jungle Lodge, is priced at $2,840.

as we'd encourage them to gather things before they go and take it with them, we found that it wasn't until they were actually there that they became so deeply affected," Paschall said.

First, her company started a nonprofit organization (Charities within Reach) to collectively gather hiking gear, school supplies, and other essentials that her deeply moved clients wanted to send. Now, with the nearly monthlong volunteer vacation annually, the company takes it a step further, allowing hikers to physically help out as well.

The cost for the 24-day volunteer vacation is $3,525 per person and includes meals, accommodations, the safari, and the opportunity to climb Mount Kilimanjaro.

Adventures within Reach also offers trips to Bhutan, Tibet, Nepal (see sidebar p. 71), Peru, and the Galápagos.

HOW TO GET IN TOUCH

Adventures within Reach, 2527 Broadway Street, Boulder, CO 80304, 877-232-5836 or 303-325-3746, www.adventureswithinreach.com.

assist scientists in monitoring wild przewalski horses

HUSTAI NATIONAL PARK, MONGOLIA

I have been infected with the most severe form of "Mongolia homesickness."
Often I see myself sitting on a rock in the warm sun observing
Bohemian or Paritet and their harems.
—British volunteer on Ecovolunteer's Przewalski Reintroduction Project

25 Finding anything still wild and free in this overdeveloped, overpopulated world is no small task. But deep in the Mongolian steppes, harems of wild Przewalski horses still roam freely, unbridled, unsaddled, and untamed.

Volunteers who want to help protect the biological diversity of the Mongolian steppe ecosystem and ensure that the proud, fierce Mongolian horses continue to survive in the wild can join a team of Dutch researchers who have been monitoring the horses since 1992, the year they were reintroduced into their native habitat.

Just like Genghis Khan, volunteers on this exciting field-study sleep in a traditional Mongolian yurt, ride horseback through remote primitive Mongolian deserts, and enjoy a unique nomadic lifestyle isolated from the modern world.

Suffice it to say, you won't be riding in a line of horses or have a wrangler riding in front to tighten your reins and tell you where to go. In fact, after a two-day orientation, you're basically on your own. You'll follow an assigned harem of horses for about four or five hours each day, collecting information about their location and behavior, and then you'll return to camp each afternoon to enter findings into a specially designed computer software program.

Thanks to this volunteer program, the horses, long the national symbol of Mongolia, have been able to make an amazing comeback. The *takhi* (the Mongolian name for Przewalski horses) became extinct in the wild in 1969. Luckily, zoologists and horse collectors, who for years had been intrigued by the sturdy horses' sandy coats, striped backs, and zebra-marked legs, had amassed enough Przewalskis in captivity to provide breeding stock and genetic diversity.

More than a dozen harems of horses are now roaming Hustai National Park, located about 60 miles southwest of Ulan Bator, Mongolia's modern capital city. Like in the old days, they're able to withstand the harsh Hustai winters, protect their young from the large population of wolves, and survive much as they had for centuries. And because the sacred Hustai Mountains, one of the last remaining steppe ecosystems in the world, has gained national park status, its 123,557 acres of undisturbed forests and grasslands are off-limits to development and cattle grazing.

Besides monitoring the horses, volunteers observe newborn foals, participate in bird- and other wildlife counts, and educate locals on the importance of preserving the national park and the horses. Volunteers with a gift for photography are encouraged to submit photos for an upcoming book on the flora and fauna of the region.

IF YOU GO

Although volunteer positions in Hustai are available year-round, most volunteers choose the spring, summer, and fall months, because winters in the Mongolian steppes are bitterly cold and inhospitable. Perhaps the very best time to visit is July, when herdsmen come from miles around to participate in the three-day Naadam Festival, an ancient and colorful competition of horse racing, archery, and wrestling—once called the "three manly games." The Naadam Festival started as a religious event but has evolved into a celebration of Mongolian statehood.

The horse race, with thousands of horses competing, takes place not on a track, but over high-altitude Mongolian grasslands. The race is a long-distance one, kicked off with a special song ("Giin-Goo") that all the horses know. The jockeys are children, ages 7 to 12, who wear colorful costumes. The top five winners are celebrated in poetry and song.

The wrestling events are much like sumo, and the archery competitions are waged with bows made from bark and wild mountain goat horn and with arrows decorated with vulture feathers.

Volunteers will take field trips to Ulan Bator; visit a Buddhist monastery; stay a night or two with local nomad families; and camp in the Moilt Valley, where the area's wolves are often spotted. Although volunteers should be comfortable in the saddle and be able to ride up to two or three hours a day, much of the data collecting is done on foot. You should be fit enough for hikes and long walks across remote Mongolian grasslands.

The program takes eight volunteers at a time. Ecovolunteer's Przewalski reintroduction program costs 59 euros ($85) a day, including meals, training, horses, and accommodations in a yurt (the Mongolians call them *gers);* there's a discount of 7 euros ($10) a day for volunteers staying longer than three weeks.

Ecovolunteers also offers many other wildlife and conservation projects ranging from monitoring beavers in Poland to jaguars in Brazil to giant otters in Bolivia.

HOW TO GET IN TOUCH
Ecovolunteer, Meijersweg 29, 7553 AX Hengelo, The Netherlands, 31 74 250 8250, www.ecovolunteer.org.

restore ancient mediterranean villages

PROVENCE, FRANCE

If middle-aged guys can go to baseball camp and pretend to be a member of the Yankees for seven days, I don't see why it's crazy to go spend a week building rock walls.
—Sam Williams, volunteer with La Sabranenque

26 A shopkeeper in St. Victor la Coste, a tiny medieval town in southern France, made the comment that tourists come "to take pleasure and form few attachments." La Sabranenquers, on the other hand, come to *give* to the village, and in so doing, form deep, lasting attachments with the villagers, the history, and the food, wine, and spirit of Provence.

La Sabranenque is a French nonprofit that, with the help of volunteers from around the globe, restores medieval and Roman-era villages, castles, stone paths, and walls throughout Provence (and northern Italy as well). St. Victor was La Sabranenque's first project, back in 1969, for which it won many awards for its impeccable restoration work; the organization is now headquartered in St. Victor, and this is also where volunteers live in quaint stone cottages that were previously restored by volunteers.

Using locally gathered materials, simple hand tools, and homemade mortar, the enthusiastic La Sabranenque staff, mostly architects and stone masons, train volunteers in environmentally friendly building techniques. You'll learn the same building techniques that have been used for thousands of years. You'll work with experienced stone masons who talk about "feeling the pulse of the stone" and "making walls smile." You'll restore arches, vaults, and winding paths leading to ancient wine caves where special bottles of the region's famous Côtes du Rhône are stored.

As romantic as it sounds, volunteers should have no illusions about it. The work can be backbreaking. You'll haul rocks, cut stones, mix mortar, and carry heavy buckets of water. You'll quickly learn the French word *putain,* a curse word that comes in handy when a big rock accidentally slips and lands on your toe.

But just think: It's an amazing way to get a physical workout beyond the gym. And consider the fringe benefits. French wine. French food. And lots of it.

Volunteers work roughly four hours a day, stopping in time to enjoy a sumptuous French lunch on a cobblestone terrace in the shade of cypress and fruit trees. Afternoons are free to nap, tour the French countryside, or take short train rides to such nearby villages as Nîmes or Arles, van Gogh's former stomping grounds (see sidebar this page).

Meals are home cooked and shared family style. Volunteers take turns in the kitchen, gathering eggs from local chickens, and picking apricots and figs from local trees. You'll learn how to recognize and select herbs, make artwork out of radishes, and appreciate the virtues of fresh organic food.

Two-week volunteer trips, including accommodations, three meals a day, and transportation from the Avignon train station, run $710. A one-week trip in the spring or fall costs $565.

HOW TO GET IN TOUCH

La Sabranenque, rue de la Tour de l'Oume, 30290 St.-Victor la Coste, France, 33 466 500 505, www.sabranenque.com.

DIGGING DEEP

Maybe you can't travel back in time, but you can take some time to get to know the past—on an archaeological dig. Archaeological sites around the world are always looking for assistance—and what better way to get to know about the history and culture of a place than volunteering to dig in its dirt!

Here's a sampling of the myriad possibilities:

- **Uncover the colonial Caribbean past.** With the turquoise sea, black sand, and shining sun as your backdrop, help excavate the site of a Free Black Village on St. Eustatius, one of the Netherlands Antilles' historic isles. The cost for one week is $490. *Archaeology Institute of America, c/o Boston University, 656 Beacon Street, 6th Floor, Boston, MA 02215, 617-353-6550, www. archaeological.org.*

- **Learn about Roman life (and death).** Help unearth a cluster of Roman tombs on the outskirts of the ancient city of Sanisera on the island of Menorca, Spain. The volunteer assignment involves seven hours of work a day, comprising both field and lab work. Minimum length of stay is 20 days, and the cost ranges from $1,800 to $2,300, which includes tuition, accommodation, meals, and excursions. *Ecomuseum of the Cape of Cavalleria, APDO 68, Es Mercadal, 07740, Menorca, Spain, 34 971-35-9999, www.ecomuseodecavalleria.com.*

- **Preserve Western history.** Assist Park Service archaeologists in stabilizing the adobe buildings of Kentucky Camp in Arizona, the headquarters of a 20th-century mining operation. Volunteers, who must commit to at least a month, also greet the public, answer questions, and act as general caretakers. There is no fee. *Passport in Time, P.O. Box 15728, Rio Rancho, NM 87174, 800-281-9176 or 505-896-0734, www.passportintime.com.*

- **Dig up ancient Israel.** Using trowels, dental picks, and large sifters, search through the remains of the ancient Israeli town of Zeitah, perched at the crossroads of four major ancient roadways. The fee for a five-week session is $1,450. *The Zeitah Excavations, Pittsburgh Theological Seminary, 616 N. Highland Avenue, Pittsburgh, PA 15206, www.zeitah.net.*

- **Dive amid World War II history.** Micronesia's Truk Lagoon served as a Japanese naval base during World War II. Which is why, beginning in 1944, the Americans bombarded the area, sinking more than 50 ships. Now you can scuba dive among the wrecks, observing and recording information on the lagoon's archaeology. You must be scuba-certified. The 13-day vacation costs $2,646. *Earthwatch Institute, 3 Clock Tower Place, Suite 100, Box 75, Maynard, MA 01754, 800-776-0188 or 978-461-0081, www.earthwatch.org.*

be an olympic hero

BEIJING, VANCOUVER, LONDON, OR SOCHI

The volunteer spirit continues to occupy an important place in our work to build a better, fairer, and safer world.
—Kofi Annan, former secretary-general of the United Nations

27 Okay, let's get the bad news over with first. If you want to volunteer at the Olympics, you have to fill out an application, send in a resume, and interview just like would for any paying job. Oh, and other than a free lunch during your shift, you're responsible for feeding yourself, finding a place to stay, and talking the boss who *does* pay you into letting you off the average 27 days volunteers spend in their unpaid positions.

The good news is every Olympics from Beijing in 2008 to Sochi, Russia, in 2014 needs lots and lots of volunteers to do everything from driving athletes around to picking up trash to testing for illegal steroid use. The Beijing Olympic Committee, which cut off its application process in March 2008, "hired" an astounding 100,000 volunteers for both the regular Summer Games and the Paralympic Games that followed soon after. Most, of course, were from China, but volunteers from every continent chipped in.

In general, to volunteer, you have to be at least 18 years old (19 for Vancouver), and it helps if you're fluent in more than one language. The application also leaves lots of space for listing previous volunteer service; in fact, for Vancouver's Games, which officially began taking applications in early 2008, potential candidates are strongly encouraged to put in pregame volunteer hours. One way to do it is through 2010 Legacies Now, a nonprofit organization that has been traveling around to different B.C. communities to drum up interest in, among other things, volunteering.

Which brings up a good point. Olympic Games take massive amounts of preplanning, so volunteers need to get their ducks in a row early. Volunteer recruitment begins two years before the games are held. London, which will

THE BARE NAKED TRUTH

If you believe the legend, the first Olympic Games were started by Hercules, son of the Greek god Zeus. The first *recorded* Olympic Games took place in 776 B.C., when Coroebus, a cook from Elis, won the 210-yard dash, the sole event that year, in his birthday suit.

These and other fascinating facts can be learned at the Olympic Museum in Lausanne, Switzerland. Like the modern Olympics, reinstated in Athens in 1896, the museum was proposed by a French aristocrat named Pierre de Coubertin. He restarted the Olympics because he believed that the Germans overran France in the 1870 Franco-Prussian War not because of their superior firepower but because the French were out of shape.

It took his idea of an Olympics museum a little longer to take off. But in June 1993, almost a century after the International Olympic Committee was founded in 1894, the Olympic Museum opened on the shores of Lake Geneva. *Olympic Museum, Quai d'Ouchy 1, CH-1001 Lausanne, Switzerland, 41 21 621 6511.*

post application forms in 2010, has already started a list for interested parties.

If you get chosen, you'll be trained not only in the venue for which you've been selected (ice resurfacing or timekeeping, for example) but also in Olympics history, the history of the country and culture where you're working, emergency rescue, and even service for the disabled.

In fact, forget those gold-medal-winning gymnasts and 100-meter-dash track stars. Turns out, the hundreds of thousands of volunteers who have made the Olympics run smoothly since 1896 are the real heroes.

HOW TO GET IN TOUCH

- **Vancouver (2010).** The Winter Olympics expect to use 25,000 volunteers. Applications, which went online in early 2008, can be found at www.vancouver 2010.com.
- **London (2012).** Until the Vancouver Games finish, you're a bit early to be one of the 70,000 volunteers London plans to use for its Summer Games. But you can sign up to be on a potential volunteers list at www.london2012.com/get-involved/volunteering/the-volunteer-programme.php.
- **Sochi (2014).** Stay tuned.

show the muslim world the good side of america

RABAT, MOROCCO

We've never experienced a foreign place on such an intimate level. Most
people never see the real country. They arrive, get on an air-conditioned
bus, they go to an air-conditioned resort. Not us. We sweat like locals,
eat like locals, and—the big goal—try to do something meaningful.
—Ken Budd, volunteer with Cross-Cultural Solutions

28 Chelsea O'Shea always considered herself a world traveler. She'd
Eurailed through most of Europe, studied mass communications in
Australia, and sipped rum punches on practically every island in the Caribbean.
But when she visited Rabat, Morocco, she realized how little she'd really strayed
from her Westernized comfort zone.

"Sure, it's exotic to snap my own photos of the Eiffel Tower and to eat
meat pies at an Australian rules football game, but when it comes right down
to it, Europeans and Australians dress—with a few minor exceptions—the
same as I do, practice the same basic religious and social customs, and use,
if not always the same language, at least the same alphabet," she said after a
trip to Morocco. "In Morocco, people dress in long, white robes, marry as
many wives as they can afford, and use an alphabet that makes as much sense
to me as a Rorschach ink blot."

Which is why northern Africa is a great place to volunteer. Ask any international
volunteer why they do it, and the answer is always something about being exposed
to a new lens on the world, being able to get under the skin of a country, coming
to realize that the insistent, media-driven ideology of the Western world can blind
you if you're not careful.

Cross-Cultural Solutions (CCS), a nonprofit based in New Rochelle, New York,
added Rabat to its list of volunteer opportunities in 2007. Like all CCS placements,
volunteers to Morocco's capital, a small coastal city with beautiful palaces, winding

OPEN SESAME

At first glance, Rabat is anything but regal. In fact, its crumbling gray walls and crowded streets could be called "downright ugly" by tourists unlucky enough to stumble around for days without befriending a local. Locals are quick to point out that Rabat, one of Morocco's four imperial cities, has adopted one of Islam's most important tenets: Outside beauty is unimportant; it's what's inside that counts.

What's inside Rabat is intriguing, mystical, and indeed beautiful. Inside the medina, an intriguing tangle of tiny souks, twisting streets, and craftsmen's shops, you'll see donkeys carrying anything from leather hides to pottery to giant color TVs. You'll soon learn that "*Balek, balek*" means "Make way." These donkeys stay in a special stable, jokingly referred to as a "four-plop hotel."

Each street in Rabat has a fountain, a mosque, and a bakery. Because few of the homes have ovens, each family prepares its bread dough, stamps it with the family symbol, and delivers it to the baker, who bakes it and returns it the same day.

---

streets, and fascinating souks, can choose from a variety of assignments. They can teach English skills or sports, empower women, inspire kids, or provide care for people with disabilities.

During your volunteer stay in Morocco, you'll live in the CCS home—a large house with a garden, fruit trees, and bedrooms opening onto terraces—and eat meals prepared by a local cook. You'll meet each night with other volunteers to share experiences such as Moroccan cooking classes, Arabic lessons, and visits to museums, ruins, and community shelters known as *boutainvilles*.

CCS Morocco, like all CCS projects, has a local staff, an interesting collection of folks who will make your time in Rabat especially meaningful. There's Khadija Channouf, the house manager who also happens to be an accomplished henna tattoo artist; Abdellah Ouhmouch, the program coordinator, who served as official translator on many American movies (*Spy Game* and *Rules of Engagement*, to name a few you might have heard of); Loubna Quirrou, the accountant who also teaches belly dancing; and security guard Hamid Jendane, who once played for the Moroccan national basketball team.

Cross-Cultural Solutions was started in 1995 by Steve Rosenthal, a former AT&T engineer who was so moved by a week he spent helping a Peace Corps volunteer build a medical clinic in Kenya that he couldn't get it off his mind when he returned to America. He longed to offer that same profound experience to others.

Indeed he has. Since its start in India working with children, CCS has sent more than 15,000 people on missions to better the planet. It has programs in 12 countries (including Brazil, China, Costa Rica, Ghana, Guatemala, India, Morocco, Peru, Russia, South Africa, Tanzania, and Thailand), ranging from two weeks to however long you want to stay. Three weeks in Morocco (one of several CCS placements that requires a three-week commitment), including accommodations, meals, and in-country transportation, is $2,885.

HOW TO GET IN TOUCH

Cross-Cultural Solutions, 2 Clinton Place, New Rochelle, NY 10801, 800-380-4777 or 914-632-0022, www.crossculturalsolutions.org.

babysit chimps

*Staring into the eyes of a chimpanzee, I saw a thinking,
reasoning personality looking back.*
—Jane Goodall, world's foremost authority on chimpanzees

29 If you think Tony Soprano had a dysfunctional family, wait until you hear about the chimpanzees at the Mona Foundation. There's Bongo, whose nervous condition prompted him to spend his early days at Mona rocking back and forth; Pancho, who is so obsessed by food that he uses both hands to stuff in as much as he possibly can; and Sara, who spent three years in a nasty custody battle.

But unlike the Sopranos, who brought their problems on themselves, the 11 chimps at Mona faced problems beyond their control. Captured from their *non*dysfunctional homes in West Africa by poachers, they were illegally traded to Spain, chained in uncomfortable, cramped cages, and forced to ride motorcycles, wear matador costumes, and perform other unnatural acts that their brothers back in Africa wouldn't dream of doing. In fact, one wonders, could Pancho's appearance in a McDonald's commercial (he was cast as an ambulance driver) have anything to do with his eating disorder?

Thanks to the Mona Foundation, an animal sanctuary outside Girona, Spain, the once troubled chimps are finally gaining sanity and living happy lives. At Mona,

WHILE YOU'RE THERE

Volunteers are usually given Saturdays off, which is the perfect time to explore Girona, an ancient, walled city near the French border. Although it predates the Roman occupation of Spain, Girona today has chic shops, outdoor cafés, and the brilliant nightlife you might expect in a university town. The Onyar River separates the modern city from the old quarter with its narrow lanes, wrought-iron balconies, medieval cathedrals, Moorish baths, and ancient ruins. And don't forget to explore the rest of the Costa Brava coast, dotted with small coves and natural beaches surrounded by mountains.

the rescued apes share a 17,000-square-foot natural enclosure with tall grass, a pond, ropes, and wooden structures on which to climb.

Although the foundation was legally recognized as a Spanish charity in 2001, its roots go back to 1984, when Simon and Peggy Templer, an English couple living in Breda in northeast Spain, established a small sanctuary to house chimps recovered from Spanish beach photographers. During the 1970s and '80s, it seems that wily photographers made a killing charging tourists to have their photos taken with their "pet chimpanzees."

Olga Feliu, a vet working in the area, often helped the Templers with medical care. By 1996, when the retired couple became too old to care for the chimps, Feliu was hopelessly hooked on primates and decided to continue the important work of returning chimps to as natural an environment as possible. Now serving as the foundation's director, Feliu started with seven chimpanzees that were rescued from a Valencia circus trainer who unmercifully kept them in tiny cages in the back of a truck.

In addition to rescuing apes and ending their exploitation, the Mona Foundation is dedicated to primate research (studies are being conducted on applied ethology, animal welfare, primatology, and human evolution) and public education—which is where you come in.

Volunteers are invited in for a long weekend, Thursday through Sunday, to help with everything from cleaning the chimps' sleeping quarters to preparing their meals to recording the data being studied by several teams of biologists, anthropologists, and archaeologists.

Although you'll spend lots of time observing your primate cousins, Feliu is very clear about one thing: Mona's goal is to allow the chimps to live like they did in the wild, with little or no human interaction. In other words, you won't get the chance to rock any baby chimps to sleep. What you will do is tromp around in the mud (so wear old clothes and bring boots), create enrichment devices for the chimp group to try out, and compile records from the center's observation huts and towers.

The sanctuary takes two weekend volunteers at a time. The volunteer weekend costs £370–£415 ($740–$830), depending on whether you choose to stay at the youth hostel in Girona, where you'll share a room with from 6 to 12 occupants, or the Hostal Bellmirall, where you'll get a private room filled with antiques in a home next to the cathedral. The fee includes training, four nights' accommodations, daily transfers to and from the sanctuary, and three days of lunches, usually taken outside in the sun while watching the chimps. The foundation also offers six-month volunteer positions with on-site accommodations and increased responsibilities.

HOW TO GET IN TOUCH

Fundación Mona, Centro de Recuperación de Primates, Ctra Cassá 1 km, s/n, Riudellots de la Selva, 17457 Girona, Spain, 34 972 477 618, www.fundacionmona.org, or **Mona Foundation,** P.O. Box 372, Cambridge, CB4 1ZS, England, 44 1223 210 952, e-mail: ldocherty@mona-uk.org.

AMBASSADORS FOR CHILDREN
sing to aids orphans in malawi

MALAWI

If you can't feed 100 people, then just feed one.
—Mother Teresa

30 You may not have Madonna's voice, money, or nanny to take in a Malawian orphan, but thanks to Ambassadors for Children (AFC), an Indianapolis-based nonprofit that arranges volunteer trips to this landlocked, Pennsylvania-size country just east of Zambia, you can still help.

Malawi, one of the poorest countries in the world, has nearly two million AIDS orphans, many of whom are being raised in poor, rural villages by a slightly older sibling or a grandparent. The lucky ones live in mud-and-thatch huts, have shoes to wear (but *only* on special occasions), and sometimes get to go to school. Things like electricity and running water are unheard of. As Kelly Campbell, spokesperson for AFC, says, "Because the average life expectancy is 37 and many mothers have seven or eight children, there is a lot to be done in this country."

The good news is that AFC's two-week volunteer trips to Malawi are sure to set off a lot less controversy than Madonna's adoption of Malawian orphan David Bantu.

Ambassadors for Children, started in 1998 by Sally Brown, a former flight attendant who went on to launch the world's largest travel club, supports children in 20 locations around the world.

"Our trips are for people who don't have the time to give a year to Peace Corps, but still want to help," Brown says. "These are folks who want cultural immersion, want to get to know the people of the countries they visit, but don't have time to take a year or two off. In my heart, I really believe that even in these short-term humanitarian projects, one person can make a difference."

Of course, the people most changed, she says, are the volunteers themselves. "These trips change people's entire perception. They come to realize that the world is a lot more complicated, diverse, and interesting than they ever thought possible."

GOD'S AQUARIUM

If you look at a map of Malawi, you'll notice a long blue strip running along the country's eastern border that it shares with Tanzania. That's Lake Malawi, one of the best freshwater scuba spots in the world. This crystal-clear lake, which makes up nearly a third of the country, boasts more than 1,000 species of tropical fish, 350 of which are unique to the lake. Night dives are highly recommended, as scores of large fish (locally named dolphinfish, though they look nothing like real dolphins) will surround you within minutes of entering the water.

Not only do AFC volunteers work on a wide variety of projects, from building schools in Uganda, to starting children's libraries in Jordan and Nepal, to helping women develop businesses in Belize, but participants also use their "extra allotted airline bag" to carry over medicine or hygiene kits or anything the local people tell them they need. Brown estimates that AFC has provided more than three million dollars in aid just in ten years' worth of volunteers' airline bags. If you look on their website, you'll see pictures of all sorts of items that AFC collects for children, from backpacks and pipe cleaners to washcloths and toothbrushes.

On the Malawi trips, volunteers work in Lilongwe, the country's capital, at the Mtendere Orphans Village, in the warehouses, or at medical clinics. Because there is *so* much to accomplish, volunteers may do anything from singing to an AIDS orphan, to leading his sister in an arts-and-crafts project, to distributing food to their grandmother. As spokesperson Campbell likes to point out, volunteers should "be ready for anything and everything."

Volunteers on this trip will also enjoy the undiscovered country's many wildlife parks and nature reserves, its mountains, and the beautiful sandy beaches of Lake Malawi (see sidebar this page). At the Liwonde National Park, volunteers enjoy a two-night safari, a river cruise, and several game-watching drives. "Hippos, rhinos, elephants, and monkeys come right up to your cottage," says Campbell, who has been there twice and says it's an amazing country.

Unlike Madonna, who flew into the country on a private jet, you'll probably be relying on public transportation, which means two days of traveling with a stopover in either South Africa or Ethiopia.

The Malawi trip is rated as an advanced trip (AFC rates its trips according to such things as culture shock, physical demands, quality of food and drink, and intensity of the actual work). Beginning trips, to give you some perspective, are geared for families and first-time volunteers. Because the Malawi trip, like other advanced trips, involves intense humanitarian work in an extremely poor country, you'll be called upon to overlook preconceived notions and less than Westernized conditions. On the up side, you'll have a rare chance to immerse yourself deep in a community and develop more than casual relationships.

The price for the Malawi trips is $1,699 and includes 11 nights' accommodations, most meals, the safari at Liwonde National Park, and a hearty donation to the volunteer sites.

HOW TO GET IN TOUCH

Ambassadors for Children, 1201 N. Central Avenue, Indianapolis, IN 46202, 866-338-3468 or 317-536-0250, www.ambassadorsforchildren.org.

keep hope alive under military occupation

PALESTINE

If there's one thing you learn in Palestine, it's resilience. Palestinians pick up the rubble from any disaster and get on with life. We try to follow their example.
—Bill, volunteer with Project Hope

31 This is not a vacation for the weak of heart. For one thing, there's that pesky army that keeps blowing up the very villages you're trying to help. Then there's the gunfire that makes hearing the English lessons you're trying to convey a little difficult. And there's the freezing of funds by the World Bank and most of the international community.

Your friends—well, they wouldn't be friends if they didn't try to talk you out of spending your vacation in an occupied military zone—will tell you to reconsider. But ask anyone who has volunteered with Project Hope, a nonprofit group that teaches English to kids in Nablus and the surrounding refugee camps, and they'll tell you it's the most rewarding vacation they've ever taken. Would they do it again? In a red-hot minute.

As Pulitzer Prize–winning playwright Tony Kushner said after visiting the West Bank, "Now when I read that a town is under siege, there's a good chance I know what that town looks like, what the children look like who play in its streets, what food is being served in its restaurants. This makes everything harder to bear, and in a situation like this, unbearable is good.... I long to return to this great and terrible place."

Project Hope works in Nablus and the Balata, Al-Ain, and New and Old Askar refugee camps. While their biggest need is for teachers of English (and the only qualification is that you know how to *speak* English), Project Hope also seeks volunteers to teach drama, painting, music, and dance.

Moomtastic, a video project of Project Hope, for example, produces short video clips to show the human, even funny, side of Palestine via MySpace, YouTube, and other social networking sites. Other volunteers helped Palestinians create a traveling circus called As-Sirk As-Saghir. An old, abandoned vehicle was turned into a colorful art car, complete with peepholes for Palestinian children to peek their heads through. Volunteers have coordinated the painting of art on walls, drama performances, and other art therapy projects that allow the refugee kids, 90 percent of whom suffer from trauma, to express themselves.

At last count, more than 700,000 refugees were living in the poor, crowded enclaves of the West Bank camps. In Balata alone, a 1.5-mile square, there are more than 20,000 registered refugees, many of whom are children and want to learn English.

Volunteers work at least 20 hours a week and, in their spare time, are encouraged to get involved in the local community and learn a bit of Arabic. As one volunteer says, "Nablus is supposedly a hotbed of terrorism, but the most lethal thing around here is definitely the hospitality."

For $70 a month, Project Hope coordinators will provide accommodations in a quiet, safe area. Although food is not provided, expenses in Palestine are dirt cheap and volunteers can usually get by on 10 to 20 shekels ($2.50 to $5) a day. The only significant cost to volunteer with Project Hope is airfare.

ANOTHER USE FOR THE PROVERBIAL OLIVE BRANCH

If you don't want to teach English or art, consider helping the Palestinians harvest olives. Some of the oldest olive groves in the world, some dating as far back as 2,000 years, are located in Palestine. Unfortunately, military closures and ongoing harassment have prevented some farm families from bringing their crops home. Since September 2000, more than half a million olive and fruit trees have been bulldozed and destroyed by the Israeli army. Every year, Zaytoun, a nonprofit from England that helps marginalized Palestinian farmers harvest and sell their olives, hosts trips for volunteer olive harvesters. Volunteers not only physically pick olives but also observe and negotiate safe passage for the farmers and their crops. *Zaytoun, 33 Carronade Court, Eden Grove, London, N7 8EP, England, 44 07814 477 188, www. zaytoun.org.*

SURFBOARD DIPLOMACY

In 2007, Dr. Dorian Paskowitz, an 86-year-old retired physician who has spent his life teaching others to surf, saw an article in the *Los Angeles Times* about a crowded beach in Gaza where two Palestinian surfers had but one old surfboard between them. He decided right then and there that he was going to rectify the situation. He rounded up 15 surfboards, grabbed one of his nine kids, and headed to Palestine. Unfortunately, the situation in Gaza wasn't quite as mellow as the California beach from which he hails.

Security guards at the border checkpoint told him, in no uncertain terms, "you're not going in." They warned him about the volatile security situation, told him repeatedly that nonessential goods were verboten.

Doc was not to be deterred.

"You wouldn't have me come 12,500 miles, one Jew to another?" Paskowitz told the guards. He grabbed one of the guards and kissed him. The guard promptly said, "Don't hug me, don't hug me!'"

To get away from the overfriendly old man, after two hours of badgering, the guards finally opened the gates. "To be able to go to your enemies and give them something that makes them happy," Doc says, "is a most fulfilling adventure."

HOW TO GET IN TOUCH

Project Hope, 29 An-Najah Al-Qadim Street (next to the French Cultural Center), Nablus, Palestine, www.projecthope.ps, or contact the Canadian volunteer coordinator at 110 Cumberland Street, Suite 237, Toronto, ON M5R 3V5, Canada, 416-879-8939.

turn bikes into pedal power

Every time I see an adult on a bicycle, I no longer despair for the future
of the human race.
—H. G. Wells, English writer

32 Everyone, it seems, is getting on the alternative energy bandwagon. Farmers are pushing for ethanol. Public utility companies are buying wind energy. Even Shell and British Petroleum are manufacturing solar photovoltaic panels.

In Guatemala, an innovative organization has come up with a whole new way to create energy. Maya Pedal, a nonprofit in San Andrés Itzapa, Guatemala, recycles used bicycles to build what they call *bicimáquinas*. These pedal-powered machines are being used to do everything from generating electricity to shelling macadamia nuts to sharpening metal blades. With help from engineers at MIT, they've also created bicycle-powered prototypes of a washing machine and a wood saw. And we're happy to report that their bike-powered blender is quite adept at making piña coladas and other blended drinks, something that undoubtedly comes in handy in nearby San Simón, named after the patron saint of drunkards.

Maya Pedal was started in 1997 as a way for locals, mostly descendants of the ancient Maya, to develop self-sustaining ways to generate an income. A local women's collective in town, for example, is using their bicycle blender to make organic aloe shampoo, the funds of which are used for their municipal reforestation project. A farm family in Pachay Las Lomas is using a bicycle water pump to tap a clean aquifer 100 feet underground and thereby irrigate their crops. Another family is using a bicycle-powered solar roaster to roast their coffee beans.

Of course, Maya Pedal is not above using the discarded bikes and parts it gets, mostly in 40-foot crates from Boston's Bikes Not Bombs, for their original use— getting from Point A to Point B. After all, if you're going to have a job, you've got to find a way to get there.

Only about 25 percent of the bikes are used for the pedal-powered machines themselves. The other 75 percent are sold, with the proceeds used to subsidize the bicimáquinas and Maya Pedal's many projects. Maya Pedal works with partners who might, say, train a group of indigenous women in animal husbandry, who will then go on to use a *bicimolino* (pedal-powered grain mill) to process feed for chickens that they will sell at a local market.

Volunteers, especially those with a smattering of Spanish, are extremely welcome. Maya Pedal offers housing in return for a few hours' work. Volunteers not only help design, build, and deliver the machines but also produce manuals for each bicimáquina and assist with community education, which might include installing and demonstrating the unusual machines.

Maya Pedal is not one of those volunteer vacation providers such as Global Volunteers, Projects Abroad, and Earthwatch, to name a few, that iron out every single logistical detail. Rather, Maya Pedal is a hardworking, fascinating group that can use all the extra bodies it can get. If you know how to wield a bicycle wrench, have a good sense of humor, can work with a team, and are able to live with minimal resources, consider this vacation, which is making a huge difference in the lives of indigenous populations of Guatemala.

There is no charge to volunteer with Maya Pedal.

HOW TO GET IN TOUCH

Asociación Maya Pedal, Cantón San Antonio, San Andrés Itzapa, Chimaltenango, Guatemala, 502 7849 4671, www.mayapedal.org.

help scientists research bottlenose dolphins

VELI LOŠINJ, CROATIA

> It is of interest to note that while some dolphins are reported to have learned English—up to 50 words used in correct context—no human being has been reported to have learned dolphinese.
> —Dr. Carl Sagan

33 In the 1996 remake of *Flipper*, Elijah Wood, playing a bitter teen whose parents just divorced, is sent from Chicago to the Florida Keys. Although we're supposed to feel sorry for Wood's character, it's hard to work up much sympathy for anyone sent to any area where there are dolphins.

The northern Adriatic Sea, where this volunteer vacation takes place, is no exception. Volunteers on this 12-day trip live on an island, spend their days on a boat, and hang out with one of the only animals that probably has more posters made in its honor than Jennifer Aniston.

But don't expect to swim with your research subjects—the scientists are

---

TO YOUR HEALTH

Before there were spas, the tiny island villages of Veli Lošinj and Mali Lošinj were proclaimed as "health resorts." Ambroz Haračic, a professor at the island's maritime school, began conducting meteorological studies in 1879 and published papers connecting the Lošinj climate with successful gardening. Indeed, Austrian Archduke Charles Stephen, who built the well-known mansion Morska Straza (Sea Watch) on the island, imported 200 rare plants that thrived. Then in 1885, Dr. Conrad Clark, whose son was healed of throat disease within three weeks of arriving on the island, proclaimed it a healthy climate for humans as well. People began flocking there to treat everything from respiratory problems to depression, and both towns remain popular health resorts.

---

studying bottlenose dolphins in the wild. The Adriatic Dolphin Project (ADP) began in 1987 when Italian biology major Giovanni Bearzi took his dad's inflatable boat to the warm waters of the Cres and Lošinj archipelago. He'd heard a rumor that, because of the relatively shallow water in the 36-island area, it was possible to get "up close and personal" with the dolphins, not just count them from an oceanographic vessel. From his tiny blow-up dinghy, Bearzi spent two weeks photographing and intimately observing individual dolphins, two weeks, he says, "that changed my life."

Bearzi eventually passed on the reins of ADP, the project that sprang up from his initial research, to the Blue World Institute of Research and Marine Conservation, a Croatian group. Today, the same life-changing research is being done on the ecology and conservation of the area's hundred or so resident dolphins. Research focuses on feeding behavior, population dynamics, and the impact of human activity.

From June through September, a total of four volunteers at a time work side by side with Blue World's scientists and marine biologists. You'll count dolphins, describe their behavior, record data, and at times even help with acoustic sampling. You'll also take turns shopping, cooking, and maintaining the field station in the 13th-century fishing village of Veli Lošinj. You might even help prepare reports or give tours to day visitors at the institute's Lošinj Marine Educational Centre.

Keep in mind that Blue World is not a tour company and that its scientists are not tour guides, although they're happy to answer questions, and they do provide a daily two-hour lecture on some topic related to cetacean biology.

Volunteers live with the scientists in a four-bedroom house on Rovenska Bay. The cost for the 12-day trip, which includes accommodations, meals, and membership in the institute, runs from $700 to $830, depending on the dates selected.

HOW TO GET IN TOUCH

Adriatic Dolphin Project, Kaštel 24, 51551 Veli Lošinj, Croatia, 385 51 604666, www.blue-world.org.

protect leatherback sea turtles

TRINIDAD

"Why would I want a TV if I spend every evening watching these turtles?"
—Grand Rivière native

34 The rule of thumb for travel to Trinidad and Tobago, the two-island nation off the coast of Venezuela, is that if you're looking for a place for your wild side to sneak out and play, choose Trinidad. If you just want to veg out in a hammock on a palm-fringed beach, go for Tobago.

This volunteer vacation proves there are exceptions to every rule. In Grand Rivière, a tiny village on Trinidad's north coast, the only nightlife centers around a cast of leatherback sea turtles that lumber to shore night after night to lay their eggs. The rest of the time, it's dead quiet in this sleepy fishing village on the Caribbean's southernmost island. In fact, it's so quiet that turtle poachers are able to walk up, grab any of the 300 to 400 leatherbacks that swim up to the beach each night between May and September, slice off their back fins, and turn them into turtle steak, unseen by anyone.

Although the government of Trinidad has outlawed the hunting of sea turtles and made it illegal to enter the turtle's nesting grounds at night without a guide, the leatherback population is still diminishing faster than any large animal in modern history. As late as 1980, there were 115,000 leatherback sea turtles swimming our world's oceans. Today, there are fewer than 30,000.

Suffice it to say, these magnificent creatures need all the help they can get. After dark every night in spring and summer, they swim onto the Grand Rivière Beach, dig deep nests with their back fins, lay 100 to 120 eggs, spend another 45 minutes camouflaging their efforts, and then swim back to the ocean whence they came. It's a riveting show, and one that, if we're not careful, could have a limited run.

It's bad enough that crabs and birds pick off the baby turtles before they make it into the sea, but now with developers building hotels and condominiums on many of their tropical nesting grounds, they're not having the best of seasons.

Only one in a hundred of the eggs on average manages to produce a hatchling that survives.

The locals, mostly fishermen and vegetable farmers, have finally figured out that the turtles are worth saving (for years they, too, feasted on turtle meat and eggs), but keeping guard night after night can get taxing. Most of Grand Rivière's 360 residents hold down day jobs, as well.

That's where you, as an i-to-i volunteer, come in. By helping the locals patrol the turtles' nesting ground, you can help correct the leatherback's demise. Every turtle is precious. Working with the Grand Rivière Tour Guide Association, you spend two weeks patroling the nesting beach, guarding the eggs, and learning everything you can about the behemoth reptiles that swim thousands of miles from the Arctic each year so their eggs can have a warm tropical beach on which to incubate.

Since your duties are at night, you'll have days free to tour the rest of the country, which, unlike many of its Caribbean neighbors, is not held hostage to tourism revenue. Blessed with substantial exports, including natural gas and oil, Trinidad and Tobago is able to be itself instead of a commercialized tourist's

MOVE OVER, RIO

To bring up Trinidad without mentioning its brash and sassy Carnival would be like visiting the Louvre and not checking out the "Mona Lisa." Lush anytime, with towering mountain peaks, orchid-filled jungles, and miles of beaches, Trinidad becomes irresistible during its pre-Lenten Carnival season. It has been called the greatest show on Earth. It's definitely one of the biggest parties, with nonstop parades, dancing in the streets, and fierce and joyful calypso music that starts at *j'ouvert* (that's sort of French for the "crack of dawn") on the Monday before Ash Wednesday and doesn't let up until way past midnight the next day. The costumes alone are worth a trip. Locals spend thousands of dollars turning themselves into peacocks with 20-foot tails, lions with Technicolor manes, and leather-clad devils with pitchforks. In fact, Trinidad is so famous for its costumes that Paris's Lido nightclub once commissioned a local costume maker to design one of its shows.

parody. Some of the enticements: Port of Spain, Trinidad's frenetic capital city, overflowing with multicultural heritage; the Caroni Bird Sanctuary, where scarlet ibis returning to mangrove roosts just before sunset create one of nature's most spectacular sights; and the Asa Wright Nature Center, where more than 170 species of birds have been recorded in the Arima Valley and a series of trails explore the 200-acre estate.

i-to-i, with more than 500 projects around the world, was started in 1994 by Deirdre Bounds, a 40-something British backpacker who taught English in Japan, China, and Greece before coming home to her one-bedroom apartment to wonder, "What am I going to do with the rest of my life?" She decided to go for her dream of helping others go "eye to eye" with fascinating cultures. Specializing in teaching English as a second language, i-to-i offers trips on five continents.

The two-week leatherback sea turtle trip, with accommodations and breakfast each day, runs $1,495.

HOW TO GET IN TOUCH

i-to-i North America, 190 E. Ninth Avenue, Suite 350, Denver, CO 80203, 800-985-4864, www.i-to-i.com.

assist archaeologists in transylvania

ROMANIA

"I am Dracula, and I bid you welcome . . . ."
—the Count, in Bram Stoker's *Dracula*

35 Although you're too late to excavate Dracula's Castle, there are plenty of archaeological sites in the Transylvania region of Romania that still need your help. Plus, your chances of finding one of Count Dracula's artifacts are probably better at the many ruins being excavated by volunteers from Projects Abroad, since Prince Vlad the Impaler, the 15th-century warlord whose cruelty inspired Bram Stoker's 1897 novel, probably stayed at Dracula's Castle only a night or two.

What you'd more likely find at Dracula's namesake castle, currently a popular tourist sight, is a casket containing the heart of Queen Marie, the Romanian ruler whose family lived there until 1948 when the castle was confiscated by the communist government. Marie, who loved the 14th-century castle and decorated it with fine tapestries, Romanian folk art, and elaborate gardens, requested that her heart be buried next to the castle's wooden church where she often meditated.

Projects Abroad, a New York–based organization that arranges ecologically minded trips all over the planet, has been sending would-be archaeologists to Romania since 1992. Working with a full-time staff of field archaeologists and anthropologists, volunteers have excavated fortified Saxon churches from the 13th and 14th centuries, the gardens of the Brukenthal Summer Palace, the 18th-century baroque holiday residence of a former governor of Transylvania, and the medieval castle of Nicolae Bathory II, whose heir tried to ward off old age by bathing in the blood of young virgins. Some claim this wayward princess who claimed the lives of hundreds of innocent young maids was as much an inspiration to Stoker, who spent seven years studying Romanian folklore, as Prince Vlad.

I VANT TO SUCK YOUR BLOOD

The historical Dracula, Vlad III, was neither a vampire nor a count. Even the name Dracula was an honorary title that means "son of the dragon." His father, Vlad II, was knighted by the Holy Roman emperor as a Knight of the Order of the Dragon, a group sworn to defend Christianity against the Turks. Although Vlad III was born in Transylvania, in Sighisoara, a fairy-tale town in central Romania, he didn't spend much time there. But after his dad was assassinated, Vlad III returned to his birthplace to avenge his death. One Easter, the newly appointed prince invited the nobles who were suspected of his father's murder to a feast. After a few opening jokes, he went straight to work with a sharpened stake, murdering every last one of his guests—hence his epithet "the Impaler." Stories of his gruesome revenge wound up being widely circulated, thanks to the newly invented printing press, making it perhaps the world's first tabloid news.

One of the more recent Romanian field projects is excavating the ancient tell settlements on the Danube's Bordusani-Popina. Just discovered in 1968, this Neolithic site on Ialomita Island dates back to 5000 B.C. and includes evidence of domesticated cows, pigs, and dogs buried alive in baskets.

Romanian archaeological field projects are ongoing and, besides digging and excavating, you'll be called upon to reconstruct ancient and medieval pottery, to conduct field walks to determine a site's boundary, and to write reports and proposals for new sites.

When you're not out on a field dig in Romania's rural countryside that one volunteer described as "right out of a Tolstoy novel," you'll be based in Brasov, an ancient medieval settlement surrounded on three sides by mountains. With a story rivaling anything you'll dig out of the ground, Brasov has been a strategic location since the Hungarian monarchy brought Saxon colonists to guard the mountain passes against the Tartars in the 12th century. It has historical squares, a nearby ski resort, and many interesting sights, including the Biserica Neagr (Black Church) with its six-ton bell and 4,000-pipe organ; the weaver's tower, one of seven original towers, which has been turned into a museum; and Piata Sfatului, a gorgeous square with outdoor cafés.

Projects Abroad has a strong presence in Romania and also sends volunteers to work for the *Brasov Visitor*, a local newspaper (one volunteer wrote about Romanian speed dating, for example), and for its programs in conservation, drama, and veterinarian medicine. Projects Abroad offers a wide variety of other trips from medical and dental projects in Sri Lanka to journalism in Ethiopa.

In Romania, you'll work with project manager George Andrei Ciotlausi, whose passion for mountaineering earned him the nickname "George of the Jungle," and stay with either a host family or in a small hostel next to Projects Abroad's Brasov office. Your hosts, proud and eager to show off traditional Romanian food and drink, will serve you such specialties as *ardei umpluti* (stuffed peppers), *sarmal* (cabbage leaves stuffed with meat and rice), *mamaliga* (maize porridge served with goat cheese), and apple and cherry turnovers.

The price for a one-month archaeological volunteer dig, including accommodations and meals with local families, is $2,295. A three-month stay can be arranged for $3,445.

HOW TO GET IN TOUCH

Projects Abroad, 347 W. 36th Street, Suite 903, New York, NY 10018, 888-839-3535, www.projects-abroad.com.

cultivate organic crops

OAXACA, MEXICO

These sprays, dusts, and aerosols are now applied almost universally to farms, gardens, forests, and homes. Can anyone believe it is possible to lay down such a barrage of poisons on the surface of the Earth without making it unfit for all life?
—Rachel Carson, in *Silent Spring*

36 Many of the pesticides that are banned in the United States are still being used south of the border. In Mexico, where not as many environmental protections are in place, people still eat food that has been sprayed with chemicals known beyond doubt to cause cancer.

You can help change all that by offering your time to Volunteer Adventure's Organic Farming Project. Working alongside biologists, you'll use sustainable farming methods to cultivate and harvest organic vegetables on a parcel of land just outside Oaxaca, the capital city of the eponymous state. Until the two biologists started this project in the late 1990s, the land where the project takes place was barren and dead. Thanks to their experimentation with biointensive farming techniques, however, the once infertile soil has been turned into vibrant cropland, producing a lush variety of lettuce, onions, beets, radishes, tomatoes, corn, cilantro, and parsley.

Although biointensive farming requires more labor than simply dumping chemicals on indiscriminately, it does have an upside

OAXACA CITY

Located about 330 miles southeast of Mexico City, Oaxaca is famous for its colonial architecture, unique cuisine, and nearby arts-and-crafts villages. At 5,000 feet elevation, the semitropical city is surrounded by the lush countryside of the Mexican Sierra and has indigenous archaeology and rich cultural traditions that date back nearly 3,000 years.

beyond the obvious health reasons—it requires no natural gas or petroleum and uses as much as 88 percent less water. It may be the best chance for Oaxaca, the second poorest state in Mexico, to save its farming communities, which like many small farms in America are at risk of takeover by large commercial interests that think nothing of irrigating away the local aquifer.

So far, the demand for organics in Mexico is small, and the majority of consumers don't even know what "organic food" means. In fact, 98 percent of the country's certified organic products are exported. And farmers who do farm organically take a financial risk, because state subsidies and incentives are unavailable to producers who shun chemicals. But thanks to programs like this one, farmers are starting to realize that fertilizers, herbicides, and pesticides are sickening their families and the surrounding environment, not to mention that tortillas made from the prepackaged cornmeal are not as tasty or as nutritious as the organic variety.

During this two- or three-week volunteer vacation, you'll work the soil, helping biologists clean and neutralize it through bioremediation, a process that uses live organisms to remove pollutants. You'll help prepare natural fertilizer, potting soil, and compost; plant and harvest crops; and even sell

TREE'S COMPANY

The farmland around Oaxaca is not the only thing to suffer from environmental degradation. There's a famous tree, some say the oldest one in the world, in Santa María del Tule, 8 miles away, that's also suffering from the shrinking water table. The tree, El Árbol del Tule, a Montezuma cypress, is not only the world's oldest living thing—at least according to the townsfolk, who named their town after the tree and who claim it's up to 3,000 years old—but it's also the world's widest. With a diameter of 33 feet and a circumference of 178 feet, it's big enough to wind any out-of-shape American who tries to run around it. The local schoolkids have adopted the tree and offer official tours, pointing out the images of many "creatures" hiding in the tree's knotty, twisted trunk. With pocket mirrors, they point out such figures as jaguars, squirrel's tails, former president Carlos Salinas's ears, and, for a while, the posterior of Monica Lewinsky. Although the tree looks like it's made up of multiple trunks fused together, DNA tests have confirmed that it is indeed a single tree. Locals celebrate their namesake tree on the second Monday of October by hanging beer bottles, garlands, grapefruits, and even empanadas from the tree's contorted branches.

the results at Oaxaca's weekend organic market. The ultimate goal for this project is to spread biointensive farming techniques to other communities around Mexico.

Besides cultivating your green thumb, you'll be invited to cooking and salsa dance classes, Spanish movies, social cafés, and student conversation exchanges. Or you can take daylong excursions to the Monte Alban ruins, visit *mescal* distilleries, or indulge in the region's many rock-climbing, horseback-riding, paragliding, and hiking opportunities.

The cost for a three-week package that includes Spanish lessons, accommodations, and one to two meals a day ranges from $1,690 to $1,845, depending on whether you stay with a host family (the cheaper option) or at a hostel in town.

HOW TO GET IN TOUCH

Volunteer Adventures, 915 S. Colorado Boulevard, Denver, CO 80246, 888-825-3454 or 303-785-8887, www.volunteeradventures.com.

bottle-feed lion cubs

ANTELOPE PARK, GWERU, ZIMBABWE

It was like living a wildlife documentary rather than watching it on television.
—Anita Lewis, volunteer at Antelope Park

37 If you accidentally leave the door to your thatched hut open, don't be surprised to come back after lunch and find a baby lion cub chewing on your shoelaces or pawing through your backpack. One volunteer even found a four-month-old cub sleeping cozily under his duvet.

For the three weeks (or longer if you get so captivated by Mickey, Milo, Kwali, Kwizi, or one of the other cubs that you simply can't pull yourself away) of your volunteer stint at the Lion Rehabilitation Center in Antelope Park, you will, for all intents and purposes, be the pride for these orphaned lion cubs. You'll bottle-feed them until they're able to fend for themselves, walk beside them through the wild, and take copious notes about their behavior (something their real mother probably wouldn't do) to ensure that, unlike many African lions,

WHILE YOU'RE THERE

As if hanging out with the king of beasts weren't enough, there are many Zimbabwe excursions available from Antelope Park, including:

- **Hwange National Park.** This park, with its salt pans, acacia scrubs, and grassy plains, is roughly the size of Belgium and allegedly has the densest concentration of wildlife in Africa. It's one of Africa's last great elephant sancturaries.
- **Matobo National Park.** This little known park has fascinating rock formations and hundreds of cave paintings.
- **Victoria Falls.** Better known as the adrenaline capital of Africa, Victoria Falls, situated between Zambia and Zimbabwe, offers bungee jumping, white-water rafting, and exhilarating swims through its waterfall gorges. David Livingston was the first white man to set eyes on them, upon which he promptly exclaimed that their power was so great that they must have been "gazed upon by angels in their flight."

they'll survive to produce future generations.

Of course, you don't want them to get too attached. That's why, when the cubs are 18 months old and able to stalk and hunt down prey, they're moved to locations without human contact where they can hunt (and breed) on their own.

In 1987, when Andrew and Wendy Connolly bought the 3,000-acre wildlife reserve, it had a grand total of six lions. By 1999, their innovative breeding program had managed to increase the lion population to more than 70, many of which are now gracefully living human free in the wild.

Sadly, many of Africa's lion rehabilitation programs aren't as successful. The lions either become too dependent on their human counterparts or they don't learn the skills necessary to stalk and take down prey. But the program at Antelope Park that rehabilitates captive-bred lions in four distinct stages (by stage three, the lions have no human contact) seems to be working.

And it's none too soon. In 1972, when the sequel to the movie *Born Free* was released, more than 250,000 lions roamed the African continent. Today, due to feline tuberculosis, poaching, and diminishing habitat, it's estimated there are fewer than 15,000. If something isn't done soon, this icon of Africa will no longer exist in the wild.

Volunteers on this project assist the staff in the rearing of lion cubs, from several weeks old to 18 months. They also help with animal observation and basic park maintenance. After three days' training (including essential safety tips), you will not only bottle-feed tiny cubs and walk with your pride in the wild but also conduct data on the older lions, feed the park's orphaned elephants (they were rescued and brought to Antelope Park during the severe droughts of 1991 and 1992), conduct snare sweeps, and scout the border fence (on either horse or elephant back) for holes and poachers' cuttings.

African Impact, a volunteer organization that also needs help with dolphin research in Mozambique, mobile medical clinics in Kenya, and leopard shadowing in Botswana, is headquartered at the reserve in Zimbabwe where thousands of tourists show up every year. From the original program at Antelope

Park in Gweru, the program has grown to a second site in Zimbabwe near Victoria Falls, and now a third site in Livingstone, Zambia.

A one-month volunteer position through African Impact costs $3,500 and includes lodging in a lakeside thatched hut, three square meals a day, wildlife education, and—get this—weekly laundry service and a maid to tidy your room.

HOW TO GET IN TOUCH

African Impact, P.O. Box 1218, Gweru, Zimbabwe, 263 4 702814, www.africanimpact.com.

track the spectacled andean bear

ECUADOR

Our culture depicts the personal self as existing in competition with and in opposition to nature. We fail to realize that if we destroy our environment, we are destroying what is in fact our larger self.
—Author Freya Matthew

38 Bet you didn't know there were bears in South America. The spectacled Andean bear, a shy, reclusive bear that has yet to attack a single human, is barely (pardon the pun) hanging on in the cloud forests of the Andes, a narrow strip running from western Venezuela to northern Argentina. In the Choco Bioregion of Ecuador, the bear, which is named for the white markings around its eyes, joins a long list of endangered species from the Andean kinkajou to a bird called the cock of the rock, named most likely for its showy scarlet head.

In the Intag region of northern Ecuador, surrounded by tranquil cloud forests, rugged mountains, and shadowy valleys, volunteers can help biologist and bear expert Armando Castellanos conduct important field research that will open new doors into this elusive bear's behavior and hopefully save it from extinction. The Andean bear is the only remaining short-faced bear on the planet and, according to the BBC's *Amazing Animals,* was the model for Paddington Bear, reason enough for several generations of kids to want to ensure its continuation.

After a week's orientation and training, volunteers will monitor both wild and rehabilitated bears by direct observation and through the use of radio tracking equipment. You'll be gathering data on the Andean bear's diet, behaviors, and social interaction. You'll also be watching for illegal activity such as poaching or tree cutting, and if new bears are captured during your project, you'll get in on collaring and releasing them.

Although volunteers often move with the bears, even camping at times, you will be based at the Casa de los Osos (House of the Bears), a clean but simple volunteer house near the village of Pucara in a rural farming region at the edge of the Cotocachi-Cayapas Ecological Reserve. The farmers, who grow corn, sugarcane,

The Otavalo market, one of the most important indigenous markets in all of Latin America, is a mere two-hour bus ride from the Casa de los Osos. It's quite a spectacle: squealing pigs, clucking chickens, cotton-candy machines, Andean pipe music, and nonstop bargaining, exchanging, selling, and socializing in Quechua, the native tongue. You can find everything from armadillo shell guitars to colorful sweaters and mats to bars of magical soap that will allegedly ward off jealousy. There's a cockfighting pit and a covered market bursting with tropical fruit and vegetables. The Otavaleño Indians, who run the market and are easily identified by their embroidered blouses, ponchos, beaded necklaces, and calf-length trousers, are known for their exquisite textiles and weavings, now sold at markets all over the world. On Saturday, by far the busiest day, the Otavalo market is like a circus, but if you go during the week, you can visit the famous weavers working on backstrap and Spanish looms.

and tree tomatoes by hand, are extremely welcoming, often offering *puro,* a potent local moonshine made from distilled sugarcane, and a chance to practice Spanish to the rotating cast of volunteers. Meanwhile, Celia, the foundation's Ecuadorian cook, provides three meals a day, mostly vegetarian fare made with local fruits and vegetables.

In your free time, you can join in on small fiestas thrown in local villages, take a short bus ride to the Apuela hot springs, or relax in an outdoor hammock listening to frogs or admiring the stars. Occasionally, volunteers will request movie night, where you'll gather on the couch around a beat-up laptop with a bowl of popcorn.

The Andean Bear Foundation likes volunteers to commit to a minimum of four weeks. They are happy to accommodate shorter stays, too, but because of the importance of accuracy in data recording, volunteers who come for shorter stays can only accompany others on their expeditions through the beautiful cloud forests and *paramos.* The cost for a four-week volunteer gig is $500 (one week is $120) and includes transportation to and from Quito, lodging, and meals.

HOW TO GET IN TOUCH

Fundación Espíritu del Bosque, Guipuzcoa 439 y Coruña, Quito, Ecuador, 593 2 2504 452, www.andeanbear.org, e-mail: volunteer@andeanbear.org.

conduct biodiversity surveys

WARIA VALLEY, PAPUA NEW GUINEA

New Guinea is an intoxicating cocktail of stone age and space age, natural history and human history, biodiversity and culture diversity, rubbing alongside one another in a harmony I've rarely experienced elsewhere.
—Rob McCall, biologist with *BBC Wildlife* magazine

39 More than half of the world's tropical forests have already been destroyed. And if the industrial logging companies keep insatiably hacking away, the 85 percent of Papua New Guinea's population that depends on the country's rain forest for food and sustenance is going to be as extinct as the thousand-year-old trees the large-scale logging companies are systematically eliminating.

The Zia tribe of Papua New Guinea's Waria Valley recently joined hands with Coral Cay Conservation (CCC), a British nonprofit dedicated to protecting endangered tropical forests and coral reefs, to figure out a way to save their rain forest. The Zia realized that the short-term gains reaped from mining and logging licenses do nothing to ensure their grandchildren's future and that many of the promises made by the international logging companies have not been honored.

CCC (with the assistance of its volunteers and local partners) has a long history of helping protect natural resources, including creating marine reserves and building a research center at a World Heritage site in Belize. As David Bellamy, president of CCC, says, "We try to put our planet back in working order by providing countries with the information they desperately need to protect and sustainably use their tropical forests and coral reefs."

Volunteers on four-week stints to the remote jungles of Papua New Guinea (the nearest road is 100 miles away) not only collect baseline biodiversity data on wildlife and vegetation but also help the tribespeople create sustainable livelihoods and assist with community projects such as water and sanitation improvement. Anybody know how to build composting toilets?

TRICK OR TREAT

Halloween has nothing on Papua New Guinea's Highland Shows. Held each summer, the Highland Shows feature tribal costumes made of everything from snakeskin to dog's teeth and human hair. The costumes, called *bilas,* are treasured possessions, handed down from generation to generation. Each tribe has its own bila, a ritualized decoration that can include pierced noses, face paint (a little pig's grease gives it a sheen), and headdresses made from pig tusks, bird quills, and cowrie shells. The replacement value for some of the more elaborate bilas is estimated at more than a thousand dollars.

While that might sound steep, consider the Huli Wigmen of Tari, whose bilas include giant, three-cornered headdresses made from their own hair. Young wigmen take special care of their hair, letting it grow until it's finally long enough to be cut and woven with brightly colored daisies, parrot feathers, and fur from the cuscus, a cat-size marsupial. The crowning touch is the plume from New Guinea's bird of paradise, a bird originally believed to be a messenger from heaven.

The climax of the Highland Shows is the *sing-sings,* which, for those of you who don't speak pidgin, means "dance performance." Each group dons its bila and dances to the chanting, hand clapping, and foot stamping of its tribe. Acoustic accompaniment is often provided by bamboo flutes and lizardskin drums called *kundus.*

Competition in the sing-sings is fierce. Tribes come from all over Papua New Guinea, some walking four or five days just to get there.

It all goes back to the 1950s, when the Australian government, temporary administrators of the country that shares an island with Indonesia, decided to put an end to ongoing tribal feuds. They staged a giant get-together and invited all the tribes. It was a smashing success and the beginning of an annual tradition that alternates between Goroka in even years and Mount Hagen in odd years.

All told, there are 700 different tribes in Papua New Guinea. For years, the tribes remained separated, unknown not only to the early traders, planters, and missionaries who had settled much of the coast but to each other, as well. Campfires seen across the mountain were believed to be lights from the gods. Those in the most remote areas weren't even discovered until the late 1930s when an Australian miner, in search of an elusive metal, found the tribesmen instead. In fact, the first white man to fly a plane into the mountains was such a curiosity that the tribesmen insisted on feeling his genitals to make sure he was human.

As Papua New Guinea's economy changes, so do its cultural traditions. Even the Highlands Show is not immune. Face paint that was once applied with hibiscus twigs is now administered with store-bought brushes. New rules prohibiting costumes made from tinfoil, plastic, and Styrofoam had to be added. Even vendors hawking T-shirts and sun visors are as common at the show as Asori mudmen wearing massive helmets made from mud and fiber.

Step one, of course, in protecting Papua New Guinea's fragile rain forest, the third largest in the world, is figuring out all the species being endangered by large-scale logging. Volunteers, using mist nets and bucket traps, capture, identify, and measure the thousands of species (some that haven't ever been recorded before) before releasing them back into the wild. Volunteers are also needed to help locals build ecolodges, establish community nurseries, and plant such crops as rice, taro, onions, and beans. They also aid in developing sustainable livelihood projects such as small-scale chicken farming and bamboo furniture making.

Volunteers sleep in hammocks, lulled to sleep by thousands of tree frogs, insects, and singing worms. They travel by canoes or rafts made from banana trees to the small villages where they work. There's no electricity or running water, and mosquitoes will be a constant torment. But think of it this way: Where else can you live in a rain forest, save an ecosystem, and hang out with tribesmen wearing bones and sulfur-crested cockatiel feathers? Four weeks of this, including lodging, meals, training, and local transportation, is yours for $1,380.

HOW TO GET IN TOUCH

Coral Cay Conservation, 1st Floor Block 1, Elizabeth House, 39 York Road, London, SE1 7NQ, England, 44 20 7620 1411, www.coralcay.org.

assemble wheelchairs for land mine victims

CAMBODIA

You don't have to have a college degree to serve. You don't even have to make your subject and verb agree to serve....You only need a heart full of grace. A soul generated by love.
—Dr. Martin Luther King, Jr.

40 Rarely does a day go by when not a single person in Cambodia steps on a land mine. All too often it's a child, often a young boy, who ends up losing his life or, if he's lucky, only a limb or two. Cambodia, a country the size of Missouri, has more citizens with missing limbs (60,000) than any other country. And unfortunately, another four to six million land mines (that's one for every two citizens) are yet to be removed. The problem, of course, is that land mines are cheap (around $3) to install, but expensive ($1,000) to get rid of. The United Nations estimates that it will take as long as a hundred years to clear this scarred and war-battered country of all its land mines.

The good news is that in Siem Reap, the gateway to the country's celebrated Angkor Wat temples, land mines have been removed and tourists are piling in. But because foreigners, as so often happens in impoverished countries, own most of the hotels and tourist restaurants (for a while, most profits from ticket sales to Angkor Wat went straight into the pockets of Sokimex, an international petroleum company), the locals are still suffering.

Globe Aware, a Dallas-based nonprofit agency that organizes volunteer trips to 12 countries, sends volunteers to Cambodia to assemble wheelchairs for the country's large population of land mine victims. In doing so, they work alongside locals—an important component of all Globe Aware trips. In addition to building these much needed wheelchairs out of recycled parts, volunteers

A CONVINCING ARGUMENT FOR THE MINE BAN TREATY

A decade ago, representatives of two-thirds of the world's nations came together in Canada to sign the Ottawa Treaty, an agreement to stop the manufacture and use of land mines. The United States was among those that refused to sign and still hasn't added its signature. Perhaps we should send U.S. leaders to a small museum in Siem Reap that Aki Ra, a former Khmer Rouge soldier, has built. Nowhere is the argument for the ban of land mines more convincing.

Orphaned at age 9 (his parents were killed along with two million other Cambodians by Pol Pot's army), Ra was conscripted into the same army that blew up his parents. His job was to lay land mines, hundreds of them, every day. To atone for his wrongdoings, Ra and his wife, Hourt, have adopted several dozen land mine victims, most of whom are children. They pay for their schooling and purchase prosthetic limbs when they're able. And he has spent 13 years personally removing land mines and other ordnance by hand.

In 1999, Ra founded the Cambodian Land Mine Museum, a living testament to the indiscriminate harm land mines can do. Money from donations to the museum, which features piles and piles of different types of land mines and a deactivated test field, go for education programs. "My mission in life," he says, "is to make my country safe for my people." *Cambodian Land Mine Museum, 6 miles from Siem Reap on the potholed road to Banteay Srei, 885 012 630 446.*

also visit the floating village on Tonle Sap Lake, experience a Cambodian wedding, and see the astonishing Angkor Wat temples that are often called the eighth wonder of the world.

But more rewarding than viewing the architectural masterpieces is the chance to present the wheelchair you assemble to the person who will use it. You'll also learn a few words of Khmer, share English skills with Buddhist monks, visit a land mine museum (see sidebar this page), see the Killing Fields, and take Cambodian cooking classes.

Globe Aware was founded in 2000 by Kimberly Haley-Coleman with two principles in mind: to promote both cultural awareness ("We think it's best to recognize and appreciate a culture, not try to change it," Haley-Coleman says, adding that they have intentionally chosen programs in locations least like our own) and sustainability. She also recognized the need for one-week volunteer vacations for busy Americans who, as she says, "have among the least vacation time among developed nations." Her own volunteering efforts with Volunteers for Peace and Habitat for Humanity were rewarding, but she knew most folks couldn't spare three or four weeks off work. "Our goal is to get Westerners, particularly North Americans, to think beyond their normal cultural context," she says.

Volunteers stay in a simple guesthouse and participate in teambuilding exercises and a cultural scavenger hunt, in addition to building wheelchairs. The price tag for a week in Cambodia is $1,200, which includes meals, accommodations, donations to the community, and on-site travel. Weeklong extensions can be added for $350.

HOW TO GET IN TOUCH
Globe Aware, 7232 Fisher Road, Dallas, TX 75214, 877-588-4562, www .globeaware.org.

do underwater reconnaissance

ANDAVADOAKA, MADAGASCAR

Amazing, impossible to describe, unlike anything or anywhere I have
ever been—a true experience of a lifetime.
—Nicola Reeve, volunteer with Blue Ventures Expeditions

41 You might have heard of Andavadoaka, a tiny fishing village on the
southwest coast of Madagascar. In 2007, it won a prestigious award
from the United Nations for creating the world's first community-run octopus
protection area.

But other than the prize—an award that took village leaders all the way to
Berlin—not many have heard of this remote village that, on a good day, gets seven
hours of electricity. Just getting there can be an adventure. You either hitch a ride
with a commercial fishing boat from Le Havre for a ten-hour sail or take a taxi from
Antananarivo, the capital, to Morombe and then from Morombe to Tulear, which
during the rainy season can take days.

So it's no wonder that Blue Ventures Expeditions, a London-based nonprofit
that uses volunteers at its research field station in Andavadoaka, suggests a minimum
stay of six weeks. You can opt for less if you're insistent, but the first ten days to
two weeks are spent in training, both in PADI scuba certification (volunteers will
receive Advanced Open Water Certification and have opportunities to reach Rescue
Diver and Diver Master, if they so desire) and in marine science education, so
between that and the near-impossible journey
getting there, three weeks is a drop in the
bucket, giving you a mere seven days
to conduct underwater surveying.

Of course, keep in mind
that training, like beauty, is in
the eyes of the beholder. All
training is done on the beach
(isn't anything done "on the

beach" worth doing?) and in the ocean where you'll participate in fish, coral, and invertebrate "spotting sessions." You'll learn to identify marine species, calculate fish populations, and collect precise scientific data. In your spare time, you'll compete in nightly volleyball tournaments and beach olympics, take sunset swims, hike through baobab forests, and ride in zebu-drawn carts.

Blue Ventures Expeditions was started in 2003 by Alasdair Harris, a marine biologist who wanted to not only conduct important marine research (it's estimated that 80 percent of the species on the Grand Récif de Tuléar, the world's fourth largest reef, can be found nowhere else) but also help locals reap the benefits of conservation. Harris and his rotating team of volunteers enlisted the local Vezo, "people of the sea," to help in saving octopuses, sharks, and, of course, their reef. With Blue Ventures's help, local villagers have developed alternative sustainable livelihoods, including aquaculture businesses and a community-owned ecolodge.

Expect to pay £1,147 ($2,300) for a three-week volunteer vacation or £1,765 ($3,530) for six weeks; this price includes lodging and meals, scuba certification, marine science training, and use of scuba equipment. You bring a mask, fins, and a wetsuit. Volunteers stay in comfortable, self-contained wooden cabins situated on a coral outcropping overlooking the beach and the blue lagoon. All revenue raised is channeled back into the conservation of threatened coral reefs and other marine resources that local communities rely upon for survival.

WALKING THEIR TALK

Blue Ventures Expeditions is all about saving the planet. And they're fully aware that bringing people from all over the world to Madagascar contributes to carbon dioxide emissions. Those planes, after all, don't fly cheap when it comes to carbon emissions.

To offset the carbon emissions created by their volunteers, Blue Ventures estimates the amount of CO_2 emitted for every mile traveled by plane. Once they've calculated each volunteer's carbon footprint, they match the value to a project that reduces carbon emissions. A recent project building energy-efficient stoves and solar stoves, for example, reduced carbon emissions by 2 tons per year per stove. All these stoves were locally produced and reduce both carbon emissions and (by 70 percent) the amount of wood it takes to heat homes. Additionally, all Blue Ventures offset programs help to alleviate poverty, educate local communities, and protect local habitats.

A HALLUCINATORY PLACE

French explorer Philibert de Commerson wrote in 1771 that Madagascar was "a naturalist's promised land." He said, "Nature seems to have retreated there into a private sanctuary, where she could work on different models from any she has used elsewhere." Irish writer Dervla Murphy dubbed it a "hallucinatory place." Let's just say that Dr. Seuss would have had a heyday here, drawing flora and fauna he'd never find anywhere else except in his own imagination. Primate enthusiasts like Madagascar's 50 species of lemurs, the spry, wide-eyed relatives of monkeys that went extinct everywhere else but there. Birders could dull pencils making lists of vangas—birds that rival Darwin's finches for diversity.

Madagascar also has more than half the world's chameleons, with their weird, swiveling eyes and body-length tongues. And it is the only home of the leaf-tailed gecko, which looks like lichen until disturbed, at which time it opens a blood-red mouth and screams like a Dallas Cowboy cheerleader. Madagascar has 1,000-odd species of orchids, freakish giraffe-necked weevils, and a peculiar elephant's foot that looks like a gourd with arms. There are white sifakas (lemurs that get their name from the worried "she-fahk" they scream out when confronted) and fossa (pronounced "foosh") that look like a cross between a mongoose and a mountain lion.

HOW TO GET IN TOUCH

Blue Ventures Expeditions, 52 Avenue Road, London, N6 5DR, England, 44 20 8341 9819, www.blueventures.org.

fix kids' teeth on top of the world

NEPAL

*Serving the children of Nepal at this clinic gives me hope that some
things are right in the world.*
—Amy Simper, volunteer with Himalayan Dental Relief Project

42 Ever since Nepal opened its mountains to tourists in 1964, climbers have been flocking to this gorgeous country between China and India. Thousands of trekkers come each year, some to scale 29,029-foot Mount Everest—a journey that costs nearly $95,000 by the time you throw in equipment, Sherpas, and the $25,000 government permit that's required—some to climb the country's other mountains, eight of which top the list of the world's highest peaks. While no one can dispute that climbers bring much-needed tourism dollars into the country, they also bring candy, which the kids of Nepal willingly snatch up. Most of the children don't speak English, of course, but they all know the word bon-bon, and they use it at every opportunity.

The problem is that Nepal, the poorest country in Asia, has only something like 250 dentists. Needless to say, that's not enough for a population of 25 million. Many of those exuberant, bon-bon-chewing kids have major dental problems. Their parents have jack-o'-lantern smiles.

Himalayan Dental Relief Project (HDRP), a Colorado- and Kathmandu-based nonprofit organization, provides free dental care to impoverished children and families of Nepal, many of whom live in remote mountain villages. Working with charity-run schools and orphanages, HDRP sets up field clinics that provide such dental services as cleanings, tooth restorations, extractions, and, most importantly, toothbrush instruction. And you don't have to be a dentist to volunteer. Nonmedical volunteers manage the long lines of patients, keep records, sterilize instruments, and spend time making the boys and girls feel special.

What you *do* need to be is willing to hike for up to three days to get to some of these villages, many nothing but a cluster of huts surrounded by potato fields and gardens. And it helps if you're good at keeping track of yaks. Yaks, of course, carry the bags, but when they wander off, as yaks are known to do, with all the expensive dental equipment, it can be a little unnerving. And suffice it to say, you won't have the normal dental office comforts of ergonomically designed furniture, pleasant music, and efficient lighting. In fact, you'll probably be sterilizing equipment in outside pressure cookers. But the children, many of whom walk for two hours to get to these field clinics, could care less. They're as excited about seeing the gleaming instruments as they are about getting their cavities filled.

As Heidi Baier, an HDRP volunteer who got engaged on a volunteer trip to Nepal, says, "Our backs are sore, our eyes feel strained, and we dream of hot showers and soft beds. Yet the immediacy of what we are doing and the vibrancy of these tough kids touches each of us deeply. It is some of the best days of my life."

The Himalayan Dental Relief Project was started in 2000 by a Denver dentist, Dr. Andrew Holecek, and his then wife, Laurie Mathews, the former director of Colorado State Parks. Since its founding, HDRP has expanded to India, Vietnam, and Guatemala and has treated 24,000 children with $4.4 million of donated dental care. Holecek, who still treats patients in Denver six months out of the year, is also a Buddhist scholar, serving on the faculty of the Ngedon School of Buddhist Studies, and is founder of Death College, a school for studying the practice of death and dying from the Tibetan perspective.

The average price for a three-week expedition is $3,500 and includes airfare from a gateway city (usually San Francisco or Los Angeles), all meals, and lodging.

HOW TO GET IN TOUCH

Himalayan Dental Relief Project's trips are organized by **Global Humanitarian Expeditions,** 602 S. Ogden Street, Denver, CO 80209, 800-543-1171 or 303-858-8857, www.humanitariantours.com.

save the rain forest

Destroying rainforest for economic gain is like burning a Renaissance
painting to cook a meal.
—Edward Wilson, American biologist

43 Most tourists go to Peru to see Machu Picchu and learn about the ancient Inca. That's a lucky break for this volunteer vacation. The more camera-toting tourists who head for Machu Picchu, the less who tromp through the jungles of the Amazon Basin, the most diverse ecosystem in the world. In fact, Puerto Maldonado, where the ProNaturaleza butterfly farm is located, escaped development for just long enough that most of its natives understand and carefully guard the complex relationship between all animals (not just the human ones) that live down the Madre de Dios and Tambopata Rivers.

If you'd like to join them in conserving their unique spot on the planet, consider one of the following volunteer opportunities.

ProNaturaleza Butterfly Conservation Project. If you're one of those people who keeps a list of butterfly sightings the way some Audubon types keep lists of birds, this is the project for you. Since 2002, ProNaturaleza, a prominent Peruvian conservation organization, has been running a riverfront butterfly farm near the Puerto Maldonado airport. The farm, formerly named Tropical Insects and now called Japipi, was started six years earlier by a couple of self-taught scientist-entrepreneurs who raised and sold butterflies (this southern Peruvian rain forest has more than 1,230 species) to museums, zoos, and private collectors all over the world.

Volunteers assist in butterfly research studies and in environmental education programs. Being located so close to the airport, the center stays quite busy with tours and butterfly walks. Japipi's volunteers are trained by the center's scientists to find caterpillars and their feeding plants in the wild. Volunteer packages with the ProNaturaleza Butterfly Project can last anywhere from one week to three months and include personalized training, field manuals, excursions, and, in the case of longer packages, even field trips to nearby protected regions such as Tambopata National Reserve, Bahuaja Sonene, and Manu National Park. ProNaturaleza, which was formed in 1984 to protect and find sustainable uses for Peru's natural resources, seeks volunteers for field projects all over the country.

ProNaturaleza, Box 18-1393, Calle Alfredo León 211, Miraflores, Lima 18, Peru, 51 1 447 9032 or 51 1 241 7981, **Butterfly Center** 51 1 264 2736, www.pronaturaleza.org.

Reserva Ecológica Taricaya. With the highest canopy walkway in the Peruvian rain forest (125 feet tall), this 1,200-acre reserve run by Projects Abroad seeks volunteers to assist with their important conservation work. Several species like the black spider monkey and the white-chested capuchin monkey became extinct before the group, led by Oxford biologist Stuart Timson, started the place from scratch in 2001, but now they're working hard to save the endangered side-neck turtle, black caiman, and other rain forest species. One of the reserve's biggest jobs is educating the 18 ethnic groups that live in the Madre de Dios (and others who settled here in the early 1900s to farm rubber trees and Brazil nuts) how to live sustainably rather than destroying the forest. They're experimenting with alternative food sources and have pilot farms for growing many of the plants being destroyed in the rain forest. The palmiche frond, for example, a popular roofing material, can be grown right at the center. The Taricaya Center, located about an hour's boat ride on the Madre de Dios River from Puerto Maldonado, has an animal release program (jaguars, margays, and anteaters are just a few of those now free to roam their protected habitat), a turtle protection project, a pilot mahogany farm, a medicinal plant garden, and much more. Volunteers build and monitor trails (30 miles since its founding), patrol the reserve, help on the experimental farms, and record such wildlife as giant anteaters, pumas, black jaguars, red howler monkeys, green anacondas, white-lipped peccaries, a dwarf caiman (fully grown at only 3 feet), and more than 350 other species. You'll live with up to 30 other volunteers (and a resident spider monkey) at the Taricaya Center. One month's stay is priced at $3,445.

Projects Abroad, 347 W. 36th Street, Suite 903, New York, NY 10018, 888-839-3535, www.volunteer-conservation-peru.org.

teach music in ghana

ACCRA, GHANA

We each disappeared as individuals. We were no longer sick or well, able or disabled. We were players in a deeply human mystery; a story older than time. And, oh, how we played!
—John Glock, fiddle player

44 Talk to any veteran volunteer and invariably you'll get some variation on the following sentiment: "I started out in the hope of giving to others, but found out I was the one getting the most." Nowhere is that more true than in Ghana, where Travellers Worldwide sends volunteers to teach music—although no one is quite clear who is teaching whom. Volunteers, who work in one of several primary schools in the Asylum Downs suburb of Accra, end up learning more from the children, who seem to have music in their souls.

In Ghana, kids sing and dance on the way to school, on the playgrounds, in the classroom, and pretty much any time they're not sleeping. But because of budget shortfalls, formal music education has been dropped from most school's curriculums. Keyboards, drums, and other instruments sit in classrooms unused.

LIVING THE HIGHLIFE

The signature music of Ghana, a joyous and complex genre known as highlife, emerged in the 1880s as a fusion of rhythms from the West African coast with music from North America, the Caribbean, and even Portugal, which gets credit for introducing the guitar to West Africa. For years, highlife, with its interesting rhythms, distinctive guitar styles, and harmonious medleys of guitars with brass and woodwinds, ruled dance floors across much of West Africa, and today it has spread across Africa, indeed all over the world. At last count, Amazon.com listed 53 CD selections of Ghanaian highlife. One of the most popular, *The Guitar and the Gun,* was recorded in the early 1980s during Ghana's civil war. Although most of the recording studios and music clubs were shut down, Bokoor Studio managed to keep highlife rolling with this now classic album.

Therefore, anyone who can play an instrument, sing, dance, or even hum "do-re-mi" is extremely welcome. But watch out—Ghanaian children will likely ask for your autograph and inquire as to whether or not you're a pop star.

Like many countries in Africa, Ghana has young people who live in garbage dumps, thousands of AIDS orphans, and families who can't even remember the last time they had enough to eat. But at the Madonna Primary School, one of the places where you'll likely be placed, or Great Lamptey-Mills Institute, a school in the Muslim sector of Accra, nothing matters but the beat. Poor, rich, old, young—they're all one, jiving to Ghana's magical rhythms.

And talk about coming home with more than you left with! Because music offers an instantaneous avenue for connecting with someone from a different culture, get ready to come home with lots of new entries in your address book. And expect to make lifelong friends, not to mention returning with a whole different way of looking at the world.

For example, "Ghana time"—which is when someone says, "See you at 10 a.m.," but really means "See you sometime tomorrow"—just might be a better way to face life. In Ghana, the pace of life is slower and more relaxed. Above all else, Ghanaians are dedicated to having fun. Even at the busy city markets, where crowded stalls sell everything from CDs of Ghana's signature highlife music to pigs feet, there are DJs blasting music and encouraging people to dance, dance, dance.

Travellers Worldwide, which arranges these volunteer teaching positions in Ghana, is a Sussex, England–based, company that specializes in volunteer vacations throughout Asia, Africa, Europe, and Latin America. Volunteers can do everything from coach basketball or cricket to work with crocodiles or leopards.

Prices for the Ghana trip vary depending on how long you stay (two weeks is £795 or about $1,590; three months, £1,795 or $3,590) and include accommodations, most often with a host family, and all meals.

HOW TO GET IN TOUCH

Travellers Worldwide, 7 Mulberry Close, Ferring, West Sussex, BN12 5HY, England, 44 1903 50295, www.travellersworldwide.com.

provide elbow grease for an international peace center

GLENCREE, IRELAND

All we are saying is "give peace a chance."
—John Lennon

45 Back in 1972, when English paratroopers shot 14 unarmed civil rights demonstrators in Derry, Ireland, and the Irish Republican Army killed 134 British soldiers, the idea of peace in Northern Ireland seemed unthinkable. After decades, even centuries, of disagreements, all anybody could do was throw up their hands.

But on July 31, 2007, the unthinkable happened. The last British troops from Operation Banner, an emergency deployment that began in 1969 and lasted 38 long years, pulled out of Northern Ireland, officially drawing a curtain on Ireland's years and years of conflict.

In a world where conflict threatens from every side, the "unthinkable lessons" learned in Northern Ireland offer hope to the rest of the world. And nowhere is this hope more alive than at the Glencree Centre for Peace and Reconciliation, a peace center in the valley of Ireland's Wicklow Mountains.

The center, which promotes the idea that nonviolent solutions must be pursued as actively as hatred, stands as a beacon of possibility. At one time, the structure was a British army barracks, built in the early 1800s to hunt down holdout guerrillas from the Irish Rebellion of 1798. During World War I, it housed German prisoners of war.

Founded two years after the violence of Bloody Sunday, the peace center was started by folks from both sides of the fence who came together with the conviction that there had to be a better way than violence, intolerance, and sectarianism. Today, the center offers a broad range of programs in such subjects as interpersonal conflict resolution, mediation, group facilitation skills, peace vs. war journalism, and understanding the dynamics of conflict. They also offer advice, training, and

"I DO" AGREE TO HONOR AND LOVE AND SEND VOLUNTEERS TO ALL CORNERS OF THE PLANET

Global Volunteers, one of the first organizations to send do-gooders on volunteer projects, was started back in 1979 because of a honeymoon. In December of that year, Michele Gran and Bud Philbrook were planning a barefoot honeymoon cruise in the Caribbean. "It was the era of the Vietnamese boat people," Philbrook recalls. "Michele didn't feel right about playing while people were on the same waters, fighting for their lives." So they compromised: five days at Disney World, Philbrook's childhood dream, and five days in rural Guatemala, helping villagers obtain funds for a much-needed irrigation project.

After the local newspaper wrote a story about their unusual honeymoon, people started hounding them for info: How can we do the same things? In 1984, Bud and Michele established Global Volunteers to provide people with an opportunity to make a difference in the lives of others around the globe. Since then, they've hooked up volunteers with hundreds of projects, from building schools in Ghana to caring for orphans in Romania to teaching English to kids in China.

---

insights to actors in other global conflict zones, most notably South Africa, Haiti, the Middle East, Sri Lanka, and Colombia.

"Glencree is led by people who don't have the answers, but are looking together for the questions," says Ian White, director of political and international relations at the center.

Global Volunteers, a St. Paul, Minnesota–based, nonprofit that organizes volunteer vacations in 20 countries, sends volunteers to Glencree for one- and two-week stays to help the organization wage peace. Like most nonprofits, the Irish peace center is sorely understaffed and underfunded. So volunteers roll up their sleeves to take care of the center's day-to-day maintenance. They paint, plant, weed, assemble, spiff up, set up, and do whatever else is necessary to generally free up the hardworking staff to focus on the important job of facilitating peace. Volunteers live at the center and enjoy the center's pastoral, peaceful setting.

In their free time, volunteers can go pub hopping (several pubs and cafés are a short bus trip away in Enniskerry), berry picking, and heather or wildflower gathering. Also nearby are the 18th-century Powerscourt House and Gardens, the seaside town of Bray, and, of course, Dublin, where they can tour the Guinness

TANKS FOR THE MEMORY

City traffic in central Belfast still parts from time to time for armored military Land Rovers. But instead of soldiers peering out the roof hatch for snipers and car bombs, the occupants are stag parties scouting for the next pub or tuxedoed high school students on their way to the Irish equivalent of the prom. Such novelty limos, snatched up as military surplus, are the last trace of Operation Banner, which began in August 1969 on the same weekend hippies gathered in upstate New York for the Woodstock Music Festival.

Brewery, Trinity College with its Book of Kells, and the Christ Church Cathedral. Glencree is also happy to arrange a special guided trip to Belfast, where volunteers can meet with and learn from local people representing both sides of the Irish conflict.

The trips cost $2,595 and include meals and overnight accommodations at the Glencree conference facility.

HOW TO GET IN TOUCH

Global Volunteers, 375 E. Little Canada Road, St. Paul, MN 55117, 800-487-1074 or 651-407-6152, www.globalvolunteers.org, or **Glencree Centre for Peace and Reconciliation,** Glencree, Enniskerry, County Wicklow, Ireland, 353 (0) 1 2829711, www.glencree.ie.

GESUNDHEIT! INSTITUTE

clown around in russia

ST. PETERSBURG AND MOSCOW, RUSSIA

Perhaps nonsense is another instrument of compassion more able to compose human connections where there once were none. We create these clown communities to redistribute the abundance of these forces— also forms of food and medicine—worth more than gold, impossible to count and available to all living species.
—Kathy Blomquist, clown participant on a Patch Adams humanitarian clown tour

46 There are two measly requirements to participate in Patch Adams's annual humanitarian clown missions to Russia: First, you have to love people, and second, you have to wear a red rubber nose on the plane from Washington, DC, to Moscow.

For 25 years, Patch Adams, the doctor played by Robin Williams in the eponymous 1998 movie about his life, has been leading clown delegations to Russia. Volunteer clowns of all ages, sizes, and persuasions spend two weeks spreading frivolity in Russian orphanages, hospitals, prisons, mental institutions, and nursing homes. They also clown around in subways, hotels, restaurants, and city streets. The idea, says Adams, is to promote joyful living and relieve suffering, something that isn't limited to public institutions.

Volunteers spend a week each in Moscow and St. Petersburg, spreading, as Adams says, "as much fun and love as is humanly possible." Other goals for the yearly trip he leads with his brother, Wildman, are to help volunteers find their inner clown selves, experience group intimacy, and expose themselves to the discrepancy between rich and poor.

Besides doing all that, volunteers will also visit the Kremlin and Red Square while in Moscow, a city that just celebrated its 860th anniversary, and Palace Square and Nevsky Prospekt in St.

Petersburg, a city often described as the Venice of the North (see sidebar p. 31).

"In a culture where money determines values, and decisions are based on 'net worth,' an investment into clown missions might appear foolish, trivial, and temporary," says Kathy Blomquist, one of Adams's volunteer clowns. "One might argue that sending food, medicine, or money better addresses the needs of the poor. But for me, it's the permission to get closer than most, led by children over obstacles that become a game heading right into someone's heart."

Besides the annual sojourn to Russia, Adams, who has been involved in what he calls "clown healing work" for nearly three decades, leads clown posses to every continent on the planet except Antarctica. His "nut-workers" have built medical clinics in Central America and taken their merry madness to Afghanistan, Cambodia, African refugee camps, Romanian AIDS

CLOWN NOSES FOR ALL

Angelina Jolie, who was made an honorary citizen of Cambodia by the king of that poverty-stricken nation, financed one of Patch Adams's clown missions to Cambodia. Other interesting tidbits about the quixotic doctor, who claims he'll spend the rest of his life correcting misperceptions from the 1998 blockbuster movie about his life, include:

- In the movie, the real-life Adams played the part of a catatonic patient with his arm in the air.
- He owns 12,000 books and subscribes to 120 periodicals, including *Food Insect Newsletter*, *Experimental Musical Instruments*, and *Funny Times*.
- After attempting suicide at age 18, he made two decisions: to serve humanity in medicine and to "never to have another bad day."
- After obtaining his M.D., he moved into a house with 20 adults (3 of whom were physicians) and children. Over the next 12 years, they treated 1,000 people per month, with 5 to 50 overnight guests at any one time—all for free.
- He writes to people on death row trying to figure out "what makes a beautiful little baby into a murderer."
- He named one of his two sons Atomic Zagnut Adams.
- Although eBay sells them for much more, you can buy a 2-inch soft foam clown nose for a mere 39 cents at www.zymetrical.com.

orphanages, and tsunami relief camps in Sri Lanka.

This two-week Russian trip costs $4,625 and includes airfare from Washington, DC, hotel accommodations, meals, all bus rides, the train to St. Petersburg from Moscow, and $150 that Adams adds on so that his Russian friends and orphans can join in the fun. He also recommends reading at least one book on Russian history, and as many books by Dostoevsky, Tolstoy, Chekhov, and Turgenev as possible.

"And, of course," says Adams, "you can do all of this [clowning and spreading joy] for free in your hometown."

And just in case you don't want to go all the way to Russia, and don't necessarily want to don a clown nose, you can volunteer at Adams's Gesundheit! Institute in rural West Virginia—perhaps gardening, cooking, building, or housekeeping. Volunteers are typically needed at Gesundheit! from April through October with a minimum commitment of one month. If you don't have all that time, opt for the Visitor Weekend Program, which might comprise such service work as ecological restoration, construction, or grounds maintenance. Either option is free.

HOW TO GET IN TOUCH

Gesundheit! Institute, P.O. Box 50125, Arlington, VA 22205, www.patchadams .org. For information about the trip, contact **Wildman Adams,** 6855 Washington Boulevard, Arlington, VA 22213, 540-298-4589.

help start a cottage industry in el salvador

ZONA ROSA, EL SALVADOR

> I never knew the true meaning of passion until I started organizing the humanitarian missions to El Salvador. Something deep within just bursts open and your heart overflows when you give of yourself and help the less fortunate.
> —Cindy Paulus, AAI leader of many missions to El Salvador

47 Twelve years ago, American Airlines flight attendant Nancy Rivard looked around an aircraft and asked a simple question. "I'd see empty space in the overhead bin, empty space underneath in freight, empty seats, and I thought, why can't we use this to help others?"

At first, airline executives balked. Wouldn't work, they said. Would be a logistical nightmare, they claimed. Would add too much weight, they feared.

But Rivard wouldn't take no for an answer. At first, she did her "good deeds" on the QT. Gathering soap, shampoo, and other hotel freebies, she'd secretly drop them off at a Bosnian refugee camp or a poor orphanage in Central America. She escorted a little girl who needed heart surgery from Guatemala to New York. She adopted a girl in Sri Lanka and lived with Indians in the Andes.

EATING IN EL SALVADOR 101

The signature food of El Salvador is the *pupusa* (poo-poo-suh), a thick, hamburger bun–size tortilla filled with everything from refried beans and cheese to meat, vegetables, and pork rinds. *Pupusarias*, establishments serving the popular fat tortillas with a side of *curtido* (cabbage, carrot, and onion salad), line the streets of San Salvador, as well as rural roadsides.

Two other Salvadoran specialties are *mango verde* and *atol shuco*, a bluecorn pudding that's not only delicious but also famous for curing hangovers.

"I looked closely at those ahead of me on the corporate ladder," Rivard says. "They were nice people, but didn't seem to have a higher purpose in their lives. Asking myself how I could contribute led to a vision of the travel industry—because of our unique airline privileges—leading the charge in fostering communication between different cultures." She even wrote an in-flight video script introducing her idea of "traveling to make a difference."

In 1996, Rivard started Airline Ambassadors International (AAI) for airline employees to use their pass privileges to help children around the world. Today, AAI, made up of flight attendants from 12 airlines, takes donated supplies to 52 different countries. Rivard's recruits, in addition, have assisted tsunami victims in Thailand, turned a junkyard in El Salvador into a sewing village, built a medical clinic in Haiti, and taken wheelchairs to a teaching hospital in Hanoi.

AAI also organizes humanitarian aid missions on which everyday civilians "ride along" to help with their groundbreaking work. The team for a recent AAI trip to El Salvador, for example, included a corporate manager, an artist, a nurse, a singer, and a seven-year-old boy who took cards and pictures to the orphans from his first-grade class back home. AAI organizes three to ten missions per month to countries in Central and South America, Asia, and Africa.

"I am convinced that most people want to make a difference, but simply don't know how to get involved," Rivard explains. "We read about problems in Afghanistan, starvation in South Africa, or an earthquake in El Salvador, and besides writing a check to the Red Cross or UNICEF, we just don't know how to respond. What Airline Ambassadors does is match ordinary people with actual world needs."

On the El Salvador trips, which run dozens of times a year, the whole family is invited along. Offering a wide array of projects, volunteers can play with kids in an orphanage, take sewing machines to a village of 146 houses that AAI (in conjunction with the Kiwanis Club) built on a former dump of rusted-out cars, help out at a medical clinic in Santo Tomás, or help local artisans start cottage industries. Ana Ligia Mixco Sol de Saca, the First Lady of El Salvador, is even on AAI's board of directors, along with Patch Adams (see pp. 131–133), Desmond Tutu, and former UN secretary Robert Muller.

On your downtime in El Salvador, you'll also have the chance to visit coffee plantations, Mayan ruins, volcanoes, villages that grow sugar cane, and some of the best surfing beaches on the planet.

Airline Ambasssadors has service projects in 45 countries, many of which invite non-airline employees.

AAI trips vary in cost but always include airfare, accommodations, sightseeing, ground transportation, and donations to the projects. On Class A projects, where most volunteers start, you stay in a four- or five-star hotel and do a little "tourism" along with your humanitarian duties; for these trips, you'll pay roughly $100 per day. On Class B trips, the most common type, you stay in a smaller boutique hotel, spend three to five days delivering aid, and pay from $60 to $80 per day. On Class C, which often involves responding to a disaster, sleeping in a tent, and traveling by horseback or jeep to a remote location, you'll pay less than $60 a day.

HOW TO GET IN TOUCH

Airline Ambassadors International, 418 California Avenue, P.O. Box 459, Moss Beach, CA 94038, 866-264-3586 or 650-728-7844, www.airlineamb.org.

take kids hiking in the land of the morning calm

GWANGYANG, SOUTH KOREA

This is a place where we enjoy hearing the earth revolve.
—Kim Weon-gil, Korean poet

48 Mountains make up 70 percent of the rugged 600-mile peninsula we call South Korea, making it one of the most mountainous countries in the world.

Like most of the country, Gwangyang, a town of about 140,000 on the southern coast, is surrounded by peaks—in the case of Gwangyang, the mountains are Baegung, Gayasan, and Gubonghwasan. And while most of the kids of Gwangyang see these beloved mountains outside their windows each day, they don't get a lot of opportunities to explore their bounty. Their parents, busy contributing to South Korea's newfound economic boom, work long hours, many at the giant steel mill built on its own island in Gwangyang's port on the South Sea. Gwangyang Steel Works is the largest steel mill in the world, producing 15 million tons of steel a year. In fact, 300,000 tourists a year flock to Gwangyang just to see the innovative company that produces steel coils for bridges, cars, and refrigerators.

Volunteers for Peace, a Vermont-based nonprofit that enlists volunteers for more than 3,000 United Nations–sanctioned community projects around the world, sends recruits to a children's center in Gwangyang, where rural kids do not have the same cultural advantages as their urban kin. And so, volunteers not only lead kids on hikes throughout their mountains, but teach them to cook, speak English, make art, and create theater pieces.

In fact, if you're the independent sort who always wanted to, say, produce a comic book with pint-size cartoonists or have your stage adaption of "Goldilocks and the Three Bears" acted out, this would be a good project for you. The children's center has lots of kids who need care after school, as well as many from the under-eight set who need care all day. And if you're a soccer fan, all the better. Thousands of

In Korea, festivals are huge. On the Lunar New Year (known elsewhere as the Chinese New Year), for example, families make a grand pilgrimage to home-towns to pay a visit to their ancestral graves. People line up for hours when bus and train tickets go on sale for this annual three-day holiday. They also stay up all night (they believe their eyebrows will turn white if they don't), keep all the lights on in their homes (to greet the new year with bright and awakened eyes), and eat *songpyon* (full-moon rice cakes stuffed with sesame, bean, chestnuts, and Chinese dates).

Near Gwangyang, like in many regions in Korea, there are regional festivals. Some of the more popular ones are:

Baegun Medicine Water Festival. During this festival, held during the wakening of the frogs, the city of Gwangyang's prosperity is prayed for at the Okyong temple. Festivalgoers sing folk songs, drink medicinal water, and perform a water ceremony.

Big Tug-of-War. This 300-year-old festival divides folks into two groups that tug on a rope and pray to the god of the sea for a large harvest of fish.

Jeoneo Fish Festival. Held where the Seomjin River meets Gwangyang Bay, this festival includes lots of herring and shellfish and the singing of the Catching Jeoneo Song.

Gwangyang tots dream of growing up and playing for the Cheongnam Dragons, the town's soccer club that recently won the closest thing Korea has to the Superbowl—the Korean FA Cup.

If you opt for hiking up Baegung, you can tell your young charges the legend of the nine bad dragons that, according to the story, lived in a lake that in A.D. 864 became a Buddhist temple. Before Doseonguksa, the fabled national monk of the ancient Silla dynasty, showed up, the nine dragons wreaked havoc on the area. But then Doseonguksa pushed all but one of them out of the lake. That ninth dragon, an unusual white dragon and the most stubborn of the lot, required a bit more aggression. Doseonguksa finally had to blind him with a stick before boiling the water in the lake to make him flee with his friends. The temple was built on the smoldering charcoal left from the fire, and the 7,000 camellia trees around the old temple site were planted to restore the weak energy left from the fire.

Or you can hike with the kids up to the four mountain fortress walls that were used for training monk soldiers during the Japanese invasion. Or to the Jungheungsa temple that has a stone lantern with two carved lions, a stone pagoda, and a stone Buddha.

Suffice it to say, your options are unlimited.

At night, you'll stay at a house in the Children's Center with other volunteers, trade cooking duties (although the center will provide the lion's share of your meals), and have free time to explore

A $250 registration fee to Volunteers for Peace covers room and board. You'll also need to pay a mandatory onetime VFP membership of $20.

HOW TO GET IN TOUCH

Volunteers for Peace, 1034 Tiffany Road, Belmont, VT 05730, 802-259-2759, www.fvp.org.

CHAPTER

3

learning retreats

Travel is fatal to prejudice, bigotry and narrow-mindedness,
all foes to real understanding.
—Mark Twain, American humanist, satirist, and writer

If you'd rather travel with a notepad than a swimsuit, this is the chapter for you. It has 27 trips with a strong cerebral component. Some of these trips are led by college professors, scientists, museum curators, or top experts in a particular field of study. Others are offered by locals whose firsthand knowledge of, say, herbal medicine or single malt whisky is light-years ahead of anything you could find in a book.

One could argue that any trip outside your own country, beyond your own comfort zone, qualifies as a "learning retreat." When you're in a foreign land, even simple things like translating road signs or converting dollars into local currency require mental gymnastics.

All we know is that learning, despite the bad rap it sometimes gets in school, is one of the most exciting pursuits on the planet. So, yes, the vacations listed in the next few pages will definitely challenge your brain, but more importantly, they'll also stretch, illumine, and grow your soul.

read between the lines at a french house party

MEDITERRANEAN FRANCE

Books make sense of life. The only problem is that the lives they make sense of are other people's lives, never your own.
—Julian Barnes, in *Flaubert's Parrot*

49 With a view of the Pyrenees upon opening the shuttered windows of your 300-year-old stone farmhouse, you'll spend five sumptuous days drinking red wine, eating food from local farmers' markets (olives, cheeses, pâtés, melons, and eggplants, to name a few), and studying a list of books that only an eccentric British literature major and her actor partner could come up with.

In their series of "Books and Drama" getaways, Moira Martingale, an English journalist, and Christopher Masters, who studied acting at the London Academy

NEARBY EXCURSIONS

The nearest big city is Carcassonne, a UNESCO World Heritage site and France's second-most-popular tourist city. Dating back to the sixth century (with possible remnants as far back as 3500 B.C.), this stunning city, being so close to the border with Spain, has endured countless invasions and has a fascinating history that involves popes, bloodshed, royal marriages, and everything in between.

Also near Domaine St. Raymond is Rennes-le-Château, a small hilltop village with a lavish old church that was so expensively decorated (with tropical gardens, exotic animals, imported wines, and an extensive international library) by the priest, Father Saunière, a poor nobody until he found some mysterious documents, that it's rumored he found the Holy Grail. Dan Brown, author of *The Da Vinci Code,* of course, capitalized on the rumors. In a different twist, many in the area still believe Jesus settled here after escaping from Jerusalem and that his descendants populate the village.

MOVE OVER, CHAMPAGNE

About 1531, some hundred years before Dom Pierre Pérignon was even born, the monks of Abbey St. Hilaire in Limoux developed a groundbreaking method of making sparkling wine. By sealing the bottle before fermentation was complete, natural bubbles were created. Although wine producers from the Champagne region (where Dom Pérignon and another Benedictine monk supposedly invented champagne) pooh-pooh this notion, Péri- gnon did pass through Limoux (and, according to the vintners there, purloined their secret) before becoming the cellar master at St.-Pierre d'Hautvillers, where his remarkable discovery was allegedly made.

Limoux vintners, pros at winemaking but hopeless at marketing, call their sparkling wine Blanquette. It's made with a blend of Mauzac, Chenin Blanc, and Chardonnay grapes and is a heck of a lot cheaper than the "real stuff," which as far as Limoux is concerned is nothing but a pale imitation.

of Music and Dramatic Arts, lead book discussions with such unique themes as "Literary Cross-Dressing" (a female author writing from a male perspective and vice versa)," "Getting Gothic" (think *Frankenstein* and *Catcher in the Rye),* and "Code Breakers and Time Lords" (hey, what's wrong with joining time travel with mysteries?).

Besides five or so books, you'll also study a play—handpicked by Masters, an accomplished actor and director who recently retired to France—that complements the literary theme. If your group of bookworms is so inclined, you might even get the chance to act out the play or one of the novels.

But there's never any pressure. As Martingale says, "While we welcome literature scholars, the course is aimed at anybody who loves books. Think of it as your local book group being airlifted to France."

Yes, you'll discuss themes, characterization, and the personal and social impacts of the books, but you'll be doing it between goblets of amazing local wines, periodic dips in the pool, and rousing games of *boule,* the French version of Italy's bocce.

Domaine St. Raymond, the country estate where the charming duo holds their workshops, is in the Languedoc region of southern France. The weather is near-perfect, the Mediterranean beach is just an hour away, and the fields of sunflowers will remind you of a one-eared artist we won't bother to name.

Domaine St. Raymond has its own chefs, a swimming pool, gardens, tennis courts, and bikes you can borrow to follow the nearby Canal du Midi, a centuries-old tree-lined waterway between the Mediterranean and the Atlantic.

In addition to the "Books and Drama" workshops, Martingale, who owns the refurbished stone house, hosts five-day art workshops in painting, digital photography, ceramics, and, for those who want to write their own books rather than read them, creative writing.

Five-day courses with most meals run from £550 (about $1,100) and include excursions to local wineries and nearby spots relevant to your course. In "Code Breakers and Time Lords," for example, you'll take a trip to Rennes-le-Château, made famous in *The Da Vinci Code* (see sidebar p. 142).

HOW TO GET IN TOUCH

French House Parties, 11150 Pexiora, France, 33 (0)4 6894 9816, or call London office, 44 1299 896819 or 44 7900 322791, www.frenchhouseparty.co.uk.

test-drive your dream career

NATIONWIDE IN THE UNITED STATES

> The highlight of my workday is this ham sandwich.
> From now until quitting time, nothing else will be as rewarding.
> —Wally, in the comic strip "Dilbert," created by Scott Adams

50 It's not that you hate your job. It's just that it doesn't make your heart go pit-a-pat. Lately, in fact, you've been spending a lot of time wondering if your parachute might be a completely different color.

Before you tell your boss to take a flying leap, why not test-drive that job that looks so much greener?

VocationVacations, a Portland, Oregon–based, travel company, organizes mini-sabbaticals for people wanting to try a different profession on for size. For one to three days, they hook up wannabes with a mentor in one of more than 130 different careers, from chocolatier to horse trainer to Broadway producer.

"VocationVacations are a blend of reality TV meets *Fantasy Island,*" says Brian Kurth, the former telecom drone who conceived the idea for these unique "working holidays" while stuck in a Chicago commute. "It's a pragmatic way to kick the tires of a new career without giving notice. You can read books and do online research, but this is a way to actually touch and feel a job you often dream about."

Admittedly, a one- or three-day apprenticeship is barely getting your toes wet, but Kurth has some pretty impressive success stories in only three years of business. Twenty percent of alumni have either made the leap to their dream job or are well on their way, including a former insurance claims adjustor who now works at a talent agency, an air traffic controller who now owns a bakery, and a couple of executives who just bought a vineyard in Oregon.

While 25 percent of Kurth's vocationers are just flirting—getting a cheap thrill being a bread baker or playing Magnum P. I. for a few days—75 percent are serious about testing the waters of a new career.

"Many of us have the mind-set that mentors are for 20-somethings. We think that once you get that degree or start that career, you're set for life, that it's too late to make radical career moves," Kurth says. "VocationVacations lets you shake it up, turn it upside down, and take a new job for a whirl."

Kurth has hand-culled the mentors, sometimes going out specifically to find, say, a cheesemaker or a TV producer. The website now has a page requesting mentors who'd like to get involved in the program. Mentors do get paid, so it's a good deal for all.

Here are just three examples:

Wake up and sell the coffee. Duncan Goodall, owner of two quirky bohemian coffee shops in New Haven, Connecticut, is passionate about entrepreneurship. "When you own your own business, you control your destiny. You might work just as hard, but you structure the job to fit your lifestyle, not the other way around," says the Yale-educated business consultant who was successfully climbing the corporate ladder when he realized he wasn't happy.

Now, he can take his two daughters to the park whenever he wants, and on Fridays—his day to babysit the younger one—he simply straps her to his chest and takes her with him. "The running joke around here is, 'It takes a coffeehouse to raise a child.'"

On VocationVacations' two-day "Coffeehouse Owner" package, Goodall shows java mogul wannabes the ropes of owning a small business, specifically a coffee business. He sees his job as part cheerleader ("Entrepreneurship is awesome," he beams) and part paperless coffee shop manual.

Admittedly, two days isn't enough time to master it all, but Goodall trusts that at the very least he'll help vocationers avoid the mistakes he made ("Every one in the book," he claims) in buying an existing shop and opening another from scratch. Depending on a vocationer's interests, the 9-to-4 sessions may cover anything from how to position and promote a coffeehouse to where best to place the espresso machine.

Channel your inner Stella (McCartney). When Mercedes Gonzalez, owner of New York's Global Purchasing Group and VocationVacations' mentor for fashion buyers and designers, was young, she read an article about job dissatisfaction. "I couldn't believe it. It said 80 percent of the people in the workforce hate their job. I swore that was never going to happen to me."

After a two-year stint in premed studies (wasn't for her), a degree in economics, and one day on Wall Street, she decided to follow her heart straight into the fashion business. And love it she does. "I even love the bad parts," she says. "And I want others to love it, too." Which is why she agreed to be a mentor to aspiring fashionistas.

But watch out. Many of the vocationers who have mentored under Gonzalez are now running their own shops or starting their own fashion labels—and much faster than they expected. In only three short years, Gonzalez has three amazing success stories: a realtor who just opened her second clothing store, a D.C. policeman who opened a children's clothing store, and a financier whose line of shoe designs has already been recognized by several fashion magazines.

"I crack the whip," Gonzalez jokes. During her two-day mentorship program, vocationers attend fashion shows and industry parties and learn how to merchandise designers, forecast trends, and review samples.

Uncork a second career. You can talk Pinot Noir with the best of them and know exactly which Chardonnay to pair with seared salmon. In the back of your mind, you've always wondered, What if I bought that little farm on the outskirts of town and planted, you know, just a few grapes?

Larson Family Winery, which hosts a two-day Wine Maker's VocationVacation on its 100-acre vineyard in Sonoma County, can fast-track your dream. Not only does this winery, which has been in the Lawson family since the 1800s, grow grapes and make wine, but it also has a crushing facility, a bottling line, and a bunch of awards for its stellar Pinot Noirs, Chardonnays, and Cabernets—not to mention a great lawn for playing sunset bocce.

Says Becky Larson, who owns the winery with her husband, Tom, "There's a great reward in being able to live off the land and in being able to raise our three children here, but make no mistake, we're farmers." Which means dealing with Mother Nature and the vagaries of the market.

This is one of the benefits of taking a VocationVacation before quitting your day job. It's easy to romanticize a career, to fantasize about how perfect it is, but by test-driving it first, you get the inside scoop on both the good *and* the bad. Depending on the season, the inside scoop at the Larson Winery might involve monitoring for grape pests, sampling leaf tissue, working the bottling line, or even donning rubber boots and stomping grapes.

With 250 mentors in more than 30 states, VocationVacations provides one-to three-day dream job immersion holidays that include lunches, a journal, and "before" and "after" sessions with a certified career coach. Prices range from $549 (cheesemaker) to $2,149 (pit boss crew). The "Fashion Buyer/Retailer" package is $1,449, and the "Coffeehouse Owner" and "Wine Maker" VocationVacations are each $949.

HOW TO GET IN TOUCH
VocationVacations, 1631 N.E. Broadway, No. 422, Portland, OR 97232, 866-888-6329, www.vocationvacations.com.

earn your elephant driver's license

THAILAND'S GOLDEN TRIANGLE

The program is designed for those who would like to get a
feel for the unique bond between elephant and mahout.
—John Roberts, director of Elephant Camp

51 There may be no such thing as a dumb question, but if you ask "How?" during mahout—elephant wrangler—training at Anantara Resort Elephant Camp, the pachyderm you're driving is likely to come to a screeching halt. *How,* after all, means "stop" in elephant language (well, in Thai). But never fear, a quick *"pai"*—go—should catch you up to the rest of your class. Another useful word is *baen*, turn, which could come in mighty handy in an elephant camp that's located at the confluence of the Mekong and Ruak Rivers.

During the three-day mahout-training course, you'll learn to bathe, feed, and care for your assigned elephant. You'll master basic elephant commands (around 70, at last count) and how to communicate with your three-ton steed by lightly touching him or her behind the ears. From the back of your jumbo beauty, you'll also explore the forests of northern Thailand, Laos, and Myanmar, all of which are within elephant bugling distance from the camp.

The mahout training course is not for late risers. Elephants and their mahouts start their day at 6:30 a.m., when elephants are rounded up from the forest, driven back to the camp, and given a few moments for morning ablutions. From there, you'll be taught how to mount your elephant—either up the side or by leapfrogging over its bowed head—and given time to acclimate to the big beast's roll and sway.

After lunch, you'll use the movement commands you hopefully mastered during the morning session to drive your trusty mount to the Ruak River for its all-time favorite activity—river bathing. And, yes, trainees are expected to get in the water with their charges, although staying on the elephant's back would be nearly impossible anyway—especially if you happen to get Lawan, the village flirt who is never shy about showing her feelings.

"The elephants at the camp are used to working with people and, like the best teachers, are extremely patient. Like humans, elephants learn to trust people over time, so we encourage guests to hand-feed their teachers with plenty of sugarcane and bananas," says John Roberts, the British director of Elephant Camp. Each elephant, he notes, eats around 550 pounds of food a day.

At the end of your three-day workshop, you'll take a "driving test" and, if you pass, you'll get an official certificate of mahout competence. You'll also get your own blue denim mahout shirt.

Says Roberts, "I don't feel too guilty for turning less-than-competent mahouts out on the streets. So far, there have been no reports of accidents. At least not yet."

Anantara Resort's 160 acres of bamboo forest, nature trails, and riverbanks provide an ideal habitat for the resort's four elephants, all of whom came here from the Thai Elephant Conservation Centre in Lampang, 375 miles north of Bangkok.

CAN'T TAKE THE BABY ELEPHANT WALK, BUT STILL WANT TO HELP?

A hundred years ago, Thailand was home to 100,000 elephants. Now, there are fewer than 5,000, many of which don't have it as good as the elephants at Anantara Resort Elephant Camp.

Carolyn and Perry Butler, vintners from California's Napa Valley, were so moved by the elephants they met on their recent visit to Elephant Camp that they've come up with a unique way to get mistreated elephants off the street.

In addition to adopting Nam Chok, a four-year-old orphan elephant, they also bottled a special "Rescue" wine (it's a 2001 blend of Cabernet Sauvignon, Merlot, and Cabernet Franc) at their Juslyn Vineyards, with 100 percent of proceeds going to the Golden Triangle Asian Elephant Foundation. Carolyn also persuaded Italian designer Cesare Casadei to create a sexy patent leather pump with a black-and-white animal print and 3.5-inch red heel for the same good cause.

The wine can be ordered through Juslyn Vineyards *(707-265-1804, www .juslynvineyards.com)* and the shoes are available at Foot Candy *(877-517-4606 or 707-963-2040, www.footcandyshoes.com).*

In addition to the three-day mahout course, the Anantara also offers a world-class spa, a cooking school, longtail boat rides, treks to hill-tribe villages, mountain bikes, tennis courts, and tours to everything from the last spawning ground of giant catfish to the Hall of Opium to Doi Tung, a craft market where you can buy hand-woven rugs, mulberry-bark paper, ceramics, and locally grown arabica coffee.

The three-day elephant camp, complete with room and breakfast, runs $740.

HOW TO GET IN TOUCH

Anantara Golden Triangle, 229 Moo 1, Chiang Saen, Chiang Rai 57150, Thailand, 66 5378 4084, www.goldentriangle.anantara.com.

meet the people of the first nations

BRITISH COLUMBIA AND ALBERTA, CANADA

They're not lessons or sessions. We live it.
And most people are moved and inspired because they're
looking for the same things—thanks, peace, and love.
—Troy Patenaude, Meti Indian and co-owner of
Kootenay Wilderness Tours

52 You probably have heard the tribal lands of the Lil'wat, the Musqueam, the Squamish, and the Tsleil-Waututh called by their European names: Vancouver and Whistler. But make no mistake, the legacy of the aboriginal peoples of Canada (collectively called the First Nations) remains strong and vibrant in this popular mountain realm. For starters, their brand-new Squamish Lil'wat Cultural Centre in Whistler, a dramatic, three-story building with glass plank walls, will be one of the main broadcasting venues for the 2010 Winter Olympics.

But it doesn't stop there.

The aboriginal peoples of Canada offer dozens of opportunities to learn about their culture, from kayaking with a Native elder to indulging in a weekend sweat lodge to participating in a traditional potlatch. You can learn about totem poles, medicinal plants, grizzly bears, or how to walk more serenely with nature. In British Columbia alone, there are some two hundred different indigenous tribes, more than in any other Canadian province (check out www.aboriginalbc.com to see the whole picture). Although the options are immense, here are a few brain retreat possibilities for

MEDICINE WHEEL

The First Nations believe that every disease has a cure in nature. Common horsetail, for example, a nonflowering weed that resembles a fern, is often prescribed for urinary tract infections and kidney stones. Angel hair lichen is said to cure pneumonia and strep.

learning about Canada's First Nations in British Columbia and Alberta (home to 43 different tribes in three treaty areas):

Heart of the Olympics. The Squamish Lil'wat Cultural Centre, with its outdoor longhouse and Lil'wat Istken (pit house), offers ongoing programs in drum-making, basket weaving, herbal medicine, and other indigenous crafts. Located smack dab in the middle of Whistler Village and adjacent to the famous Fairmont Château Whistler and Four Seasons Resort, this stunning new cultural center also has an art gallery, a series of carved cedar canoes, and a gift shop with local-made jewelry, weavings, moccasins, and clothes.

Tourism Whistler, 4010 Whistler Way, Whistler, BC V0N 1B4, Canada, 888-869-2777 or 604-932-3928, www.tourismwhistler.com.

Vancouver Island. In Tofino, on the very west end of Vancouver Island where there's an old-growth pine forest, Tlaook Cultural Adventures—run by Tlaook, her father, and her sister, all members of the Tla-o-qui-aht tribe—will take you out in a traditional Nuu-chah-nulth dugout canoe to learn more about their culture. The most popular trip, Cluptl-Chas, goes to Echachist Island, an old summer fishing and whaling village, and ends with a salmon, crab, and *tsu-up* (sea urchin) bake on the beach, all for C$140 ($U.S.136).

If you can get in (you'll be competing with the likes of Danny DeVito, Uma Thurman, and Susan Sarandon), stay at the Wickaninnish Inn (or the "Wick," as it's known in Tofino), a gorgeous hotel where you can watch eagles, seals, whales, and, most famously, ocean storms. Tlaook's father, Joe Martin, makes masks, canoes, and Native cedar boxes at the hotel's art studio on the beach. Every room has a panoramic window facing the wild Pacific waves, a set of binoculars, a Hudson Bay blanket to wrap up in, a handmade driftwood chair, a fireplace, and a rain suit (in case you want to explore the beach). Rooms range from C$260 (U.S.$253) off-season to C$1,500 (U.S.$1,460) for a suite in high season.

Also on Vancouver Island is the U'Mista Cultural Centre (entrance fee C$6), where you learn about the traditional potlatch ceremonies of the Kwakwaka'wakw. Defying the accumulation of wealth that symbolizes modern-day capitalism, the potlatch is an ancient ritual where people gather for the sole purpose of giving of themselves—whether it be personal belongings, dances, stories, or the rights to share the best fishing hole. You'll see dance performances, hear stories, and view an amazing collection of elaborately carved and decorated potlatch masks.

Tlaook Cultural Adventures, Box 899, Tofino, BC V0R 2Z0, Canada, 250-725-2656, www.tlaook.com.

Wickaninnish Inn, Box 250, Tofino, BC V0R 2Z0, Canada, 800-333-4604 or 250-725-3100, www.wickinn.com.

U'mista Cultural Society, Front Street, P.O. Box 253, Alert Bay, BC V0N 1A0, Canada, 250-974-5403, www.umista.ca.

Secluded Rocky Mountains. For those wanting to hang out in the wild the way the First Peoples did, Kootenay Wilderness Tours offers one- to eight-day wilderness adventures in Alberta, where you'll learn to identify common plants and tracks, practice wilderness skills, and participate in powerful ceremonies with Native elders. On the four-day "Elk Runner" trip, for example, you'll take nature walks, learn to make fire with two sticks, participate in a sharing circle, smoke a peace pipe, and partake of a traditional Thanksgiving feast with a Native elder. Tours start at the Cross River Wilderness Centre, about an hour and twenty minutes by car south of Banff. The cost of the "Elk Runner" trip is C$830 (U.S.$808).

Kootenay Wilderness Tours, 428 Parkridge Crescent S.E., Calgary, AB T2J 4Z4, Canada, 877-659-7665 or 403-271-3296, www.kootenaywildernesstours.ca.

thrill to the wildebeest migration on the serengeti

TANZANIA

The wildebeest is a creature who has been put together out of spare parts.
—Alan Root, wildlife filmmaker

53 Chicago's Field Museum of Natural History knows a thing or two about creating a blockbuster. In 1977, it brought "The Treasures of Tutankhamun" to town in a coup that rang up 1.35 million admissions, to this day one of the largest turnouts for a touring exhibition. And if you haven't already heard about the $17 million it spent to buy and restore Sue, the world's largest intact T. Rex skeleton, the question is: Where have you been the last ten years? The venerable lakefront museum that was originally created as permanent repository for artifacts from the World Columbian Exposition of 1893 has even been known to create bidding wars to secure such exhibits as Jackie Kennedy's traveling gown collection.

But when it comes to offering field research tours, the Field Museum takes a more modest approach, offering an average of only 10 or so tours a year. Most are led by curators and scientists who work for the museum.

BARNEY'S GOT COMPETITION

When Sue's skeletal remains were snatched up by Chicago's Field Museum for $8.4 million, the biggest bucks ever spent on a dinosaur fossil, jaws of the human variety dropped. But she's proven to be a good investment. Along with such merchandise as T-shirts and Sue backpacks, the museum offers or licenses nearly a dozen Sue-themed toys, including paintable figurines and magnetic sculptures. There's even a CD called *A T-Rex Named Sue* featuring Al Jarreau and other musicians.

"Instead of offering hundreds of tours, many of which would end up getting canceled, we offer just a handful of really specialized tours," says Steve Hines, director of Field Museum Tours. "We try to make each one really special."

After the King Tut exhibit, the Field, of course, is practically required to offer an Egypt trip every year, something it's been doing for nearly three decades. Another trip that gets repeated year after year, selling out all 16 slots, is the "Tanzania Migration Safari," which follows the soul-stirring spectacle of 1.5 million wildebeests charging through the wilds of Tanzania—the largest assemblage of grazing animals on the planet. It's one place—maybe the only place left—where the human species' much chastised hegemony over the world's creatures becomes dubious.

Since 2000, this popular tour has teamed the same two staff zoologists: William Stanley, collection manager of the museum's Division of Mammals, one of the world's largest collections of mammal species, and Mary Anne Rogers, a 24-year Field Museum veteran who manages the Fish Collection. With their firsthand knowledge of the Serengeti ecosystem, these old pros provide a depth of information that travelers on other tours rarely get. Around campfires each night, Stanley regales his charges with tales about his childhood growing up in Kenya.

Because Stanley and Rogers know Tanzania so well, they're able to take each year's lucky 16 off the beaten path. Having built relationships with other scientists in the area, they're able to provide access to places not normally on the safari circuit.

During the two-week journey that's scheduled each February during the wildebeest calving season, you'll stay in a tent camp and spend two nights in the world-famous Ngorongoro Crater, a 102-square-mile crater filled with rhinos, cheetahs, and lions. "I love to see the expression on people's faces when they first go to the Ngorongoro Crater," says Stanley, who enjoys sharing his research on endangered mammals in Tanzanian forests.

The $7,495 price for the two-week safari includes accommodations, most meals, Tanzanian visas, and an opening reception at the museum itself. Participants are expected to be in vital physical condition.

HOW TO GET IN TOUCH

Field Museum, 1400 S. Lake Shore Drive, Chicago, IL 60605, 312-922-9410, www.fieldmuseum.org.

see the unreported side of modern africa

UGANDA

Uganda is the pearl of Africa.
—Winston Churchill

54 If you've caught CNN International over the past couple of years, you know that Uganda is "gifted by nature," as the country's advertising slogan goes. You've seen lush jungle foliage, rugged river gorges, and silverback gorillas with biceps as big as telephone poles.

Uganda's television blitz, created by the giant public relations firm Hill & Knowlton, is part of a whole new marketing game known as "nation branding." In order to reshape public opinion—not a bad strategy for a country whose image has been shaped largely by former dictator Idi Amin—the central African government ponied up $650,000 to H&K for coming up with the new slogan, not to mention the million-dollar CNN ad buy.

It's obviously working. Tourism is up in Uganda, with most takers coming to either raft the Bujagli Falls, climb the snowcapped Rwenzori Mountains, or—by far the most popular reason—to track mountain gorillas in Bwindi Impenetrable National Park or chimpanzees in the Chambura Gorge and Kibale Forest.

But according to Maria Baryamujura, founder of COBATI (Community-Based Tourism Initiatives), all the packaged safaris offer little benefit to the locals, 80 percent of whom live in rural areas. In fact, most of the dough generated by the big media blitz ends up in the pockets of the international corporations that are building skyscraper hotels in Kampala.

"I believe it's important to educate Western travelers about the other side of Africa, the positive side that is not often revealed by the international media," she says.

That's why Baryamujura has developed a unique tourism initiative that works with small rural communities, encouraging them to share their lifestyles, indigenous knowledge, organic food, and small-town hospitality. In other words, forget the flashy packages and go for the experience.

Her bottom-line goal is to convince Western tourists to alter their holiday behavior. "Instead of driving straight through villages in safari vans heading for national parks, why not divert to local villages, get involved, and make contact with local people?" she asks. "For most tourists, their expectation of an African village is very different from what they find. They come expecting a community filled with hungry children, adults dying of HIV/AIDS living in dirty unsanitary conditions and poverty. Tourists are usually very surprised at how African villages and people are different from the images they see on media."

Baryamujura's trips—what she calls "village tourism"—allow media-saturated Westerners to detach themselves from old-fashioned thinking and stereotypes. As she points out, "It gives them a broader view of the world, builds strong relationships, and enhances the human condition," not to mention benefiting small rural communities and helping to prevent villagers from being forced to relocate to big cities.

COBATI sets up homestay programs for visitors who want to learn about the real Uganda, whose economy has been based on small, African-owned farms since precolonial days. On a COBATI homestay, you'll get the chance to visit banana plantations, see homesteads with Ankole longhorn cattle (indigenous to Uganda for at least seven centuries), attend community weddings, stay with midwives, and visit flower farms. Perusi Karamuzi, a widow with six children, for example, opened her homestead to visitors, giving them hands-on lessons in zero grazing, beekeeping, mushroom growing, and Ugandan handcrafts.

"People are surprised that you could go to someone's home without an appointment and freely join them for a meal. They're surprised to learn that people are happy, children healthy, and the landscape is scenic," Baryamujura says.

COBATI not only sets up homestay trips but also works to encourage rural communities to see the resources that they have. Prices for a homestay trip start at less than $50 a day.

HOW TO GET IN TOUCH

COBATI, Plot 6 Collville Street, P.O. Box 7493, Kampala, Uganda, 256 (0) 41 344613 or 256 77 506747, www.cobati.or.ug.

learn business tips from the chinese

BEIJING, CHINA

If the world gives us a chance, we will return it many splendors.
—2008 Summer Olympics poster in Shanghai

55 Napoleon Bonaparte once made the comment that China was a sleeping giant that, when it finally awoke, would move the world. As it turns out, the French emperor could have had a second career as a psychic.

In the last two decades, China has become the go-to guy when it comes to business. With a population of 1.3 billion, the now wide-awake giant is the world's largest producer of steel, coal, and cigarettes, has 100 million Internet users, and has more cell phone users (360 million) than the United States has people. And as China widens its doors to the rest of the world, with its recent acceptance into the World Trade Organization and its hosting duties for the 2008 Summer Olympics, savvy business folks are realizing that knowledge of China's local business practices, laws, culture, and society is vital to business success.

World Link Education, an international organization that works with several Chinese universities, offers classes in learning Mandarin and understanding the complexities of Chinese business. Taught in English, the Chinese business course lasts five weeks (you can also opt for a shorter, language-only course) and combines classroom lectures with company seminars and on-site study trips of a variety of Chinese businesses. If you're interested, free guided tours to such tourist hot spots as the Great Wall, Summer Palace, Lama Temple, Tiananmen Square, and the Forbidden City are also available on the weekends.

Guest lecturers from China's prominent business and economic universities cover the nation's history from a marketing perspective, its political climate, recent reforms, and the seemingly murky waters of Chinese business etiquette. Professor Gao, one of several key lecturers, won the Chinese National Book Prize in 1988 and was recognized by Harvard Business School for his business and marketing skills.

WHEN IN CHINA . . .

Recently, the Chinese government put out a list of "Eight Honors and Eight Dishonors" to express what President Hu Jintao called the "socialist concept of honor and disgrace," for instance, "Do strive arduously," "Don't wallow in luxury." Here are a few of our own honors and dishonors for doing business in China:

- More than being proficient in Mandarin, patience is the skill most needed. The Chinese are old pros at knowing when foreigners are under tight deadlines, and they use that to their negotiation advantage.
- Defer to age. Progress aside, China is still very much a hierarchical society, and age trumps almost everything. For example, the eldest representative should be allowed to enter and leave the room first.
- Don't count on the Internet. Even with more than 100 million users, there are still major Internet obstacles. The thousands of Chinese ideographs don't always translate to a computer keyboard, and there's always that sticky little problem of the "Great Chinese Firewall": government censorship.
- Avoid China during the Lunar New Year. Tradition demands that every Chinese return to his or her traditional home for the holiday, so you'll be vying with millions of travelers on every conceivable mode of transportation.
- Though the official Chinese language is Mandarin, spoken by more than 70 percent of the population, there are more than 200 other Chinese languages.
- Show up on time. Punctuality is all-important in China. Even a five-minute tardiness is a serious affront.
- Realize there are a few things you *do* understand. Starbucks, for example, is everywhere in China, as is McDonald's, KFC, Taco Bell, and Pizza Hut. In fact, in China, Pizza Hut is considered fine dining—with reservations required. And at Taco Bells, waiters wear enormous sombreros that would surely inspire anti-defamation lawsuits from the National Council of La Raza if worn stateside.

Some of the businesses you'll be invited into are the Chinese divisions of Sony, Nokia, and Microsoft; the Dragon Seal Winery, a state-owned winery that produces a mean Cabernet Sauvignon; and the Blue Zoo Beijing, a popular walk-through aquarium.

As for your Mandarin classes, you'll do seat time in the classroom, of course, but you'll also get the chance to practice with Mandarin Chinese speakers. You'll play basketball, go bowling, partake in a traditional Peking duck dinner, and even sing karaoke, all the while practicing your new Mandarin skills. While five weeks may not be enough time to master the most common 3,500 Chinese characters, you should end up being able to read and understand some news from newspapers, radio broadcasts, and television. But most importantly, you'll learn enough to keep from embarrassing yourself (see sidebar p. 161).

And while it's easy to get lost in a country with four times as many people as the United States, World Link keeps its language classes small, from five to eight participants. You'll learn to write, speak, listen, and master vocabulary, as well as get the low-down on dealing with everyday situations of Chinese culture.

Working with the Academy of Chinese Language Study (ACLS) with locations in Beijing and Shanghai, World Link has been recognized and accredited by such U.S. universities as Stanford, Fordham, and Ohio State. With residence halls right next door, you'll get free Internet access and after-class tutors, if for some reason you haven't quite mastered the phrase *Nali, nali, nin guo jiang le,* which, loosely translated, means "Please don't, please don't, you overpraise." Anything but complete and total modesty is considered arrogant.

World Link also offers classes in Chinese folk music, martial arts, painting, massage, and Chinese medicine.

The five-week Chinese business class costs from $3,370 to $4,410, depending on your choice of lodging, which include options from living with a host family to shared or private apartments to three-star hotels. Included are classes, after-hour tutors, social activities, study tours, and transfers to and from the airport.

HOW TO GET IN TOUCH

World Link Education, 1904 Third Avenue, Suite 633, Seattle, WA 98101, 800-621-3085, www.worldlinkedu.com.

master the art of blending scotch

SCOTLAND

*I love to sing, and I love to drink scotch. Most people would rather hear
me drink scotch.*
—George Burns, Academy Award–winning actor

56 If you're one of those Scotch lovers who swears by having a wee dram every now and again, you may have already made the pilgrimage to the motherland. Chances are you've visited at least a few of Scotland's hundred-plus whisky distilleries and know that if the snifter in front of you smells of peat and salt air, it comes from the Isle of Islay; if it's über sweet, it's probably from Speyside; and if there's fruit and smoke, it's likely a single malt from the Highlands.

Now, thanks to the Glengoyne Distillery near Loch Lomond in the Scottish Highlands, 15 miles north of Glasgow, you can extend your whisky education even further. This prestigious distillery invites whisky pilgrims in for one of two classes in learning how to blend Scotch. They call it "getting inside the barrel."

The two-hour "Master Blender" class runs £25 (about $50) and teaches aspiring stillmen how to create their own blend. Not only will you sample award-winning 17-year-old single Highland malts and visit the bonded warehouses, but you'll also go home with a self-made, 100-milliliter bottle of your own blend.

Or, if you're ready for your Scotch Ph.D., sign up for the "master class," which includes nearly a whole day of whisky tasting, touring, talks, and personalized

IN GOOD COMPANY

If you get goose bumps from a full-frontal whiff of Glengoyne's 10-, 17-, and 29-year-old single malt Scotch whiskies, you're not alone. Some of Glengoyne's famous imbibers have included the late Queen Mother Elizabeth, Alanis Morissette, Ozzy Osbourne, Eminem, Ryder Cup captain Sam Torrance, and members of the Eurythmics, Coldplay, Pink Floyd, the Pretenders, and REM.

blending. At the end of this class, which costs £100 ($200), you'll leave with a 200-milliliter bottle of your own making, a personalized bottle of ten-year-old single malt Highland Scotch, a certificate, and a cellar book.

In both classes, you'll visit the former Manager's House, including the Sample Room, its walls lined with whiskies at different stages of maturation; the Club Room, designed by the hip Glasgow design firm Timorous Beasties (known for its surreal and provocative textiles and wallpapers, the firm got its name from the Robert Burns poem "To a Mouse"); and the Board Room.

Although it began operations long before (when distilleries evading the taxman hid in secret coves of the Highlands), Glengoyne Distillery has officially been making Scotch whisky since 1833. It's just down the road from the 15th-century Duntreath Castle, with its medieval stocks and dungeons, near the area where Scotland's own Robin Hood—Rob Roy—valiantly fought the British aristocracy. Often considered the "most scenic distillery in Scotland," Glengoyne gathers its water from a 60-foot waterfall gliding down from the Campsie Hills.

But watch out. Bill McDowell was a news editor at *The Herald* (Glasgow) when he first signed on for a master class. He fell so "head over heels" with the distillery, the whisky, and the folks who make it that he ditched his prestigious news job to become a Glengoyne stillman.

If you don't want to make the drive down scenic A81, Glengoyne graciously offers its own helipad. If you're just interested in a simple wee tasting tour, offered every hour on the hour, you can simply show up. But if you want to take either class, it's imperative to call ahead for reservations.

HOW TO GET IN TOUCH
Glengoyne Distillery, Dumgoyne, near Killearn, Glasgow, G63 9LB, Scotland, 44 1360 550 254, www.glengoyne.com.

bone up on orangutans

BORNEO AND SUMATRA

Orangutans don't just pack their bags and move somewhere else.
They stay, and they die.
—Ian Singleton, scientific director of the
Sumatran Orangutan Conservation Programme

57 Other than that futzy old Aunt Clara, orangutans are the closest relatives we have. We share 96.4 percent of the same DNA and, like us, they live alone (as opposed to the other great apes, which live in family groups), have nine-month pregnancies, and have youngsters that cry, throw tantrums, and even, according to BBC News, play charades.

Unfortunately, they're not expected to survive (at least not in the wild) through the rest of the century. In fact, their habitats in Borneo and Sumatra are shrinking by the hour thanks to poachers, palm oil manufacturers, and developers who think nothing of cutting wide swaths through the pristine rain forests where they live. Until the 1990s, these red-hued apes were widespread across Asia, but now the only populations left outside zoos are on the islands of Borneo and Sumatra. Because they live in the jungle canopy, building intricately woven nests in the trees where they live and play, they've not been so hot at adapting to nonjungle life.

To see and learn about the habitats of the remaining 60,000 orangutans, sign up for an educational safari with World Primate Safaris, the only safari company to specialize in primates, period. Besides three to four yearly trips to Borneo and Sumatra, this British company, which donates part of its profits to the preservation and conservation of our endangered cousins, offers tracking safaris for gorillas in Uganda and Rwanda, lemurs in Madagascar, chimpanzees in Tanzania and Uganda, and other primates elsewhere.

In Borneo, you'll visit the Sepilok Orang Utan Sanctuary, a 15-square-mile swatch of virgin rain forest where you can watch previously captive orangutans being fed, and Danum Valley, a conservation area with leopards, elephants, and Sumatran rhinos, as well as orangutans.

LION AND TIGERS AND BEARS, BUT NOT FOR LONG

In Sumatra, the orangutan population is shrinking by a thousand a year. Some scientists suggest they could be extinct within ten years. Unfortunately, they're not alone. Indonesia, in fact, has more endangered species than any other country in the world. According to the International Union for Conservation of Nature and Natural Resources, there are 128 mammals and 104 birds, as well as many reptiles and insects, that are steadily losing ground in Indonesia. The clearance of just 250,000 acres of Sumatra's primeval forest means sure, if not sudden, death to 50,000 monkeys, 9,000 siamang, 600 gibbons, 15,000 hornbills, 200 tigers, and 100 elephants. Also in dire straits are the clouded leopard, the flying squirrel, the sun bear, and the Sumatran rhino.

In Sumatra, you'll tube down the Tangkahan River, shower under a jungle waterfall, swim with elephants, and visit Gunung Leuser National Park, part of one of the world's largest rain forests. Roughly the size of Belgium, this 6.5-million-acre ecosystem supports more than 2,000 apes, 320 species of birds, and the largest flower in the world—the Rafflesia Arnoldi, which grows up to three feet across and smells like rotting meat. The Leuser ecosystem is also the last place on Earth where orangutans, Sumatran tigers, rhinos, clouded leopards, and elephants can be found in one place.

The "Borneo and Sumatra Explorer" trip, often led by British zoologist and renowned wildlife photographer Nick Garbutt, costs £2,750 (about $5,500) and includes all accommodations and most meals. Although you're liable to get wet any time of the year (it *is* a rain forest, after all), the best time to visit is March through October.

HOW TO GET IN TOUCH

World Primate Safaris, 11 Crescent Place, Kemp Town, Brighton, BN2 1AS, England, 866-357-6569 or 44 1273 691 642, www.worldprimatesafaris.com.

find out what's really going on behind the headlines

AFGHANISTAN

Travel and tourism has become one of the world's largest industries....
What might be possible if the vast community of globe-trotters joined
together, agreeing not to give our money to governments that torture and
abuse their citizens?

—Jeff Greenwald, travel writer

58 Ever since Soviet tanks rolled into Afghanistan in the late 1970s, the demand for tours to this war-torn country has pretty much dried up. Even Kabul, the capital and largest city with four million people, has very few surfaced roads, and the existing infrastructure can barely support the country's sagging population, let alone a bunch of tour buses.

Yet, despite this country's inhospitable headlines, it's still an important archaeological crossroads, thanks to the historic Silk Road and the country's National Art Gallery, which, despite losing 92 percent of its holdings to Taliban bombs, still contains important artifacts spanning 12 centuries.

Plus, there will always be foreign tourists who wonder, What's it really like?

For these folks, there's Global Exchange, a not-for-profit human rights organization in San Francisco that organizes trips behind the headlines. Unruffled by reports of kidnappings, beheadings, and shootings, Global Exchange figures that once you actually crouch in a home destroyed by rocket fire, walk the potholed streets, and meet real people who may not be the ones making the headline news, rather the ones directly influenced by the day-to-day realities of that news, you'll have a better sense of the challenges faced by people around the world. Since 1989, the group's Reality Tours have taken participants to four continents to meet union leaders, work alongside laborers at farmers' cooperatives, discuss terrorism with Afghan college students, and witness the effects of globalization worldwide. Participants learn about women's struggles in

Afghanistan, the impact of oil exploration on Ecuador's indigenous communities, the implications of fair trade in Tanzania, the struggle for peace and justice in Palestine and Israel, and events in many other headline-grabbing destinations.

The idea behind Global Exchange's trips is that travel can be a force for change and, if done right, can even positively influence international affairs. It calls its tour groups "delegations" and its clients "citizen diplomats," and its alumni are encouraged to stay engaged upon their return home by organizing "teach-ins" and writing letters to the media.

While the appeal of such trips might seem limited, Malia Everette, director of the Reality Tours, likes to points out that, in contrast to the mainstream travel industry, Global Exchange did not see a decline in numbers after 9/11. Instead, some members of the American public, fed up with what many considered the exaggerations, myths, and downright lies perpetuated by the media, remained hungry to discover what's really true. These people want a new vantage point from which to view U.S. foreign policy.

"I know that places like Club Med exist for a reason. We all need someplace, occasionally, to just zone out," Everette says. "But it's not reality. It's not reality when the only locals you meet are the ones serving you your drinks."

Global Exchange organizes Reality Tours to more than 30 countries in Latin America, Africa, Asia, and the Middle East. All are coordinated by locals working in the host communities who gladly dispense information about, depending on the trip's theme, the area's history, politics, economy,

---

GONE FOREVER

The world gasped in horror when, in March 2001, Taliban rulers in Afghanistan destroyed two giant Buddhas that had withstood 1,500 years of earthquakes, drought, and onslaughts of Genghis Khan's armies. The colossal sculptures were located in Bamiyan, an important religious site about 80 miles northwest of Kabul. By the fifth century, Buddhist monks had built temples, monasteries, and a honeycomb of caves into Bamiyan's towering sandstone cliffs. The Buddhas, also sculpted out of the cliffs, stood 120 feet and 175 feet tall and flanked the east and west ends of the town, which was a major oasis on the Silk Road. The Buddhas, visible to travelers from miles away, were blown to bits, said the Taliban, because Islam decrees that no human forms can be depicted in religious settings.

---

religion, government, health care, education, and environment. Before you go, you'll get an information packet, a recommended reading list, and an education outline.

In Afghanistan, Global Exchange delegations help Afghans rebuild their lives after decades of civil war. You'll meet with students from Kabul University and women doctors providing health care to rural communities. You'll see the challenges that Afghan women are facing, hear their stories firsthand, and learn how you can support their efforts. Among others things, you'll learn about micro-lending projects and visit the Red Cross Rehabilitation Clinic for land-mine victims, a newly built school for girls, a prostitute rehabilitation project, and the National Art Gallery and History Museum.

The ten-day trips to Afghanistan cost $1,750 and include transportation within the country, shared room accommodation, trip guides, translation of all programs, admission fees, reading materials, two to three meals daily, visas, program fees, and an experienced trip leader.

HOW TO GET IN TOUCH

Global Exchange Reality Tours, 2017 Mission Street, No. 303, San Francisco, CA 94110, 800-497-1994 ext. 261 or 415-255-7296, www.globalexchange.org.

explore the wonders of the panama canal

PANAMA

I took the isthmus, started the canal and then left
Congress not to debate the canal, but to debate me.
—Theodore Roosevelt, about his decision to take
Panama from Colombia

59 Every year, more than 200 cruise ships float through the Panama Canal, along with 26,000 other vessels hauling everything from steel ball bearings to automobiles. Each of the locks that move the ships through this skinny waistline of Central America releases enough fresh water daily to supply the water needs of a city of 150,000 (26.7 million gallons a day). To say it's one of the world's great engineering feats (it took ten years and 250,000 people to build, including 5,609 Americans who lost their lives) is an understatement.

History buffs and engineering enthusiasts interested in learning more about the famous canal that Jimmy Carter finally turned over to Panamanian control in 1979 might consider taking an educational cruise straight into the heart of things. Here are a couple of possibilities, the second of which combines the canal with a trip to Costa Rica:

M/V *Coral Star*. Because the 115-foot luxury liner called the *Coral Star* has only eight staterooms (maximum passenger load is 16), you get the onboard naturalists, biologists, and historian guides pretty much to yourself. Plus, with that kind of teacher-student ratio, you'll master your lessons so quickly there will be ample time leftover to dive, fish, and explore Panama's secluded tropical beaches.

On the intimate "Two-Ocean Expedition and Canal Transit"—one of many trips offered on the *Coral Star*—you'll swim in both the Pacific and the Atlantic, visit the indigenous tribes of the Darien Rain Forest, snorkel the Las Perlas Archipelago, explore the old haunts of adventurer Sir Francis Drake, and hike the old Camino Real.

GREEN PANAMA

Panama, besides having Central America's best shopping, dining, and night-life (especially Casco Viejo, Panama City's resurgent historical quarter), is an ecotourist's dream. And that's partly because of the United States, which is not something that can often be said when it comes to the environment. The United States permitted very little development in the Canal Zone—not because it cared overmuch about healthy land and rivers, but because the canal requires monstrous amounts of fresh water. Every large ship that makes a transit needs 52 million gallons from Gatun Lake, and having a virgin rain forest that generates lots of rain was vital for canal operations. Therefore, the Panamanian rain forest still has hundreds of species of birds (Espirito Santo Gold Mines is one of the world's top places for bird-watching) and an impressive variety of everything from orchids to ocelots. With 15 percent of its land in national parks, Panama's biosphere is one of the world's most extensively protected.

Bocas del Toro, an archipelago of 68 islands that stretches along the western edge of Panama's northern coast, has four species of endangered sea turtles (hawksbill, leatherback, green, loggerhead), endangered mammals such as Central American tapir, all five species of big cats (jaguar, puma, ocelot, jaguarundi, and margay), barely explored mountains and rivers, coral gardens, and lots of colorful characters you'd expect to find in a Humphrey Bogart film.

You'll get an up close and personal understanding of the history of Panama, while also learning about Panama's unique cultures, wildlife, economy, and geography. You'll also learn the whole bloody history, including the French failure to build a canal in the 1880s, the problems of digging through thick tropical forests (not to mention a spine of rugged mountains), and the tropical diseases that, we're happy to report, are now quite manageable.

The M/V *Coral Star* is elegantly appointed with mahogany and teak. The seven-day cruise costs between $3,500 and $3,700 (based on double occupancy) and includes all meals and excursions.

M/V *Coral Star*, 5150 Highway 22, Suite C-10, Mandeville, LA 70471, 866-924-2837, www.coralstar.com.

National Geographic Expeditions. Passing through the legendary Panama Canal is a highlight of National Geographic Expedition's "Wonders of Costa Rica and

HISTORY LESSON

At the time President Theodore Roosevelt persuaded Congress to construct a canal to link the Atlantic and Pacific Oceans, Panama was a province of Colombia—a petty fact that didn't deter Roosevelt, who merely dispatched the gunship U.S.S. *Nashville* in 1903 to Panama to stop the Colombian troops from quelling the "revolution" that had been planned by Roosevelt and a handful of prominent Panamanian families. Within a few weeks, a treaty was signed and a 50-mile-long, 10-mile-wide swath of Panamanian land was America's for the digging.

An S-shaped isthmus with roughly the same land area as South Carolina, Panama has a lot of things going for it: It's outside both hurricane and earthquake zones, the tap water is safe (something you can't say about every Central American country), the U.S. dollar is the de facto state currency (the balboa, Panama's official tender, is rarely used), English is widely spoken, and it has the same biodiverse rain forest that transformed Costa Rica into an ecotourism mecca.

---

the Panama Canal" cruise. The round-trip journey begins in San José, Costa Rica, aboard the M.V. *Sea Voyager,* a 60-passenger vessel that carries a fleet of Zodiac landing craft, snorkeling equipment, and kayaks. In the company of a diverse team of experts—from naturalists to geologists—you'll skim along the beautiful coastlines of Manuel Antonio and Corcovado National Parks, search for wildlife in Costa Rica's rain forest, and explore the wild, primitive Osa Peninsula. During the dramatic two-day canal transit, you'll travel by Zodiac to Gatun Lake (the source of the canal's water power) and join local guides for hikes through the tropical forests of Barro Colorado Island. The price tag for this 8-day expedition starts at $4,240.

National Geographic Expeditions, 1145 17th Street, N.W., Washington, D.C., 20036, 888-966-8687, www.nationalgeographicexpeditions.com.

train to be a geisha

A geisha is like Prozac for your soul.
—Geisha client

60 A hundred years ago, there were as many as 80,000 geishas in Japan. But few today are willing to undertake the years of training in dance, music, and clever conversation that's required of Japan's elite female entertainers. Nevertheless, thanks to Arthur Golden's best-selling book *Memoirs of a Geisha* and Rob Marshall's movie based on the book, geisha "transformation" services are all the rage in the ancient temple town of Kyoto.

If you'd like to do more than simply paint your face, don a kimono, and trip around in 4-inch-high clogs—the extent of most of these "geisha for a day" gimmicks—you can sign up for a weeklong geisha training program offered once a year by four veteran geishas at the international School of Geisha. Granted, you'll still be a rank *maiko* (geisha trainee) at the end of your seven days, but the training you'll receive offers one of the best glimpses into the many traditions of the Japanese culture. Geisha culture exists for the sole purpose of preserving the traditional arts.

By studying this icon of Japan, you'll learn about the tea ceremony, an ancient ritual that aims to unite the server and those being served. You'll learn about kimonos, flower arranging, ceramics, storytelling, Japanese theater and dance, and, most importantly, how to access your inner depths.

Says Olga Manichiyo, one of the creators of the unique geisha class for

GEISHA ALTERNATIVES

Since it's probably too late for you to become a full-fledged geisha (serious students start as early as age ten) and harness the peace and tranquility that comes with the territory, maybe you should skip all that and go for added lifespan instead. According to Japanese legend, if you boil an egg in the Owakudani Crater (near Mount Fuji), you'll add seven extra years to your life.

DOs AND DON'Ts OF JAPANESE *SADOS* (TEA CEREMONIES)

- **Don't be late.** The Japanese are consumed with punctuality. If one of their trains runs even a few minutes behind schedule, conductors hand out "late passes" for workers to explain to their bosses.
- **Ditch the shoes at the door.** Slipper etiquette requires that guests remove their shoes and don slippers on entering someone's house.
- **Take a gift.** Whenever you visit someone's home, bring a gift—something like food or flowers.
- **Eschew politics.** Don't look for Jon Stewart to tape *The Daily Show* at a Japanese tea ceremony anytime soon. Talking about politics is strictly prohibited. Instead, you should stick to admiring your host's choice of flower arrangements and utensils.
- **Pay attention to tea etiquette.** Putting your lips against the prettiest part of the tea cup is strictly verboten. And before imbibing your tea, turn the bowl a full 180 degrees.

Westerners, "By inquiring into the forbidden world of geisha, women unfold their inner character and develop a beautiful mind."

In addition to mastering the secrets of a geisha's allure, the training includes tours of local temples, culinary excursions, and a chance to see the Land of the Rising Sun in a way only locals normally get to see it.

And you won't be the first American to study geishahood. According to the school, Jackie Kennedy underwent geisha training to hone her skills as a presidential wife, and Liza Dalby, an anthropology doctoral student, entered the so-called world of willows and flowers for her dissertation on the Japanese geisha. Dalby's three-year training earned her the geisha title Ichigiku of Pontocho and prompted hundreds of geisha fantasizers to consult her for advice.

The school offers six-week and six-month trainings in London in addition to the yearly weeklong sessions in Japan.

HOW TO GET IN TOUCH

School of Geisha, Castle Place, 141-145 Kentish Town Road, London, NW1 8PB, England, 44 (0) 20 7754 5472, www.schoolofgeisha.com.

study tectonic plates

ICELAND

The man who feels smug in an orderly world has
never looked down a volcano.
—Anonymous

61 If you're a serious geology buff, you probably have a life list of geology must-sees that undoubtedly includes an erupting volcano, an active geyser, a continental glacier, a fjord, a caldera, a limestone cave, a slot canyon, a varve, a layered igneous intrusion, and the like. More than likely, you've already marked off a few of these geologic destinations on your list: Arizona's Meteor Crater and the Grand Canyon, perhaps, or Michigan's banded iron formation and Utah's Waterpocket Fold, or maybe Wyoming's Devil's Tower and Australia's Ayers Rock.

Eventually, as items on your list get checked off and you add new ones, you'll be struck with the desire to witness a tectonic plate up close and personal. Plate tectonics, scientists now agree, directly or indirectly play a role in every single geologic process. The Earth's plates, as they continually collide and separate, keep us at her mercy and astound us with violent displays of volcanoes and earthquakes. While we have no control over plate-tectonic processes, gaining knowledge about them at least helps to even the playing field.

The Geological Society of America (GSA) offers an annual expedition to Iceland to study and observe plate tectonics. This highly volcanic country, which straddles the Mid-Atlantic Ridge, is literally being pulled apart, offering scientists a natural laboratory for studying the relatively new theory of plate tectonics. It's one of the few places on Earth where you can actually see the plates separating. Granted, it's only half an inch or so a year, but it's enough to keep such volcanoes as Hekla, Krafla, and Surtsey (see sidebar p. 176) erupting and spouting.

The Iceland trip is one of several geoscience field trips offered by GSA. In 2007, for example, 17 lucky takers spent nine days in northern China studying the fossils of recently discovered feathered dinosaurs. And in 2008, the Geological

Society is offering trips to study the volcanoes of Costa Rica and Nicaragua and the geology of the Canadian Rockies, the Salmon River, and the Grand Canyon.

Not only do these "GeoVentures" open windows to the world's most spectacular geological sites, but they also allow participants to hang with other geology aficionados. After all, it's not just everybody who wants to spend an afternoon discussing the pros and cons of rifts or fissures.

On the Iceland trip (it's officially called "Iceland: Plate Tectonics Alive: Learn about Geoscience on a Midocean Ridge"), you'll spend eight glorious days visiting volcanoes, hearing professional lectures on Iceland's unique geology, witnessing icebergs and glaciers, and learning about geothermal power. Reykjavik, Europe's northernmost capital, also happens to be one of the world's cleanest cities because ingenious Icelanders have harnessed their plentiful supply of geothermal energy to supply nonpolluting heat and electricity. You'll also get plenty of time to soak in Iceland's numerous hot springs and learn more about the Vikings who were memorialized in the 40-some Icelandic Sagas, written in the 13th and 14th centuries and studied still today by the country's school children. Filled

---

NEW KID ON THE BLOCK

On November 14, 1963, off the southern coast of Iceland, some fisherman noticed black smoke bubbling up from the sea. At first, they worried their boat was on fire, but soon it became apparent that the boat was just fine—it was some lava erupting from one of Iceland's many underwater volcanoes. By the next day, a tiny new island had emerged in a dramatic fire-and-brimstone birth. This new piece of real estate was named Surtsey after Sutur, the Icelandic god of fire. Surtsey continued to spit up lava for 3.5 more years, until eventually the new island grew to a square mile in area.

Because Surtsey is above sea level and not too far from shore, scientists were able to study the eruptions and related tornadoes, waterspouts, hail, and lightning, opening a perfect lab for studying the evolution of a new land. In 1965, it was designated a nature reserve. The same year, three postage stamps were issued that continue to be a sought-after prize for philatelists everywhere.

---

with amazing heroes and epic battles that would definitely give J. R. R. Tolkien a run for his money, the sagas were originally written off by historians as mythology, but now, after archaeologists have begun catching up, are proving to be surprisingly accurate.

The eight-day trip costs $3,197, including accommodations, most meals, local guides, professional lectures, and all activities. Although the trip is designed for science teachers and includes some instruction in how to teach the science of plate tectonics, GSA is happy to include anyone with an interest. One quick phone call to the leader should do the trick.

HOW TO GET IN TOUCH

Geological Society of America, P.O. Box 9140, Boulder, CO 80301, 303-357-1005, www.geosociety.org/geoventures, or **Holbrook Travel,** a travel company that specializes in booking trips for zoos, colleges, and professional organizations, 3540 N.W. 13th Street, Gainesville, FL 32609, 800-451-7111, www.holbrooktravel.com.

learn about medicinal plants with andean shamans

BOLIVIAN AND PERUVIAN ANDES

Cultural anthropology made leaps and bounds when it moved
from the sphere of observer to observer-participant.
To truly experience the ancient traditions of these lands,
we go to be in it, to be a part, not apart.
—Alan Leon, proprietor of Sacred Heritage Travel

62 Wait until Willard Scott hears about this.

High up in the Andes, where there's no running water, no Hilton hotels, and nary a hospital, there are tribes whose elders stay strong and active long after they turn one hundred. Cancer is almost unheard of, mental health is taken for granted, and disease means there's something wrong with the person's "intention," not the body.

In part, these tribes are healthy because their diet comprises homegrown and organic local food that's grown on land that has been prayed over for thousands of years. But maybe it's also because they consult with shamans who know a thing or two about herbal remedies. For thousands of years, the Kallawaya, who practice ceremonial healing in the Bolivian Andes near Lake Titicaca, have traveled throughout South America healing and gathering knowledge of herbs and ceremonies. For centuries, they served as doctors to Incan royalty, having at their disposal a unique vegetable and mineral pharmacy. They were known as "keepers of the science."

Thanks to Sacred Heritage Travel, a company run by Alan Leon, an American who has worked with Andean and Amazonian priestesses and healers, it's possible for Westerners to find out what their highly educated medical doctors are missing. "The Western techno culture, dysfunctional and cut off in so many ways, has much to gain by simply being in the presence of the sanity of an ancient lineage," Leon says.

THOSE KALLAWAYA

The name Kallawaya is a Spanish derivative of the Quechua or Aymara words *kolla wayas,* which mean "carriers of the grass." For centuries, the Kallawaya were nomads who traveled South America collecting herbs and accumulating healing techniques. Many Westerners reported amazing healings after chance encounters with this revered tribe, including a crippled child who could not be cured by modern medicine but walked perfectly after drinking a potion presented by a Kallawaya shaman.

In 2005, UNESCO, the Central Bank of Bolivia, and the Vice Ministry of the Culture of Bolivia published a book called *Kallawaya: World Recognition for a Science of the Andes,* about the Kallawaya recognizing their unique contribution and profound knowledge of medicine, pharmacology, and symbolic curing. As Carmen Beatriz Loza, the author of the 180-page book, says, "There is an urgent need to safeguard this part of medicine, but also a system as a whole that is immersed in a thousand-year-old culture."

In 1991, Leon was traveling in Peru, sleeping in a stone hut with a family of high priests who had never received foreign visitors. Deep in the night, he and the entire family all woke up at the exact moment having had the same dream. After celebrating for a couple of days (the dream meant a treasured family member had "come home"), they urged Leon to "bring the people." They said it was time to pass on their ancient knowledge to outsiders.

Although there are many "sham shamans" prancing around South American cities, giving seminars and claiming ancient wisdom, Leon works with 22 healers who have an unbroken ancient lineage from the Inca/Quechua, Aymara, and Kallawaya heritage. There's nothing contrived or sensationalized. These healers stay near the land and near their villages, passing down wisdom that was passed down to them.

Sacred Heritage Travel offers a variety of trips introducing Westerners to shamans of the Australian, Andean, and Amazon rain forest cultures. All South American trips include a full day at the sacred site of Machu Picchu.

At the 15-day "Amazon Rainforest Herbal Camp," you'll work with two native healers, collect herbs, ride in a covered canoe next to pink dolphins, and be offered the chance to experience ayahuasca, a psychotropic healing herb.

On the 15-day "Andean Kallawaya Healers" trip, you'll four-wheel the shores of Lake Titicaca and the peaks of the Royal Range; stay in traditional villages; visit megalithic temples, La Paz's witches' market, and other sacred sites; get your cocoa leaves read; meet with local *yatitis* (native Aymara shamans); and participate in many ceremonies and rituals.

The "Amazon Rainforest Herbal Camp" runs $3,300, the "Andean Kallawaya Healers" trip $3,200, and both include all in-country transportation, lodging, guides, ceremonies, entrance fees, airport taxes, and more than half of your meals.

HOW TO GET IN TOUCH

Sacred Heritage Travel, 5395 E. Camino Cielo, Santa Barbara, CA 93105, 866-233-7600, www.sacredheritage.com.

break into bullfighting

SALAMANCA, SPAIN

All my life, I thought learning to *torear* was a secret,
a closed society, a forbidden guild. Now, there's a way in.
—Joe Escalante, musician and student of the
California Academy of Tauromaquia

63 A bull weighs half a ton and at full tilt can run 850 yards in 90 seconds. So even though you think you've got the balls to run with the bulls in Pamplona, it might behoove you to get in a few bullfighting lessons first.

The California Academy of Tauromaquia, the first school in the United States for studying the science of bullfighting (yes, it requires geometry as well as grace and mental discipline), takes matador-novitiates to Spain every summer to study *toreo* in the country where it's most famous. The five-day class includes training in bullfighting techniques, visits to historic bull ranches, front-row seats to several big *corridas* (that's Spanish for "bullfights"), and all the history, art, food, and wine that goes along with Castilian Spain.

Salamanca, the stunning city where the workshop is based, has been a university town since 1218, when Alfonso IX of León decided his kingdom needed a college. You'll hear the same cathedral bells and walk the same cobblestone streets and narrow alleys as Cervantes, Cortez, and Columbus, all

SKULLDUGGERY

One of the original buildings at the Universidad de Salamanca has three skulls embedded into the wall. On one skull is a sculpted frog, the university's unofficial mascot. For centuries students have offered traditional prayers there for good luck. If the frog doesn't work for your bullfighting needs, you'll be happy to know that all 225 of Spain's *plazas de toros* (bullfighting rings) have hospitals for the wounded and, even though several popes have threatened excommunication to bullfighting devotees, chapels where *toreros* can receive the Holy Eucharist.

A BUNCH OF BULL

Pamplona is a sleepy town in the hills of northern Spain, waking with a start once a year in July for the seven-day feast of St. Fermin in honor of the town's first bishop. Although bands play, town folks jig, and everyone dresses in immaculate white linen, the highlight of the festival is the daily bull run, which is photographed and reported around the world. Every single day of the festival, six snorting, stomping bulls are set free to storm 850 yards of cobblestone streets from Pamplona's Hill of St. Vicente to the city's bullring.

Thousands of fleet-footed "bullfighters" gather at Town Hall Square each day to attempt to outrun the bulls. Although Ernest Hemingway, who visited the bull run half a dozen times or more between 1922 and 1959, is partly responsible for the event's massive popularity, it's a well-known fact among locals that he never actually ran it himself.

On the other hand, if the madness of Pamplona seems a bit too much, you can always fight bulls at Terceira, in Portugal's Azores. Every weekend from May to October, bulls are let loose on the island's main roads, but they're graciously tethered to a rope and guided by several strong men. You can get as close or stay as far as you dare.

of whom spent time at the university. In fact, it was at Salamanca's Convent of San Esteban, one of two convents in the city (the other, Las Duenas, is famous for its delicious tea biscuits baked daily by cloistered nuns), where Christopher Columbus studied his plans before initiating his trip to the New World. Salamanca also happens to be the capital of the *campo charro,* a region with wide meadows and oak woods where Spain's most important bull ranchers breed the country's most-revered bulls. It's where famous bullfighters Belmonte, Manolete, and El Cordobes trained before they were man enough to don the sequined silk jackets and make the million-dollar salaries (although El Cordobes liked to say, "I was taught, not by a master, but by the bull").

The course consists of theory classes and *tientas*—(gulp!) face-to-face encounters with real livestock. The good news is that first-time *aficionado prácticos,* which is what you will be, are relegated to fighting yearling heifers. Tientas, taught by professional toreros, are considered a service to the ranchers, who see it as a way to test out young, pedigreed bulls for their pluck and dexterity before siccing them on celebrity matadors.

According to Coleman Cooney, founder of the school, students train in the classic manner, one-on-one with experienced instructors who run the horns. There's video analysis, lessons on bullfighting culture, and instruction in the anatomy of bulls, all of whom are carefully bred for fury and style. Each night you'll return to your three-star inn on Salamanca's Plaza Mayor, a tree-lined, porticoed plaza dominated with tapas bars and a hopping nightlife scene.

The bullfighting workshop in Salamanca costs $2,200 and includes all ground transportation, training, equipment, ranch visits, and accommodations.

HOW TO GET IN TOUCH
California Academy of Tauromaquia, Rancho Santa Alicia, Valle de las Palmas, Baja California Norte CP, 20002 Mexico. 619-709-0664, www.bullfightschool.com.

learn to gamble like bond— james bond

MONTE CARLO, MONACO

A dollar won is twice as sweet as a dollar earned.
—Fast Eddie Felson, in *The Color of Money*

64 Monte Carlo has opera and ballet companies, a symphony orchestra, and an Oceanographic Museum that was directed for many years by none other than Jacques Cousteau. But the reason people flock to this scenic principality between the French Alps and the Mediterranean is plain and simple: They like to gamble.

Monte Carlo's casinos—unlike their American counterparts where you're liable to spot everyone from homeless vagrants trying to alter their luck to your Great Aunt Myrtle—cater to the rich, the famous, and the tuxedoed. Tennis shoes are strictly out.

Two of Monte Carlo's five famous casinos run gambling courses, the most exclusive of which is the Casino de Monte-Carlo's "Initiation Super Privée." Hosted at night in the pricey Cabaret Salon, the course lasts 2.5 hours and offers instruction in European roulette, Punto Banco, and blackjack. It's taught by skilled croupiers and includes cocktails, gaming chips, and your own personal gambling diploma.

Just getting in the door of the Casino de Monte-Carlo's gaming halls can be an expensive proposition (though anyone who's dressed properly and carries a passport can wander into the sumptuous, two-story entrance hall, with its ring of stately columns and public slot machines). Built in 1878 by Charles Garnier, the same architect who designed the Paris Opera House, the lavish baroque casino charges a minimum stake of 80 euros ($118), for example, in the Salles Privées (Private Rooms).

It doesn't really matter, though—all of the halls are sights to behold, with stained-glass windows, elaborate sculptures, Bohemian crystal chandeliers, and Boucher-style frescoes and bas-reliefs.

QUEEN FOR A DAY AND 25 YEARS

The Grimaldi family, whose affairs have been the fodder of tabloids since 1956 when American actress Grace Kelly gave up her film career to marry Prince Rainier III, has ruled Monaco since 1297 when it took over the principality that's slightly smaller than Central Park by disguising themselves as monks and murdering the rulers.

Kelly met the prince in 1955 when she was in France for the Cannes Film Festival. Although rumors were rife that the prince-to-be was mainly worried about a 1918 treaty with France that required him to produce an heir or lose the realm, she consented to marry the wife-hunting prince within a year after their meeting. Alfred Hitchcock, upon hearing about the engagement, quipped that he was "very happy Grace had found a good part."

When the future Princess Grace set sail from New York's Pier 84 with her family, bridesmaids, poodle, and over 80 pieces of luggage, more than 400 reporters applied to sail along, hoping to report on the "wedding of the century," as it was widely known.

It was a fairy-tale romance...until 1982 when her sports car plunged off one of the gardened cliffs behind Monaco.

A tour of the princess's favorite places are as good a way as any to see the postage stamp–size country. These sites include:

- **Monaco Cathedral.** On Avenue St.-Martin, the main drag, you can visit the late 19th-century Romanesque-Byzantine cathedral where Princess Grace and Prince Rainier were married, and where they, along with many other Grimaldis, are now buried.
- **Palais du Prince (Prince's Palace).** The 17th-century palace, which was completely repainted and decorated for the April 19, 1956, wedding, is open for guided tours when her son, Prince Albert, is absent (if the flag is flying over the palace, he's home). From the palace, you can enjoy not only spectacular views of the city, the Italian border, and the harbor with the world's biggest yachts, but also watch the Changing of the Guard that takes place every day in front of the main entrance at five minutes before noon.
- **Princess Grace Rose Garden.** Princess Grace loved flowers (she was president of Monaco's garden club), and she no doubt adored this public garden, filled with 4,000 magnificent rosebushes. Upon her death, the prince changed its name in her honor.
- **Oceanographic Museum,** established in 1910 by Grace's grandfather-in-law, Prince Albert I, houses two floors of collections, including a 66-foot whale skeleton, ships' models, and a giant aquarium with rare species of marine life from all corners of the world.

Don't expect to rub elbows with any of the 30,000 Monégasques, as Monaco's citizens are called, because they're forbidden from gambling. On the upside, they do get free education, lavish social services, and the chance to make a very good living catering to the chi-chi set that *are* allowed to throw dice.

Instead, you'll be gambling next to Arab oil magnates, tennis stars, famous actors, yachters, and other millionaires who have second homes in the fairy-tale city, because even part-time citizens are exempt from paying taxes.

The gambling classes run from 9,700 euros ($13,500) for the daytime "European Initiation" that is held in the Touzet and Médecin Salons and initiates gamblers to the European way of gambling to 12,300 euros ($17,000) for the nighttime Cabaret Salon—note that the price tags are the same whether you're an individual, couple, or group of up to 30 people. Monte Carlo, not surprisingly, also offers classes in Formula One racing, diamonds, and expensive perfumes.

Before you make a run at the tables, remember to mutter Monaco's national motto, "Deo Juvante." It means "With God's Help."

HOW TO GET IN TOUCH

Casino de Monte-Carlo, Place du Casino, MC 98000 Principality of Monaco, 377 9216 2000, www.casinomontecarlo.com.

learn swahili while saving the black rhino

NANYUKI, KENYA

In Kenya you've got the chance to remember
what the world is really like.
—Actress Joanna Lumley

65 Note to Asians: Try Viagra instead.

Since 1970, the Kenyan black rhinoceros population has dwindled from 20,000 to a measly 400—largely because of this crazy belief in many parts of Asia that rhino horns, ground into powder and dissolved in liquid, possess aphrodisiacal qualities.

We'll give it to you that their massive horns make handsome dagger handles, another popular use, at least in Yemen, but do you really want to drive this magnificent beast that's been around for 35,000 years to the brink of extinction just for the sake of your sex life?

Despite massive efforts by conservationists, rhino poachers—standing to gain $1,400 per pound for ground-up African rhino horn (the Asian variety can reap 12 times that much)—continue to figure out ways to nab rhinos, chainsaw off their horns, and supply the voracious Asian appetite.

That's where Linus Gatimu and Dr. Geoffrey Wahungu come in. With the help of the Earthwatch Institute, a Massachusetts-based nonprofit that supports research projects in 150 countries, these African scientists are conducting ongoing rhino field research at a fenced-in, scout-patrolled sanctuary in Kenya where 88 percent of the remaining black rhinos live. They're gathering information about these shy, elusive creatures, studying their habitat and trying to determine the best way to ensure their survival.

Straddling the Equator along the Laikipia plateau, the Sweetwaters Black Rhino Reserve, only 140 miles north of Nairobi, is one of several reserves now being employed throughout Africa to keep poachers out and endangered animals safe.

WHERE'S DR. DOOLITTLE WHEN YOU NEED HIM?

Rhinos are not the smartest tacks in the tool chest. They're slow witted, unpredictable, and finicky—at their best, like your average two-year-old. Do one tiny thing to rile them and they'll charge at you full speed with their massive horns thrust forward.

Except, that is, for Morani, one of 45 black rhinos that live on the Sweetwaters Game Reserve. Even though *morani* is a Maasai word that means "warrior," he's anything but. When he was a baby, Morani was found wandering near his mother who had been killed by poachers in Amboseli National Park. He was eventually brought to Sweetwaters, where he now lives a life of quiet leisure in his own 100-acre enclosure, protected by armed guards. He's tame enough that you can feed him out of your hand and have your photo snapped beside him—if you can stand the smell.

Also at Sweetwaters Game Reserve, you'll find:

- Carol, a tame warthog, who doesn't sing "Hakuna Matata," but does enjoy greeting visitors to the compound.
- Sweetwaters Chimpanzee Sanctuary, a 200-acre chimp haven only 15 minutes from the research camp. Visitors can take a 30-minute boat ride down the Ewaso Nyiro River through the chimps' habitat. Initiated in part by the Jane Goodall Institute, this colony of orphaned and abused chimps is being rehabilitated, and they are being taught to fend for themselves.
- Growing populations of elephants, giraffes, Cape buffalo, hippos, olive baboons, zebras, Thomson's and Grant's gazelles, impalas, hartebeests (Kongoni), Beisa oryx, elands, bushbucks, reedbucks, steinbucks, porcupines, bush babies, hare, lions, leopards, spotted hyenas, black-backed jackals, mongooses, aardvarks, cheetahs, ostriches, black-bellied and Kori bustards, secretary birds, Von der Decken's hornbills, yellow-billed and Marabou storks, golden crown cranes, helmeted guinea fowl, crowned plover, white bellied go-away-birds, red-billed oxpeckers, little bee-eaters, grey-capped social weavers, long-tailed widowbirds, speckled mousebirds, African pied wagtails, malachite kingfishers, superb starlings, and lilac-breasted rollers.

And you can help. Earthwatch sponsors educational trips to the reserve that teach students about the black rhinoceros and its habitat, as well as giving the research scientists assistance in rhino patrol, vegetation measurement, and other necessary jobs. On this 15-day Earthwatch expedition, you'll master GPS tracking skills, take a crash course in Swahili (many of the scouts and guards speak little English), and learn to identify footprints of not only rhinoceros but also aardvark, hippo, elephant, and dik-dik (a kind of small African antelope).

Most of your work will be on foot in a classic African savanna with tall grasslands, whistling acacia woodlands, and magnificent views of snowcapped Mount Kenya. On your scouting missions, you'll have a good chance of seeing what in Africa is known as the "Big Five"—lion, leopard, rhino, elephant, and buffalo—and you'll learn to identify the many tree and shrub species that make up the savanna.

Each evening, you'll return to the Sweetwaters Reserve Research Center, where you'll gather around an open veranda and campfire for amazing meals of Nile perch, *nyama choma* (grilled meat), and *ugali,* a traditional Kenyan dish made with milk, cornmeal, and water. If you're lucky, you might even sample some Kenya cane, a potent African spirit, or be challenged by the reserve's scouts to a campfire soccer game.

The 15-day "Saving Sweetwaters Rhino" expedition costs $2,850 and includes meals and accommodations in thatched huts.

HOW TO GET IN TOUCH

Earthwatch, 3 Clock Tower Place, Suite 100, P.O. Box 75, Maynard, MA 01754, 978-461-0081, www.earthwatch.org.

OXFORD UNIVERSITY

study at the world's oldest english-speaking university

OXFORD, ENGLAND

A summer in Oxford is perfect for the arousal of fantasy.
It is a city full of quaint suggestion, evocations, exceptions,
where there are surprises around every corner.
—Jan Morris, travel writer

66 You don't have to be a Rhodes scholar to study at Oxford University. Thanks to the university's Department for Continuing Education, anybody can take classes at this prominent institution.

The "Oxford Experience," a residential summer program, is designed for nonacademics who want to spend a week learning about, say, global warming or Victorian fiction while hanging out in the city Oscar Wilde, one of the university's many famous students, said was the "most beautiful thing in England."

Only an hour from London's Paddington Station, Oxford and its legendary skyline, known as the "City of Dreaming Spires," is a medieval dreamland, a time warp of sorts where everything from its winding cobblestone lanes to its impeccably manicured gardens is beautiful and historical.

Most of the dozens of weeklong classes offered during the Oxford Experience

IN GOOD COMPANY

By studying at Oxford, even if only for a week, you'll join an elite delegation. Among others, Oxford has educated 6 kings, 47 Nobel Prize laureates, 25 British prime ministers, 28 foreign presidents, at least 12 saints, 20 archbishops of Canterbury, and at least one pope. You'll join the ranks of Walter Raleigh, Rupert Murdoch, John Wesley, Bill Clinton, Margaret Thatcher, Lewis Carroll, Aldous Huxley, T. E. Lawrence, Oscar Wilde, C. S. Lewis, J. R. R. Tolkien, Percy Shelley, W. H. Auden, Stephen Hawking, Richard Dawkins, Hugh Grant, Dudley Moore, and Tim Berners-Lee.

RAISE A PINT

Oscar Wilde gave this bit of advice: "The only way to get rid of a temptation is to yield to it." For yielding to the temptation of British beer, consider a famous Oxford hangout such as High Street's Mitre Pub. Established in 1261, it was a favorite haunt of Wilde's during his college days, especially after curfew when he should have been sawing logs.

Even older than the Mitre Pub is the Bear Pub on Alfred Street, which was supposedly built over a bear pit in 1242. The ties on the wall are a tradition started in the 1950s by a lascivious pub owner's wife who apparently collected a tie from each student on which she bequeathed her own "private lessons."

On St. Giles, in Oxford's Merton College, is the infamous Eagle and Child—known locally as the Bird and Baby—where literary pals, the Inklings (members included J. R. R. Tolkien and C. S. Lewis), met each Tuesday for a Guinness and a smoke around the pub's old fireplace. In 1962, the famous literary society moved their meeting place across the street to the Lamb and Flag, also a hangout spot for Graham Greene and a setting in Thomas Hardy's *Jude the Obscure*.

But don't get too carried away. According to legend, Oxford was started as a monastery in the Dark Ages by a pious princess who wanted to become a nun. St. Frideswide, the princess-turned-nun, was allegedly pestered by a lecherous royal suitor who was struck blind when he attempted to enter Oxford to seize her.

---

are staged at Christ Church, perhaps the most well known of Oxford's 39 colleges. You'll get an insider's view of life inside Christopher Wren's Tom Tower, the cathedral with its famous choir, the Christ Church meadow, and other famous locales.

For five one-week sessions each summer, starting Sunday lunch through the following Saturday, Oxford offers morning classes, with afternoons free to explore this magical, misty city. You'll study under Oxford academics, live around a quad, wander through the college's amazing gardens, and take afternoon field trips with your fellow students.

In your free time, you can visit Blackwell's Bookshop (53 Broad Street, 44 (0) 01865 333 606), a world-famous bookshop that made the *Guinness Book of Records* for having the most books in one room; tour the Ashmolean Museum of Art and Archaeology (Beaumont Street, 44 (0) 01865 278 000, www.ashmolean. org), founded in 1683, with an exceptional collection of European, Egyptian, and

Near Eastern antiquities; or take a punting excursion on the Cherwell or the River Thames (although in Oxford, they call the Thames the Isis). Oxford also offers dozens of literary tours, from *Alice in Wonderland* locales (Lewis Carroll, a shy mathematics don whose real name was Charles Dodgson, came up with his stories for the daughter of the dean, Alice Liddell, and her sisters while rowing them down the Thames) to the haunts of C. S. Lewis and J. R. R. Tolkien. Or if you prefer, you can tour settings from the *Harry Potter* movies, many scenes of which were shot here.

Oxford's Department for Continuing Education also offers daylong and weekend classes. The daylong classes, again open to anyone, cover a world of topics from archaeology to Haydn's piano music to Nietzsche's philosophy. There's even one that will finally answer that ever present question about "God and the Meaning of Life." The weeklong Oxford Experience seminars cost £980 (about $2,000), including lodging and meals, while the shorter classes range from £39 (about $80) to £204.50 ($418) for the weekend courses.

HOW TO GET IN TOUCH

Department for Continuing Education, University of Oxford, Rewley House, 1 Wellington Square, Oxford, England, OX1 2JA, 44 (0) 1865 270360, www.conted .ox.ad.uk.

visit vanishing cultures and legendary treasures by private jet

WORLDWIDE

Wealth is not his that has it, but his that enjoys it.
—Benjamin Franklin

67 Several times a year, the National Geographic Society—founded in 1888 to increase geographical knowledge of the world—puts together an epic educational opportunity: a private jet expedition to the most precious, treasured, and legendary natural and cultural wonders around the globe.

Those who fork over $56,950 for a trip simply entitled "Around the World by Private Jet" are treated to a 24-day life-changing adventure. You swoop into Peru, Easter Island, Samoa, the Great Barrier Reef, Cambodia, Tibet, India, Tanzania, Egypt, and Morocco (to name some of the highlights) aboard a custom-designed Boeing 757. You explore 12 UNESCO World Heritage sites, among them Machu Picchu, Angkor Wat, the Taj Mahal, and the Pyramids of Giza.

Perhaps even more impressively, participants are shown sites by experts who are legends in their own right. Imagine Louise Leakey, the youngest of the Leakey fossil-hunting family, telling you how she and her mother, Dr. Meave Leakey, unearthed the skull of *Kenyanthropus platyops* in Kenya, or Dr. Zahi Hawass, the world's foremost Egyptologist (and National Geographic Explorer-in-Residence), taking you behind the scenes in Giza. Plus, all of the trips feature a National Geographic expert who accompanies you the entire way—Peter Hillary, who, with his famous father, the late Sir Edmund Hillary, became the first father and son to summit Mount Everest, is scheduled for the February 2009 departure.

If you're so inclined to indulge in one of these extraordinary educational journeys, you'll not only be transported by a private plane with 88 seats instead of the standard 228, but you'll avoid the hassles of commercial flying. Indeed,

PLANES, TRAINS, AND BOATS

Okay, so we already filled you in on the plane part. Here is a pint-size sampling of National Geographic Expedition's train and boat adventures:

- **The Baltic's Historic Waterways.** Aboard the *National Geographic Explorer,* explore the magnificent cities of the Baltic Sea, from Stockholm to Gdansk to St. Petersburg, with stops in the medieval old towns of Lübeck, Riga, and Tallinn and a special visit with Novel Prize Laureate Lech Walesa. 16 days, $10,390–$19,280.
- **Panama Canal.** See pp. 170–172.
- **Sailing the Greek Isles.** With the spray of the Aegean splashing your face, you'll discover the beauty and ancient mythology of the Greek Isles. Your transport is the elegant, three-masted S.V. *Panorama,* which speeds you from timeless Cycladic villages on the jewel-like isle of Sifnos to the beautiful island of Santorini and the ancient sanctuary of Delos, birthplace of Apollo and Artemis. 9 days, $4,980–$6,290.
- **Trans-Siberia Rail Journey.** Roll across two continents and eight time zones on the world's longest and most legendary rail journey. On board the deluxe Trans-Siberian Express, travel from Vladivostock to Moscow, stopping to explore Mongolia's capital, cruise Lake Baikal, and visit monasteries and museums in some of Siberia's most fascinating cities. 17 days, $13,650–$18,340.

the plane's long-range capabilities and ability to land in smaller airports afford unmatched flexibility; the group sets its own schedules, flying direct and avoiding layovers.

Furthermore, the accommodations on this brand of National Geographic journey are ooh-la-la. In Siem Riep, near Angkor Wat, for example, you'll be staying at the famed Raffles Grand Hotel d'Angkor, built in 1932 in French colonial style; in the Elephant Bar sip a Sidecar where Somerset Maugham once imbibed. In Tanzania your abode for the night is the Ngorongoro Sopa Lodge, overlooking the spectacular Ngorongoro Crater and the diverse wildlife—including the endangered black rhino—that roams the crater floor. And in Marrakech, Morroco, you'll stay at the premier Sofitel Marrakech, with its immense, garden-bedecked swimming pool, its own Turkish steam bath, and gleaming marble everywhere.

But then maybe we're getting off point. All National Geographic journeys, even the ones that normal folks can afford, are focused on learning, on expanding horizons. They're led by the top experts in the field—the ones you've read about in the yellow-bordered magazine and seen on the National Geographic Channel; folks who rule their worlds of anthropology, archaeology, biology, history, photography, filmmaking, and general exploration of the world.

Launched by the National Geographic Society in 1999, National Geographic Expeditions offers nearly 100 amazing education travel opportunities each year, on which you can learn about everything from Italy's hidden treasures to Mongolia's nomadic cultures to the American Southwest's unique geology to Southern Africa's incredible wildlife.

Prices for these multiday trips range from $2,595 for the Bryce, Zion, and Grand Canyon National Parks expedition to the golden price tag of the "Around the World by Private Jet" trip.

HOW TO GET IN TOUCH

National Geographic Expeditions, 1145 17th Street, N.W., Washington, D.C. 20036, 800-966-8687, www.nationalgeographicexpeditions.com.

trek through the sinai with the bedouin

SINAI DESERT, EGYPT

No man can live this life and emerge unchanged.
He will carry, however faint, the imprint of the desert,
the brand which mark the nomad. . . . For this cruel land can
cast a spell, which no temperate clime can match.
—Sir Wilfred Patrick Thesiger, author of *Arabian Sands*

68 A few years ago, *Wired* magazine coined the phrase "going bedouin," which basically means working anywhere with a laptop and cell phone, paying for "office space" with lattes and muffins.

While the tribe of "bedouins" described by *Wired* is growing exponentially, the original Bedouin, the nomads of the Middle East, are shrinking in number, unappreciated by their governments and lured by tourism developers (sometimes with funding from the U.S. Agency for International Development) to bus tables and carry bags in upscale Red Sea resorts.

In the Sinai, though, the Bedouin are hanging in there, thanks in no small part to Emma Loveridge, a British theology student who, while doing Ph.D. research at Sinai's St. Catherine's Monastery (see sidebar opposite), fell in love with the nomadic culture and decided she wanted to do what she could to preserve it.

In 1990, Loveridge began offering small tours to the Sinai Desert, giving people the opportunity to walk and live with the Bedouin she'd grown to love. Although conceived as a hobby, a way to keep her hand in the Sinai, Wind, Sand, and Stars (so named for the Antoine de Saint-Exupéry book that depicts the French pilot's 1935 crash in the Libyan desert) became so successful that Loveridge now employs a staff of three and sends up to 50 groups a year to visit the hundred Bedouin families she works with.

SACRED PLACE

St. Catherine's Monastery, where Emma Loveridge completed her Ph.D. in early Christian art and manuscripts, is revered as the site of Moses' encounter with the burning bush. There's even a bush—supposedly the same one—which you can take pictures of. It now has a fire extinguisher next to it, though whether to deter the overexuberant or to provide irony is unclear.

More interesting than the ancient bramble, perhaps, is the monastery's rare collection of Christian icons and ancient manuscripts, dating back to the fourth century and outnumbered only by those in the Vatican. Ten to fifteen Greek Orthodox monks run the place, which stands in the shadow of Mount Sinai. Until this century, this remote outpost, the world's oldest continuously inhabited monastery (completed in 550), could be reached only by camel, a ten-day trek from Cairo. Visitors were hauled up in a basket pulled through a trapdoor.

From the monastery, you can climb the 3,750 steps up Mount Sinai that were said to have been cut by a single Byzantine monk in the fifth century as an extraordinary act of penance. At the top, along with tea stalls and souvenir hawkers, you'll be able to see Egypt's highest peak (8,642-foot Mount Catherine), where, in the eighth century, monks guided by a dream supposedly found the body of St. Catherine of Alexandria, which had been taken there by angels after she was martyred for refusing to renounce her Christian faith.

"The Bedouin had a desire to keep their families together, using their desert skills rather than have them break up and leave for the cities," says Loveridge, who is now an ordained minister in the Church of England. "I wanted to help Bedouin people maintain their own culture, while keeping in contact with my own."

The Sinai Desert is located in northeastern Egypt, situated at the crossroads of Asia and Africa, a vast and barren triangle of land between the Red Sea and the Gulf of Suez. Like most deserts, it's devoid of anything familiar. The things that give you credibility at home—your job, the money in your pocket, your Armani handbag—are useless in the desert. Instead, you come face to face with silence, reality, and ultimately yourself.

On Loveridge's eight-day desert treks, you'll live with Bedouin families; ride camels with them through barren desert valleys, dry washes, and sandstone cliffs; camp with them under the stars; share meals of Bedouin bread, goat cheese, and mint tea; and hear tales around the campfire of the fig path, the thoria star, and how Bedouin mothers naturally immunize their infants against scorpion bites.

You'll also visit St. Catherine's Monastery and (if you're able) climb to the top of Mount Sinai, perhaps the only place in the world where Christians, Muslims, and Jews agree on something—that this remote desert outcrop is where Moses was given the Ten Commandments.

Because Loveridge is fluent in Arabic and the local Bedouin dialect, as well as understanding the Sinai's endless history and how to survive in a remote desert environment, she has been called on to organize geological surveys, consult on countless TV and movie documentaries, assist with academic research projects, and even help 25 army chaplains run a 2,000-mile desert marathon to raise money for a children's hospital.

Prices vary depending on the length and the journey, but start around £860 ($1,700) per week.

HOW TO GET IN TOUCH
Wind, Sand, and Stars, P.O. Box 58214, London, N1 2GJ, England, 44 (0) 0870 757 1510, www.windsandstars.co.uk.

study astrophysics

GENEVA AND PARIS

> Larry: "Okay. You know how they say in certain
> museums history comes alive?"
> Rebecca: "Yeah."
> Larry: "In this museum it actually does."
> —From *Night at the Museum*

69 In the 2006 blockbuster hit *Night at the Museum,* the exhibits at the American Museum of Natural History (AMNH) spring to life, wreaking havoc upon a newly recruited night watchman played by Ben Stiller. Perhaps a better way to bring the 138-year-old institution to life is to sign up for one of its AMNH Expeditions.

Offering unique itineraries to all continents of the globe, AMNH Expeditions books in-depth educational tours with rare access to some of the world's most remarkable places. Think Mekong Delta, Syria, Nagorno-Karabakh. Wanna sketch the Serengeti? Attend an arctic symposium on global warming?

Since 1869, this stellar museum has not only displayed many wonders of the natural world and foreign cultures but also spearheaded their discovery. Every year, the museum conducts about a hundred scientific field expeditions. Museum logbooks are laden with reports from Franz Boas in the North Pacific, Theodore Roosevelt in South America, Robert Peary at the North Pole, and Margaret Mead in the South Pacific.

In fact, legend has it that it was Mead, dragging friends along on her research trips to Polynesia, who started the whole idea of "educational travel." Since Mead's days, AMNH Expeditions has transported more than 20,000 museum members to far-flung destinations on all seven continents. Led by the museum's own curators and research scientists, AMNH Expeditions are designed for curious adventure travelers with a scholarly bent. They provide access and depth of information that most commercial tour packages can't match. On an "Egypt: Treasure of the Pharaohs" trip, for example, museum members were treated to a farewell dinner with Mrs. Anwar Sadat.

Just as Margaret Mead lived among indigenous tribes in Samoa, AMNH travelers spend time with the Navajo, sleeping on floor mattresses in traditional hogans, and witness tribal mask dances in Mali, Africa. Or you can follow the footsteps of Roy Chapman Andrews, who found troves of dinosaur fossils across Mongolia's Gobi desert.

On the "Private Access CERN: Astrophysics in Paris and Geneva," you'll spend a week at the world's largest particle physics center exploring the connection between cutting-edge cosmology and string theory. The trip—led by **Dr. Michael Shara**, AMNH curator for astrophysics, and **Dr. Michelangelo Mangano**, senior scientist in the Theoretical Physics Unit at the European Council for Nuclear Research (CERN)—begins in Paris with a gala dinner at the Musée Nationale d'Histoire Naturelle. From there it's off to Geneva, where you'll study particle physics, high-energy particle collisions, and their application in a variety of fields. You'll also visit the Observatoire de Genève.

AMNH Expeditions are not cheap. The prices range from roughly $2,995 for a five-day "Kingdom of Monarchs'" trip to central Mexico to $22,475 (starting price) for "Earth Orbit," a rare behind-the-scenes tour of space facilities in the United States, Russia, and Kazakhstan, including meetings with astronauts and cosmonauts, a chance to try out a zero-gravity simulator, and a front-row seat to the launch of a Soyuz spacecraft. The CERN Astrophysics trip is $7,450 and includes accommodations and some meals.

HOW TO GET IN TOUCH

American Museum of Natural History, AMNH Expeditions, Central Park West at 79th Street, New York, NY 10024, 800-462-8687, www.amnhexpeditions.com.

study marine biology on the great barrier reef

QUEENSLAND, AUSTRALIA

> My first view—a panorama of brilliant deep blue ocean,
> shot with shades of green and gray and white—was of atolls and clouds
> .... Here was a tremendous visual spectacle, but no grand musical
> accompaniment; no triumphant, inspired sonata or symphony. Each
> one of us must write the music of this sphere for ourselves.
> —Charles Walker, U.S. astronaut

70 If you're a scuba diver, Australia's Great Barrier Reef is your mecca, the very tip-top of your to-do list. At 1,250 miles long, it's like nonstop coral all the way from New York to Kansas City. It's the world's largest living organism and the only one that can be identified from space. With 2,000 species of fish, some 400 species of coral, and more than 4,000 invertebrates, this extravaganza of color can best be described as an underwater Mardi Gras.

That's the exciting news. The not-so-exciting news is that, like all coral reefs, it's endangered. Some scientists give it as few as 50 years. Warming ocean temperatures cause coral bleaching, a process that expels algae, sucks the coral of its sugar, and leaves behind nothing but coral polyp skeletons. So if you have any desire to study coral reefs or reef biology or anything that depends on this 1981-designated World Heritage site, you'd be wise to get a move on.

AustraLearn, a Westminster, Colorado–based, company that sends college kids to study at Australian, New Zealand, and South Pacific hot spots, offers ten-day to two-week learning trips to the Great Barrier Reef. Administered by the Centre for Marine Studies at the University of Queensland, these courses are geared for college students, but will happily admit anyone with a year or more of college credit under their belt—no matter what their age. Oh, yeah, there's one other

LAND OF AUS

Forget koalas and kangaroos. Here's a trio of even more interesting facts about Australia.

- **Australia is the only country in the world to immortalize a convicted criminal on its ten-dollar note.** Francis Greenway, a British architect convicted of forgery and sent to Mother England's "newest" penal colony, received his pardon in 1819 when the colonial governor, Lachlan Macquarie, fell in love with Hyde Park Barracks, a building Greenway designed to house fellow convicts. Greenway designed many buildings in Sydney's "Rocks" area, including the elaborate Conservatorium of Music that was originally built as the governor's stable. His picture now graces Australia's ten dollar paper note.
- **Sydney's prestigious Opera House pays tribute not only to the arts but also to the country's strong gambling industry.** When Australia decided to build the Opera House on Sydney's Bennelong Point, it hosted a competition for architects around the world. Danish architect Joern Utzon won the contract, bidding the building at $7 million, and then resigned from the project nine years later when costs skyrocketed, thanks partly to a million-plus Swedish tiles that had to be set by hand. Not easily discouraged, the cunning Australian government held a lottery to raise the remaining funds. The 4.5-acre complex took 15 years and a final price tag of $66 million to complete. The Opera House Lottery is still in effect today.
- **Australia's most famous painting resides not in a fancy art museum, but in a bawdy bar in Melbourne.** It's called "Chloe," and it's a full-length nude by French artist Jules Lefebvre that made headlines around the world when it was first unveiled at the 1880 Melbourne International Exhibition. Tourists flock to the little bar that now houses the famous oil.

teensy requirement—your GPA, no matter how long ago it was acquired, needs to be at least 3.0.

Unlike some so-called learning vacations that focus more on vacation than learning, these trips are for students who really care about the Earth and its oceans. You'll be asked to take a test, write a paper, and, more importantly, take the message back home that global warming is a serious issue, one that each and every one of us must address.

Every summer, the Centre for Marine Studies offers six ten-day to two-week courses in such topics as Coral Reef Ecosystems, Tropical Marine Invertebrates, Physical-Biological Oceanography, and Marine Neurobiology. These courses are scientific field studies, meaning you work at a research field station, not in a turgid, stuffy classroom. Yes, you'll get a few lectures in the morning and evening, but most of your time will be spent in the field (in this case, the Coral Sea).

In the ten-day "Coral Reef Ecosystems" program, for example, you'll conduct research alongside internationally recognized scientists on such topics as coral bleaching, photobiology, population genetics, and fish ecology. You'll learn to use state-of-the-art remote-sensing devices and how to interpret satellite data.

Since Heron Island Research Station, one of four research stations manned by the prestigious University of Queensland, suffered a devastating fire in March 2007, you'll most likely work at Moreton Bay Research Station until Heron Island can be rebuilt. All of UQ's research stations are located on pristine islands in the Great Barrier Reef, and you'll bunk right next to scientists and professors in dorm-like facilities and eat with them while having heated discussions on which threat is biggest: overfishing (especially with dynamite and cyanide), land-use issues (sewage and industrial sludge), or the global warming–induced coral bleaching.

Cost for the ten-day "Coral Reef Ecosystems" course is A$3,650 (about U.S.$3,200) and includes tuition, transport, accommodations, and meals.

HOW TO GET IN TOUCH

Centre for Marine Studies, Level 7, Gehrmann Building, Research Road, University of Queensland, Brisbane, Queensland, 4072 Australia, 61 7 3365 4333, www.cms.uq.edu.au, or **AustraLearn,** 12050 N. Pecos Street, Suite 320, Westminster, CO 80234, 800-980-0033, www.australearn.org.

walk in the footsteps of
alexander the great

Great Alexander wept, and made sad mone,
Because there was but one world to be wonne.
—Robert Hayman, *Quodlibets Book II*

71 Peter Sommer, a British archaeologist who in 1994 retraced Alexander's march from Troy to the battlefield of Issus, may very well be one of the world's best messengers in telling the great man's story. Not only did he spend 14 weeks walking the very route on which Alexander led 40,000 men, but he has produced travel articles, books, and a BBC documentary about the great general who never lost a battle.

"Who could not be intrigued by a man who inspired his soldiers to march for 12 years, beyond the known ends of the Earth?" Sommer says. "Having studied his campaign in libraries, I wanted to get out on the ground and see how the landscape with its mountains, rivers, and deserts shaped his strategies and determined his route. I wanted to see it up close for myself."

And now you can, too. Two years after Sommer's epic reenactment (without the pillaging and town besieging, of course), he started a travel company to lead archaeology tours to the country he had fallen head over heels for. For more than ten years now, he has been leading tours to showcase Turkey's ancient civilizations and soaring mountain landscapes complete with history lessons about the guy Colin Farrell was never meant to play.

Once a year, Sommer leads (yes, he personally escorts it himself) a 19-day "In the Footsteps of Alexander the Great" trek across Turkey's Anatolia covering the first leg of the great leader's extraordinary 22,000-mile journey.

Leading his guests through time, Sommer introduces them to the lives of the people who inhabited Alexander's tumultuous world. He takes them to Troy, where the great one ran naked around Achilles' tomb; Ephesus, where on the night of

Alexander's birth, a madman burned the temple of Artemis to the ground; Didyma, where his victory over the Persians was first prophesied; and Istanbul, where the Alexander sarcophagus lies today—although Sommer is the first to tell you that the white marble coffin is not "the Great's," but most likely belongs to a gardener named Abdalonymus who used his final resting place to pay homage to his protector.

"Turkey," Sommer beams, "has more and better preserved Greek and Roman archaeological sites then Greece and Italy combined. The landscape is simply riddled with ruins, many of which are virtually untouched. You can stroll through an olive grove, stumble upon a Greek temple, and have the place all to yourself."

In addition to the epic journey that's repeated once a year, Peter Sommer Travels offers a half-dozen archaeological *gulet* cruises along Turkey's three main seas. Gulets, Byzantine-style wooden yachts handmade in Turkey from Taurus Mountains pine and mahogany, are comfortable, stylish, and perfect for sailing the Lycian shore. And, yes, Sommer accompanies guests on most gulet tours, too.

The 19-day "In the Footsteps of Alexander the Great" tour runs £3,195 (about $6,500).

EAT, DRINK, AND BE TURKEY

Besides being an archaeological paradise of Greek, Roman, Byzantine, and Ottoman treasures, Turkey also happens to have one of the world's preeminent cuisines. From an array of soups and meze (traditional Turkish appetizers) to olives and meat and fish dishes, Turkish cuisine is painstakingly prepared from simple, fresh ingredients seasoned with herbs and spices grown locally. Oregano, marjoram, and thyme grow wild along Turkey's Mediterranean coast.

For liquid nourishment, try *raki,* a potent anisette that clouds over when water is added, giving it the popular name "lion's milk"; *meyve suyu,* freshly squeezed fruit juices (particularly orange and pomegranate); or *ayran,* a yogurt whipped with water.

And centuries before Starbucks cornered the market, Turkey was famous for its coffeehouses.

SAILING THE LYCIAN SEA

When he's not following Alexander the Great's footsteps, Peter Sommer is usually leading gulet tours along the Lycian coast of southern Turkey. In 1810, British Admiral Francis Beaufort was the first to survey this unspoiled coastline with its soaring limestone mountains, hidden bays, and Byzantine, Greek, and Roman ruins. As one of the first shipping routes between Constantinople and Jerusalem and, in more modern times, between Greece and Egypt, this lovely coast has attracted sailors from Anthony and Cleopatra to St. Paul. In fact, the world's oldest shipwreck, the *Ulu Burun,* dating back to 1350 B.C., was found here in the mid 1980s, a veritable time capsule from the Bronze Age with tons of copper, lapis lazuli, a wax book, and a golden scarab belonging to Egyptian queen Nefertiti. Suffice it to say, the Lycian Coast is a great place to sail.

Many archaeological sites cling to the coastline within easy access. From the deck of your gulet, you can see giant tombs carved out of the cliffs to resemble Greek temples. On Gemiler Island, an easy place to moor, you can explore a small Christian community with five churches from the Byzantine era. Nearby is Kaya Koy, a ghost town abandoned by Greek inhabitants in 1923. The fishing village of Ucagiz, a harborage dating back 2,500 years, has a fifth century necropolis (city of the dead) on one side and a Byzantine town that came a thousand years later on the other.

Said inveterate Middle East traveler Freya Stark (who also followed in the footsteps of Alexander the Great, in the 1950s):"There are not so many places left where magic reigns without interruption...and of all those I know, the coast of Lycia is the most magical."

HOW TO GET IN TOUCH

Peter Sommer Travels, 96 Monnow Street, Suite 2, Monmouth, NP25 3EQ, England, 44 1600 888 220, www.petersommer.com.

become spellbound by italian art

ROME, FLORENCE, AND VENICE

Art enables us to find ourselves and lose ourselves at the same time.
—Thomas Merton, Catholic mystic

72 Mention the word gap in America and the ubiquitous fashion retailer comes to mind. In England, however, the "gap" is the 15 months after secondary school before a student begins university. Savvy students use this all-important "gap year" to further their education *outside* the classroom. They might volunteer to build homes in Mexico, climb the peaks of Nepal, or raft Chile's great rivers.

Those who want to build a foundation for their next four years of education might elect to sign up for a six-week gap-year course with Art History Abroad (AHA). Since 1973, this mind-expanding company from Suffolk, England, has been training young eyes to appreciate Italy's art, sculpture, and architecture. But more than opening doors to hidden Italian treasures, AHA's mission is to produce cultivated minds. As its director, Nicholas Ross, likes to say, "We see students' minds as fires to be kindled.

"Even though our aim is to enlighten people to the world of art, our tutors inevitably draw connections between art, philosophy, music, literature, or history, so, effectively, we teach Civilization," says Ross, who has been leading the company since 1983.

And now, AHA also offers two-week art history courses that anybody, of any age, can take. But if you don't have time to fall in love, steer clear. AHA's tutors, as they call themselves, teach with such infectious gusto that the end result is a life of endless devotion. To art. Of all kinds.

During your course, you'll see the cream of Italy's masterpieces, eat at local cafés that haven't yet made the guidebooks, and romp with 20-somethings who still believe anything is possible.

Art History Abroad has a penchant for the back street and side door. Ross, for example, carries a sketchbook to explain ideas that don't translate well into words and has a gift for recognizing the best channel for imparting his passion. In

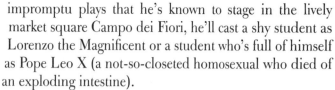

impromptu plays that he's known to stage in the lively market square Campo dei Fiori, he'll cast a shy student as Lorenzo the Magnificent or a student who's full of himself as Pope Leo X (a not-so-closeted homosexual who died of an exploding intestine).

Although Ross can't lead all the tours (the company takes 300 lucky folks to Italy each year), he's also a genius at finding (or maybe he draws it out?) and employing tutors with wit, warmth, and intelligence, all of whom can make the local sounds, colors, and languages spring to life. You'll almost think you're in Renaissance Florence with the Medici family or partying with Casanova in the 18th century or maybe even standing with the crowd in a Michelangelo painting. "It was so refreshing and exhilarating to meet people who had such a love for the arts," says Rebecca Udy, a recent partipant. "We re-enacted gladiator fights in the amphitheater in Verona, pretended to be wealthy Medicis in their palaces in Florence, and imitated sculptures by Michelangelo and Donatello. It was six weeks of absolute heaven."

Thanks to many years of friendship and AHA's collective "insider information," you'll be admitted to many places not open or evident to the public. Whether it be embassies in Rome, artists' studios in Florence, or poets' palaces in Venice, you'll be the ongoing recipient of Italy's boundless generosity of spirit. All tours include a private visit to the Vatican museums unencumbered by camera-snapping tourists, including Michelangelo's Sistine Chapel, Raphael's Stanze, and the sculpture court.

HEADS UP

One of the little-known "sideshows" that AHA tutors will likely introduce you to is the pickled monks' heads at Venice's Il Redentore Church. It's a Capuchin monastery founded during the plague of 1575. The Venetian Senate promised that if the city would be spared, the doge would, once a year, cross the Canale della Giudecca on a bridge of boats to give homage to the Redeemer. As for the pickled noggins, the monks of Il Redentore believed that everything given by God should be used in his worship, including the recycling of body parts.

You'll stay in pensions and B&Bs, all owned by families that have been friends of the program for years. You'll be treated to such entertainment as rugby matches in Rome, or Puccini's *Turandot* in the ruins of Caracalla's baths, or tutors reading from the diaries of Marco Polo at an outdoor Venice café.

AHA offers a couple of two-week options. Northern Italy, with four nights in Venice and five each in Florence and Rome, is £2,500 ($5,100) and includes accommodations, entry to all museums, enlightening tutors, entertainment, attractions, and breakfast each day. The Southern Italy option, with the same inclusions, spends four nights in Sicily, one night in Reggio, two days in Naples and Amalfi, and five days in Rome and also costs £2,500 ($5,100). Or you can elect to do both for £4,600 ($9,380). AHA can also tailor-make a private itinerary with Ross as your leader.

HOW TO GET IN TOUCH

Art History Abroad, St. Andrews Castle, 33 St. Andrews Street South, Bury St. Edmunds, Suffolk IP33 3PH, England, 44 1284 774772, www. arthistoryabroad.com

visit research stations on the lost continent

ANTARCTICA

The ice was here, the ice was there,
The ice was all around:
It cracked and growled, and roared and howled,
Like noises in a swound.
—Samuel Taylor Coleridge, *The Rime of the Ancient Mariner*

73 When former vice president (and Nobel Prize winner) Al Gore organized Live Earth, an all-continents concert held July 7, 2007, to raise awareness about global warming, he wasn't quite sure how he was going to stage a show in Antarctica. After all, the Earth's seventh continent is 98 percent ice, averages below-zero temperatures, and has a grand total of 4,000 human residents, one for every 1,000 square miles—and that's in the summer when most of the research stations are fully staffed. In the winter, as few as a thousand scientists man the stations. Thank goodness he heard about Nunatak, the hottest rock group in Antarctica. Or should we say, the only rock group in Antarctica.

Nunatak, a Greenlandic word that means "mountain popping out of ice," consists of five researchers with the British Antarctic Survey who, by day, research evolutionary biology and climate change. By night, they're the house band at Antarctica's Rothera Research Station. The concert that kicked off outdoors in temperatures of −10°F played to a sellout audience of 17 people, the entire population of the Rothera base.

If you'd like to hear Nunatak, or perhaps just learn about the planet's most untouched and isolated continent, sign up for an Antarctic expedition that combines some of the world's most spellbinding scenery with talks by some of the world's foremost Antarctic experts. Here are a couple of good ones:

National Geographic Expeditions. Aboard the *National Geographic Endeavor* or the *National Geographic Explorer*—ice-class expedition ships accommodating 110 and 148 passengers—you'll explore the spectacular Antarctic Peninsula. A magical, mountainous realm, the peninsula is, as far as Antarctica is concerned, the most populated spot on the continent. Indeed, in summer the human population swells to 3,000, not including tourists. On this 15-day adventure you'll be accompanied by a diverse team of experts, including naturalists and undersea specialists who will give you the ins and outs of Antarctica and its wildlife. They'll explain how Weddell seals make unique sounds called echolocation, to detect objects and prey with sound waves; why leopard seals are near the top of the Antarctic food chain (only the orca is higher); and how the Adélie penguins use a type of gang handshake to help family members identify each other.

You'll cruise aboard Zodiac landing craft in search of leopard seals deep beneath the water's surface, kayak around icebergs, and walk ashore amid thousands of penguins, including gentoo, Adélie, and chinstrap.

But most of all, you'll have an experience you'll never forget. "Don't expect to come back home and be the same person that got on the plane and headed south such a short time ago," says Karen Copeland, a natural history expert who blogged

NO MAN'S LAND

Since 1959, when 12 countries signed what's known as the Antarctic Treaty System (at last count, it was up to 45 signatory countries), all claims on this forbidden frozen wilderness have been suspended. Antarctica, which consists of all land and ice shelves south of 60°S latitude, is politically neutral. It's set aside as a scientific preserve and protected environment, and military activity is strictly prohibited.

While the fringes of this great white wilderness are studied for their wildlife, fresh air (the cleanest of the planet), and dark winter nights (perfect for astronomers), the heart of Antarctica provides a telling barometer for global warming.

From a year-round habitat called Dome C, a rotating community of French and Italian researchers has been digging deep—more than 2 miles deep—into the crust of ice to trace the history of climate for nearly a million years. Particles of dust and air bubbles trapped in the ice establish links between greenhouse gases and shifts in weather patterns. These invisible ice signatures reveal the effects of nuclear tests of the 1940s, '50s, and '60s, the eruption of Krakatoa in 1883, and other climate changes that go far beyond the brief history of *Homo sapiens*.

And despite what some politicians might tell us, they've already confirmed that carbon dioxide levels are higher now than at any time in the past 800,000 years.

about her experiences on the January 2008 trip. "Maybe it was the ice that did it. Maybe it was the vastness, the solitude. Maybe the birds stuck out their tiny feet and said, 'Stop, look at us. We can show you how to live.'" The 15-day trip, offered several times a year, ranges between $10,250 and $17,590, depending on class of accommodation.

National Geographic Expeditions, 1145 17th Street, N.W., Washington, D.C., 20036, 888-966-8687, www.nationalgeographicexpeditions.com.

TraveLearn. With the help of this Pennsylvania-based travel company that offers educational trips complete with college faculty and in-country experts, you'll fly to Buenos Aires, and from Ushuaia, Argentina, board the M/V *Akademik Ioffe,* a working Russian research vessel that will be your floating hotel for the 10- to 19-day trip. This boat, with its staff of 53, has all the equipment you'll need for the subzero temperatures, including parkas, Zodiac landing craft, camping gear, and snowshoes, as well as a sauna, plunge pool, and complete polar library.

In addition to visiting the Antarctic research stations of Great Britain, Argentina, and Poland, you'll get a chance to camp out on the ice, visit penguin rookeries, see icebergs bigger than Cincinnati, and hear such lectures as "Antarctic Ecosystems" and "Seabirds: Ocean Wanderers" right after viewing albatrosses, giant petrels, and half a dozen kinds of penguins.

Started by college professor Dr. Edwin Williams, TraveLearn works with a network of more than 300 universities, planning trips for their alumni associations, continuing-education departments, and the general public. The organization's destinations highlight important historical and natural landmarks such as the Great Wall of China, the Great Barrier Reef in Australia, Machu Picchu in Peru, the pyramids of Egypt, Vatican City in Italy, and the Acropolis in Athens. And on each trip, there's a university professor to put it all in context.

"I want travelers to have on-site, people-to-people experiences," Williams says.

Ranging from $5,600 to $15,750, the Antarctic excursions include cruise transportation and all meals, lectures, and services aboard the ship.

TraveLearn, P.O. Box 556, Hawley, PA 18428, 800-235-9114 or 570-226-9114, www.travelearn.com.

view african masks as they were intended to be seen

DÉDOUGOU, BURKINA FASO

Who was that masked man?
—Question posed at the end of each episode of *The Lone Ranger*

74 Seeing an African mask in an American museum is like listening to Beethoven's Fifth Symphony without the first four notes. No matter how authentic the mask, how skilled the curator, or how good the commentary displayed beside the exhibit, an African tribal mask is not the same without the tribesman.

Masks in Africa are sacred, only to be worn by chosen initiates, only to be used in special ceremonies. They're used to invoke spirits, prepare for war, or celebrate the harvest, a hunt, or the passing of a loved one. To hang them on a stark museum wall detached from their full-body costumes, apart from the music and dances they were made to celebrate, is to lose the mask's very soul. And to a Bwa or Nuna tribesman, a mask without a soul is a mask without a social, religious, or moral context.

However, all is not lost. Between March and June, mask festivals are thrown all over Burkina Faso. They're usually small, hosted by such tribal villages as Boni or Pala. If you happen to hit it right (or know enough French to call Bonde Yacouba, Boni's artistic director of the Mask Societies, at 226 20 99 6 53), you can watch the ceremonies that honor the wisdom of the Bwa ancestors.

If you're uncomfortable leaving it to chance, consider booking an airline ticket to Dédougou, a town in western Burkina Faso, for the biennial Festival International des Masques et des Arts—FESTIMA, as it's popularly called. It's held in even years (2008, 2010, and so on), and African tribes from across the continent (as well as groups from Europe, Asia, and the Americas) come to demonstrate the power and mystery behind their sacred objects. More than 40 villages from such countries as Mali, Togo, Benin, Senegal, and Cameroon bring their masks complete with full-blown regalia and ritual.

DEPARTMENT OF HANDICRAFTS

Most governments have departments of finance, public works, parks, and so on. But how many governments do you know that have a Department of Handicrafts? Back in 1985, after a population census discovered that more than 500,000 Burkinabe were working in the handicraft industry and that handicrafts make up more than 20 percent of the country's gross national product, Burkina Faso's Council of Ministers set up an arts-and-crafts fair (the Salon International de l'Artisanat de Ouagadougou, SIAO), which has grown to be one of the best places (not to mention the largest) on the Dark Continent to find African arts and crafts. Held every other year (again in even years) for ten days in the capital Ouagadougou, this huge international festival displays the best of Africa's hand-woven textiles, exotic leatherwork, ethnic jewelry, colorful pottery, calabash toys, bronze, and other handcrafts from nearly all of the countries in Africa.

Just 18 miles east of "Ouaga," as the locals call their capital, in the village of Laongo, there's an amazing collection of granite sculptures. This sculpture garden was begun in the 1990s by a contingent of global artists who show up every couple of years to add new sculptures, any one of which would fit right into any world-class art gallery. It's hard to find, but just stay on the dusty road heading to Ziniare.

The good news is that you don't have to be part of a tribe to attend. More than 400,000 visitors from all over the world show up for the parades, exhibitions, forums, cabarets, and, of course, elaborate masks of leaves, fibers, clays, fabrics, feathers, straw, skins, and wood.

FESTIMA began in 1995 when a group of African students, worried that their culture was being lost to modern society, formed the Association for the Preservation of the Masks (ASAMA) to celebrate the important ancient rituals associated with masks. By 1997, the four-day mask festival was in full swing (back then, they held it yearly). Filming of the event in 2000 and its airing on African public television made the festival an even bigger event. Each festival centers around a theme ("The Mask and the Environment" or "The Mask and Pluralism," for example), and festival organizers encourage tourists who come for the event to extend their stay and visit villages in the beautiful region of Boucle du Mouhoun. Some of these villages are even happy to allow visitors to help them make masks.

The festival is free, but tickets must be purchased for some of the dancing and ceremonial events.

HOW TO GET IN TOUCH
ASAMA, BP 42, Dédougou, Burkina Faso, 226 20 52 08 36, www.festima.org.

tip a mug, quench your thirst, and trace the roots of beer making

GERMANY

. . . because without beer, things do not seem to go as well.
—Diary of Brother Epp, Capuchin monk

75 Okay, so beer was not invented in Germany. That honor goes to the Sumerians, who were making beer more than 10,000 years ago. But it is in Germany where we find both the oldest archaeological evidence of brewing (a Celtic beer amphora from about 800 B.C.) and the oldest preserved malting plant and brewhouse (in Regensburg on the Danube, dating back to A.D. 180).

So if you want to learn about beer, there are few places better than Germany, where you can find both some of the finest brew universities (yes, there are brew universities—Versuchsund Lehranstalt für Brauerei in Berlin and Weihenstephan near Munich, to name just a couple) and the world's largest beer-drinking party. Yes, we're talking about Oktoberfest in Munich, which for 16 straight days in late September and early October hosts nonstop beer-slurping in 14 monstrous tents. The Löwenbräu tent alone can seat 6,000 revelers. More than six million beer imbibers from around the world show up to listen to oompah music, quaff some suds (hic!), and gain some knowledge about the drink that's made from just four ingredients—malt, hops, yeast, and water.

Admittedly, Oktoberfest itself might not be the best venue for furthering your beer education, but there are plenty of places throughout the country that can aid in your understanding of the golden liquid's craftsmanship. At last count, there were about 1,200 breweries in Germany brewing some 2.6 billion gallons of beer a year, and Germans as a whole drink twice as much per person as Americans and 60 percent more than the average Western European.

In this country of castles and ancient fortifications, you can visit centuries-old brewhouses, where contented monks created their liquid bread, and biergartens that originated in 19th-century Bavaria when ingenious brewers, not yet privy to

THE FIRST CONSUMER PROTECTION LAW

In 1516, a mere 24 years after Columbus discovered America, Duke Wilhelm IV of Bavaria enacted the first legal standard for food production: the legendary Bavarian Purity Law. Known in Germany as *Reinheitsgebot*, it basically states that beer can contain only four ingredients: malt, hops, yeast, and water. The duke wanted his subjects to feel confident that their beer had no questionable grains or additives—some of which, his subjects complained, had hallucinogenic effects.

Still in effect today, the ordinance that was adopted by all of Germany in 1906 insures that only natural ingredients, without artificial enzymes or chemical stabilizers and enhancers, are used. In fact, beer makers in many other countries have also adopted the purity doctrine, including many microbreweries in the United States and Canada. This sets them apart from, for example, Anheuser-Busch, which recently introduced a beer with caffeine, guarana, and ginseng.

refrigeration, planted leafy linden and chestnut trees above their storage cellars to keep their creations cool. You can tour the world's oldest brewery in Weihenstephan, Bavaria, in business since 1044 and still producing beer today. Bamberg, a picturesque medieval town of 70,000, has an unprecedented nine breweries.

BeerTrips.com, based in Missoula, Montana, offers several yearly trips to German beer regions, as well as itineraries to Belgium, the Netherlands, the Czech Republic, and other beer-loving destinations. On each of their trips, carefully planned to capitalize on the cuisine and culture associated with beer making, expert brewmasters, beer writers, and home brewers lead the pack.

On BeerTrips.com's annual trek to Oktoberfest, you'll not only partake of the festival that began in 1810 when Prince Ludwig invited the whole town of Munich to celebrate his marriage to Princess Therese but also visit brewpubs across the border in Prague, sip some of Bamberg's infamous smoke-beer, and tour Ayinger Brewery, a small family-owned brewery in the shadow of the Alps that grows its own barley malt, uses water from its own spring, and consistently places first in the World Beer Championships.

The 10-day Oktoberfest trip, with lodging, daily breakfast, three beer lunches, and four dinners with beer, runs $2,595.

HOW TO GET IN TOUCH
BeerTrips.com, P.O. Box 7892, Missoula, MT 59807, 406-531-9109, www.beer trips.com.

wellness escapes

It's dangerous business, Frodo, going out your door. You step
onto the road, and if you don't keep your feet, there's no knowing where
you might be swept off to.
—Bilbo in J. R. R. Tolkien's *The Hobbit*

The word "wellness" has been slapped on everything from granola bars to hospital continuing education classes. Here we're borrowing it not because it's the perfect word, but because it's the best one we can find to sum up the vacations in this chapter. All 25 of the vacations listed are dream vacations, experiences that you can't find anywhere else.

We'll be the first to admit that not all of them are for everyone. It takes a special kind of person to want to kite-ski across a polar ice cap or to hike hundreds of miles through the Japanese mountains. For travelers who want the familiarity of, say, Bermuda or the guidebook-friendly ease of London, well, you should probably look elsewhere. But before you do, make sure there's not something here that tickles a long-forgotten fantasy, a longing you've buried under all the bills, mortgages, and important adult responsibilities.

And give a cheer—a long and loud one—for your fellow travelers who can't wait to try the new, to push the boundaries, and in the process, to make all of us "more well."

ride zip lines through a jungle of singing gibbons

BOKEO NATURE RESERVE, LAOS

I'm in Laos zipping through the air on a wire cable to my new home in a tree, as I wave goodbye to my new friends, which definitely include monkeys and a bear. This is not something I thought I would ever be able to say to myself and have it correlate to reality. But at this point, who's paying attention to reality?
—Brad Payne, recent visitor to the Gibbon Experience

76 You'll sleep in an open-air tree house 100 feet above the ground. You'll swing (or actually zip-line) through the jungle and—although this part is optional—probably beat your chest and yell, "Ah-ah-ah-ah-ah!" But don't perform the Tarzan signature yell too loud, because you might miss the vocal duets of the rare, singing gibbons with whom you'll be sharing your jungle canopy home away from home.

In 1997, black-cheeked crested gibbons, which everybody thought were extinct, were rediscovered in a remote primordial rain forest in northern Laos, just across the border from Thailand. Like much of Asia's wildlife, these candidates for *American Idol* are in grave danger. Their habitat is being logged, poached, slashed, and burned by corporate rice farms.

Although the 300,000-acre Bokeo Nature Reserve where the gibbons live is protected on paper, there was no enforcement and little incentive to see that the gibbons, macaques, giant squirrels, barking deer, Asiatic black bears, tigers, clouded leopards, and more than 400 kinds of exotic tropical birds would continue to have a safe place to live.

Enter Animo, a forest conservation organization that decided to think outside the box. Rather than offer the typical ecotour, the perennial answer to raising funds and saving wildlife, they decided to bring in tourists, all right, but instead of letting them tromp through the very ground they're trying to

JUNGLE BOOGIE

While playing George of the Jungle is certainly a once-in-a-lifetime experience, you can also feel good that you're supporting a worthy cause. All funds raised by the Gibbon Experience are reinvested to protect this biodiverse Laotian forest. Animo not only pays local forest guards for 24/7 prevention from poaching and logging, but also uses locals to cook meals and guide tourists. At last count, Animo had employed more than 40 people from Lao Loom, Lao Theung, and Lao Soung, helping alleviate poverty. As Animo likes to point out, "Our forest conservation and canopy visits generate as much income every year as a local logging company could do but once."

save, they rigged up an elaborate overhead canopy village with zip lines to get from place to place.

In fact, the only way to actually reach Animo's Gibbon Experience (and to explore once you're there) is to strap on a harness, snap on a belay, and zip from platform to platform on metal wires. It's definitely not for wimps. The longest zip line traverses 1,500 feet over a valley 300 feet deep.

But think of the view! Not only do you get panoramas of the sweeping jungle, but you get to hang out in the treetops where the animals themselves live. As the mist clears each morning, you've got a front-row seat to the daily rain-forest concert.

The tree houses where you'll stay for two nights have running water, beds (although the mattresses are barely 3 inches thick), showers, and toilets that, though equipped with normal seats, are little more than holes in the floor. All meals are cooked by Laotian chefs who zip over to your tree house three times a day with steaming bowls of sticky rice; fish soup; *laap,* a cousin to steak tartare often made from water buffalo; and other exotic Laotian dishes that they've concocted over the village fire.

The Gibbon Experience is not an easy place to get to. Even in the dry season, the road—little more than a dirt track—is muddy and full of ruts. Be prepared to get out and push and to walk, if necessary.

Wild Planet Adventures, an ecotourism company founded in 1993 that strives to provide intimate encounters with wildlife, offers a five-day "Gibbon Experience" trip complete with an English-speaking naturalist (the local guides who fly you through the air with the greatest of ease speak only Lao) and bookends at Thailand's award-winning Phu Chaisai Spa, a peaceful mountain spa in Chiang Rai with bamboo cottages and a spa whose waters are fed by surrounding mountain streams. Including all meals, lodging, and naturalist guide, the gibbon trip costs $895.

If this isn't your thing, Wild Planet Adventures offers plenty of other exciting wildlife-focused escapades around the world. Take every paddler's "dream trip" down the rivers of Costa Rica, for instance, or an ultimate nature cruise in the Galapagos, or even a spectacular diving trip in Panama.

HOW TO GET IN TOUCH

Wild Planet Adventures, 1001 Bridgeway, #455, Sausalito, CA 94965, 800-990-4376 or 415-925-4300, www.wildplanetadventures.com.

go au naturel

CAP D'AGDE, FRANCE

I've come to realize that without our clothes,
we're all just one and the same.
—Katy Regan, visitor to Cap d'Agde

77 No shirt, no shoes, no problem.

Like any good oceanside resort, Cap d'Agde in southern France has a wide, sun-drenched beach, an interesting variety of shops and restaurants, and daily activities such as beach volleyball, windsurfing, and sandcastle-building competitions. The only difference is that in Cap d'Agde, people wear nothing but their birthday suits.

Yes, the whole town of 40,000 is a nudist colony. Only to call it a "colony" is not giving the fully functioning, self-sufficient town with its own police department and doctors' offices its due. People in Cap d'Agde bank in the nude, buy groceries in the nude, and, yes, even dine out at restaurants in the nude. In fact, if you try to sneakily wear a Speedo onto its gorgeous 1.5-mile-long beach, authorities will politely ask you to either "take it off, take it all off" or to leave. Voyeurism, at least the kind where you don't share and share alike, is strictly forbidden.

At first, it can be uncomfortable. You find yourself scrutinizing every bump, every lump, every blemish. You wonder why you didn't take that New Year's resolution seriously. But before long, you start to settle in. You come to realize, "Hey, if this is how God made me, why shouldn't I be proud of it?"

Naturists, as they call themselves, talk about body acceptance and claim that hanging out in the very outfit they came with offers a refreshing kind of freedom. There's no pretending to be someone you're not. As the Naturists Association proudly proclaims on its website, "We view the nude human form for what it is: a gift of nature, dignified and worthy of respect, regardless of shape, size, age, or hue."

And look at it like this: You won't need a lot of suitcases.

Cap d'Agde was developed from scrub in the 1970s and belongs to Agde, a fifth-century walled city just a few miles inland. The resort spreads out from a large man-made harbor with a marina. While there is also what is known as "the textile section" (a neighborhood where clothing is not optional), the naturist section is completely independent, with its own boutiques, banks, restaurants, swimming pools, nightclubs, and services.

Harry Shaffer, an 88-year-old economics professor from the University of Kansas, and his wife, Betty, rented an apartment in Cap d'Agde every summer for 11 years. "It was very liberating," Betty says. "It made you realize what life could be like. The only thing is, you had to remember to put your clothes back on when you left."

Cap d'Agde, situated in the lush Languedoc region, is also close to many other wonderful French destinations. The port city of Sete, known as the "Venice of Languedoc," is nearby. This romantic town with canals and quaint neighborhoods is a great place to get Bouziques oysters and *bourride*, a French specialty of monkfish in garlic mayonnaise. The medieval fortified city of Carcassonne, a UNESCO World Heritage site on the Canal du Midi, lies 75 miles to the west. From Cap d'Agde, you're also close to Nîmes, with its Roman heritage; the bustling city of Montpellier and its Place de la Comédie, adorned with the elegant "Three Graces" fountain; and charming Arles, a labyrinth of ancient streets. And, of course, it's only a five-hour train ride from Paris on the speedy TGV.

There are four types of accommodations in Cap—apartments, villas, a campground, and one hotel. Hotel Eve, although not exactly the Ritz, has a large heated pool, a sauna, a 24-hour lounge, a staff that speaks English (because the resort caters to lots of French and Germans, English can be harder to come by elsewhere), and clean, comfortable rooms. Newbies often stay there until they can score an apartment or villa.

The campground—the original nudist colony—has more than 2,500 sites, and whether you bring a tent or rent one of the permanently parked mobile homes or chalets, you'll get a secure swipe-card to allow safe admittance.

HOW TO GET IN TOUCH

Cap d'Agde, Bulle d'acceuil, Rond-point du Bon Acceuil, BP 44, F-34305, Le Cap d'Agde Cedex, France, 33 4 67 01 04 04, www.capdagde.com. **Hotel Eve,** Impasse Saissan, BP 857, 34307 Le Cap d'Agde Cedex, France, 33 3 67 26 71 70, www.hoteleve.com. **Peng Travel,** a British company that specializes in naturist holidays, can help you book an apartment or villa, 86 Station Road, Gidea Park, Romford, Essex, RM2 6DB, England, 44 845 345 8 345, www.pengtravel.co.uk.

embark on a sacred pilgrimage

SHIKOKU, JAPAN

> What the pilgrimage took from the body,
> it gave back to the spirit tenfold.
> —Ashley Wright, recent Shikoku pilgrim

78 There are 88 Buddhist temples on the Japanese island of Shikoku, strung around the perimeter like a giant mandala. Every year, a handful of pilgrims *(o-henro-san)* make the 700-mile trek around the island to visit every single one. Many travel by bus, car, or bicycle, but the serious pilgrims, the ones who want the true gifts of this sacred journey, walk. It takes a while—a month if you're really scooting, several if you go slow enough to feel your own breath.

The trip is anything but easy. Shikoku, even though it's the smallest of the four main Japanese islands, has a spine of jagged mountains and to make it to all 88 temples takes determination, patience, and the willpower to battle fatigue, weather, and your own mind—which, at some point, is guaranteed to start jabbering, "What were you thinking? This is ridiculous! I want to go back to Tokyo, back to a hotel, back to the comfort of my own country."

Lots of people quit before they finish the entire route. But those henros who persist, the ones who battle on despite the voices, say the trip gave them "strong legs and a strong heart." The strong heart, of course, is the goal—not the muscle that pumps at an average of 70 beats per minute, but the spiritual heart that sustains their power and nourishes their soul.

Lots of henros go with a specific request—they want the answer to a failing marriage, perhaps, or the healing of a beloved child. They come to get the help of Kobo Daishi, a ninth-century Buddhist monk who, according to believers, walks with them and listens to their pleas. Engraved into the walking stick *(tsue)* that henros take on their journey is the inscription, "We two walk together." Stacks of braces and crutches near the glittery temple altars of lacquered wood and gold lead one to believe that maybe there's something to Daishi's reputation as a miracle worker.

Born in 774, Kukai (who was later renamed Kobo Daishi) is to this day revered and known by virtually everyone in Japan. He was a poet, scholar, advisor to the emperor, and master calligrapher and founded an esoteric sect of Shingon Buddhism.

Although many of today's henros are practicing Buddhists seeking enlightenment, others are simply adventurers looking for a physical challenge or outdoorsmen eager to hike the mountain trails leading to these spiritual centers. It doesn't matter. The temples and their monks willingly welcome one and all.

Henros typically carry not only the enscripted walking stick but also a small white satchel that holds a *nokyo-cho*, a special book for collecting the signatures and seals of each temple. They also wear a special outfit, a white robe-like jacket and pointy straw hat, that identifies them as one who has chosen to make this personal sacrifice.

People along the route often bow as a henro passes by or they present them with *o-settai*, gifts to help them on their journey. O-settai, usually given by people who themselves would like to make the pilgrimage but can't, are their prayers to Kobo Daishi. Henros might get candy from bus drivers, ice cream from shopkeepers, yen from old ladies working the fields.

PILGRIMAGE BY PROXY

For the right price, you can hire an agent to make the Shikoku pilgrimage on your behalf. This designated fill-in will take the pilgrimage route, say the appropriate prayers, chant the appropriate sutras, and collect the appropriate temple stamps, all the while making sure that the gods, Buddhas, bodhisattvas, and Daishi-sama know the merit should go to your spiritual bank account, not theirs.

A still easier option is to buy the O-henro-san game, created by Pin Change Company, a subsidiary of Matsushita Electrical. Scenes of all 88 temples roll by as you punch buttons on your Nintendo GameCube console.

At each temple, henros offer heart sutras, a simple chant at both the main hall and the daishi hall, before lining up to receive their seal and signature, always done in beautiful calligraphy.

HOW TO GET IN TOUCH

To get the best map of the Shikoku walking route, you can send 3,500 yen ($32) plus 870 yen ($8) postage to **Mr. Tateki Miyazaki** (15-5 Hibarigaoka, Matsuyama-shi, Ehime-ken 791, Japan), and if you ask for *Shikoku Henro Hitoriarukiu Dogyo-ninin*, he will send you his two-volume guide for walking pilgrims. It's written in Japanese, but the maps, if followed correctly, will lead you from temple to temple with minimal time on highways and maximum time with nature.

You can also contact the **Shikoku 88 Holy Places Association,** 1065-1, Zentsuji-Cho, Zentsuji City, Kagawa Prefecture 765-0004 Japan, 81 877 565 688.

Alternatively, contact the **Japan National Tourist Organization,** 1 Rockefeller Plaza, Suite 1250, New York, NY 10020, 212-757-5641, www.japantravelinfo.com.

balloon over the swiss alps

CHÂTEAU D'OEX, SWITZERLAND

> Balloonists can dawdle, lollygag, cast their fate to the wind and
> become part of the ebb and flow of nature, part of the sky itself.... In
> that silent realm, far from the mischief and toil of society, all one hears
> is the urgent breathing of the wind.
> —Diane Ackerman, in "Traveling Light," *The New York Times*

79 When Buddy Bombard was 12, his mom sat him down for a serious talk. "Buddy," she said, "life is short. Seek out towering adventures." The young lad took his mother at her word, leaving the next day for a solo 8-mile bike ride to the nearest ocean, where he hitched his first ride on a sailboat. For the next 20 years, he crewed on many sailboats, eventually helping captain three America's Cup yachts.

But by 1968, at the ripe old age of 35, Bombard began to fear life was passing him by. Sure, he'd seen many ports of the world, but he longed to see what was beneath the sea, what was beyond the port. His Dartmouth economics degree and his job as an insurance executive just wasn't cutting it.

So he offered to take over the reins of the Chalet Club, a club of wealthy skiers who had bought a railcar and outfitted it with a player piano and stewardesses, using it to take them from New York to the slopes of Stowe, Vermont, each weekend. Bombard reckoned that if these club members liked barreling down snowcapped mountains, they might be talked into jumping out of airplanes and rafting down

ELBOW RUBBING WITH THE BEST

Buddy Bombard, dubbed the "Wizard of Ahhhhhs," has plied the skies with the best of them. Here's the short list of past customers you may have heard of:

- Julia Child • Joan Rivers • Mary Tyler Moore • Jim Henson
- Kirk Douglas • Helen Gurley Brown • Malcolm Forbes

untamed rapids. Soon the Chalet Club, under Bombard's leadership, became what he called "a ski club gone berserk." His members were pushing themselves further and further afield. One of the early trips involved scouting for the Loch Ness monster. Buddy's Chalet Club became, for all practical purposes, the world's first adventure travel company.

Today, Bombard—an Air Force jet pilot, skier, scuba instructor, honored balloon pilot, gourmet, and renowned raconteur—helms his own company, one he has been running since 1977: Buddy Bombard's Europe, which specializes in ballooning adventures in Europe. When he's not working, Bombard splits his time between a home in West Palm Beach, Florida, and an estate, Château de Laborde, in Beaune, France.

Bombard still personally escorts each trip. Thanks to his long-standing friendships with some of Europe's most colorful nobility (Princess Manni Wittenstein of Salzburg and Prince Girolamo and Princess Irinia Strozzi of Florence, to drop just a few names), Bombard's guests often receive private invitations to visit ancestral estates. They dine in centuries-old castles, in private villas, in posh French restaurants, and even aboard the balloon. Guests stay at luxury hotels chosen for their local charm and historical significance.

Every January during the Château d'Oex International Alpine Balloon Festival, Bombard extends his normal "Highlights of the Alps" trip to take in the world-famous event, which features the best balloons from all over Europe. On this nine-day excursion through the Swiss Alps, three of Bombard's nine baby blue, eight-story-tall balloons catch the dawn thermals and compete in precision events with more than a hundred balloons ranging from a huge winged cow to giant frog to a hot air balloon cell phone. You'll float with this stellar fleet over quaint mountain villages and herds of black chamois mountain goats, past walled medieval castles. Many of Bombard's guests combine the trip with a ski vacation in Gstaad, where the likes of Julie Andrews and Roger Moore have homes.

Bombard currently offers eight ballooning itineraries in six European countries (Austria, the Czech Republic, France, Italy, Switzerland, and Turkey) ranging from five to ten days in length. The nine-day Château d'Oex trips for 2008 run $17,283 (with a single supplement of $1,920) and includes lodging at Grand Hotel Park, a Relais & Châteaux property, plus all meals, eight days of balloon rides, and many other cultural excursions.

HOW TO GET IN TOUCH

Buddy Bombard's Europe, 333 Pershing Way, West Palm Beach, FL 33401, 800-862-8537 or 561-837-6610, www.buddybombard.com.

snowshoe bulgaria

RILA AND PIRIN MOUNTAINS, BULGARIA

Rila's jagged peaks stab heavenwards, a shower of ice crystals
rains like glitter, like a child's snowstorm shaker.
—Morag Reavley, Bulgarian snowshoer

80 In 2007, Bulgaria joined the European Union. Before the Bulgarians could so much as trade in their levs for euros, their new European cousins began flocking in, buying up Black Sea real estate, developing spas, pouring money into newfangled ski lifts. Bansko, a short two-hour drive from Sofia, quickly became the new Zermatt.

That's all fine and good if you just want to ski. But if you're hankering to get to know this new member of the EU, to experience its true heart, to really see its wild mountain valleys, consider trading in the skis for a pair of snowshoes.

Inteco, a company run by a young Bulgarian geographer named Ivo Stoilkov, offers snowshoe tours through the Rila and Pirin Mountains. Far from the madness of the booming ski towns, these tours show off the silent, monochromatic beauty of Bulgaria's mountain ranges. Stoilkov and his strapping young guides with their bionic thighs also offer ice climbing, bear-watching (there are more than 700 bears in the Balkan Mountains), archaeological exploration (in 2004, archaeologists found several Thracian tombs, one with a fifth-century, pure gold mask), visits to monasteries (Bulgaria has more than 120, many from the Byzantine and Ottoman eras, when they were cultural and enlightenment centers), and horseback-riding tours.

On the snowshoe trip, offered in February and March, you'll spend most of your time in the amazing Rila National Park. One of Europe's largest national parks, it has more than a hundred peaks, some towering to 9,600 feet, as well as large alpine meadows, deep canyons, caves, waterfalls, and some 120 lakes, 70 of them dating back to the Ice Age. The park also has a wealth of natural mineral springs, perfect for soothing those muscles after long winter treks. In the whole of Bulgaria, there's something like 560 hot springs, so don't be surprised if this gorgeous country soon makes the short list of top spa destinations.

A ROSE BY A BULGARIAN NAME

Bulgaria produces 70 percent of the world's rose oil, a pricey product used for making perfume, chocolate, liquor, and jam. Ounce per ounce, the rare Bulgarian Kazanlak, a rose oil specially cultivated for its fragrance, costs three times more than gold; which isn't surprising when you learn that it takes more than 1,300 roses to make one gram of the precious oil.

Bulgaria's Valley of the Roses, located between the Balkans and the Sredna Gora mountains, hosts a Festival of Roses every year on the first Sunday in June, at the start of the harvest.

Kazanlak, the capital of the Valley of the Roses, is also known as the Valley of the Thracian Kings. Once a significant Thracian settlement, the area has more than 500 burial mounds, tombs, and other archaeological sites. The most famous of the tombs, the Kazanlak Tomb, a late fourth- or early third-century B.C. domed burial chamber, is a UNESCO World Heritage site with gorgeous paintings and murals from the Hellenistic era.

Crisscrossing the wild Rila Mountains is a network of ancient footpaths. In communist times, hiking was considered an ideal activity for citizens, so a well-marked system of trails linked by cozy mountain huts, chalets, and lodges was developed. One of the paths leads to a tenth-century, fresco-laden monastery. And in winter, these paths are ideal for snowshoers.

On the current incarnation of Stoilkov's eight-day snowshoe trip, which starts and ends in Sofia, you'll snowshoe to Bulgaria's famous Seven Lakes area, to the quaint traditional village of Saparevo, to a hot mineral bath in Sapareva Banya, and, of course, to the UNESCO-listed Rila Monastery, a Renaissance architectural masterpiece with elegant, whitewashed arcades and verandas, a courtyard, and a brightly painted church. You might even see a rare Asiatic jackal.

At night, by the fire in your cozy village guesthouse, you'll dine on such Bulgarian specialties as tangy goat cheese salad, deep-fried peppers with rice, and nut-studded baklava, all washed down with *rakia*, a Bulgarian plum brandy, and Melnik, the full-bodied red wine that Winston Churchill bought by the crate.

The eight-day snowshoe trip with most meals is 490 euros (about $700).

HOW TO GET IN TOUCH

Inteco, 38 Budapest Street, 1202 Sofia, Bulgaria, 359 2 831 832, www.intecotravel.com.

trek the sahara desert with a camel caravan

LIBYA

It is little wonder that the desert has been fertile ground for religion. It's a space for revelation, for big thoughts—an immense open-air temple.
—Todd Pitock, traveler to Libya's Sahara

81 The bad news? GPS isn't available in the Sahara Desert. The good news? The Tuareg camel caravans that lead this stunning trek through the Sahara's Acacus Mountains would know the routes even if you tied their iconic blue veils over their eyes.

No sooner did the United States lift its travel ban to Libya on February 26, 2004, than adventure-tour operators began sizing up the country, which has five UNESCO World Heritage sites, Neolithic rock art, grand ocher dunescapes punctuated by date-palm oases, and a long shoreline of the Mediterranean Sea.

KE Adventure Travel—a company started in 1983 by a couple of college friends who had a thing about K2 and the Karakoram Mountains (Glen Rowley and Tim Greening led the first commercial trek up Baltoro Glacier to K2 and developed trekking routes in Pakistan that have become the established classics)—became one of the first to scout the magnificent rock formations in Libya's Acacus Mountains.

Stretching 60 miles along Libya's southwest border, the remote Acacus are sculpted by wadis, dry watercourses, and orange sand dunes that press silently against the bright blue sky. KE started offering trekking and camping trips to this wild and remote desert in 2007.

On KE's ten-day trip, which begins in Tripoli, you'll trek four or five hours a day (or ride camels, which KE's Bill Smith describes as "like a gently rocking boat") along wadis between tall sandstone rocks. You'll visit Neolithic rock-art sites, some of which date back 12,000 years, and walk alongside veiled Tuareg nomads whose way of life has changed little in 5,000 years. You'll enjoy the Tuareg's proud hospitality, their mint tea, their *tagella* (bread baked in the sand), and their desert camps, lit by nothing but a chandelier of stars. To a Tuareg, a house with walls and a roof over it is a living tomb.

Before returning to Tripoli, you'll spend a day at the ruins of Leptis Magna, the best and most complete Roman ruins in the world. Originally built by the Phoenicians, Leptis Magna became a prominent stronghold of the Roman Empire and has vast public baths, circuses, temples, and colonnaded streets.

The ten-day trip, including two nights in hotels, seven nights camping, all meals, and guides, is priced at $1,790.

HOW TO GET IN TOUCH

KE Adventure Travel, 3300 E. First Avenue, Suite 250, Denver, CO 80206, 800-497-9675 or 303-321-0085, www.keadventure.com.

combine yoga and ayurveda in a beachside coconut grove

KERALA, INDIA

Yoga teaches us to cure what need not be endured
and endure what cannot be cured.
—B.K.S. Iyengar, famous yoga teacher

82 There are hundreds, probably thousands, of places you can take a yoga vacation, ranging from Ireland's Clare Island to Egypt's Red Sea to Garobapa, Brazil. But if you want to go straight to the source, the place where it all began, book a life-transforming yoga vacation in India.

One option, of course, is to visit one of India's many ashrams, but if your normal yoga practice consists of an hour after work (and that's only on the days your boss doesn't ask you to work late), you may not be ready for the discipline some ashrams require. The Astanga Ashram at Mysore, for example, segregates yogis by gender and requires a monthlong commitment.

On the other hand, two American yoga teachers from Expanding Light, a California-based yoga and meditation center, offer a less rigorous yearly yoga retreat to India. While you'll get several hours of daily yoga practice—usually on the beach, under coconut trees—you'll also consult with Ayurveda specialists who will design an energy-correcting plan for your two-week stay.

Gyandev and Diksha McCord, the yogis from Ananda Village, the Expanding Light's retreat center, host their yearly retreat at Somatheeram Ayurvedic Beach Resort, a tropical paradise overlooking the Arabian Sea. Located in the Indian state of Kerala, Somatheeram has been consistently recognized as India's best Ayurvedic resort—which is saying something in a country that has hundreds of such facilities.

After your morning *sadhana* (meditation) and asanas (yoga postures), you'll be treated to a variety of Ayurvedic treatments. Doctors will determine your *dosha* (energy) profile and prescribe a diet, herbs, exercise, and Pachakarma (basically massage designed to pry toxins from your tissues) just for you.

GREATEST SHOW ON EARTH

In 2001, Demi Moore, Richard Gere, Madonna, and other VIPs made headlines when they showed up in Allahabad on the banks of the Ganges River for Maha Kumbh Mela, a Hindu festival held every 12 years and often called "the greatest show on Earth." It's certainly the biggest. Seventy million people, most of whom camped in dusty tents along the rivers, came to wash away their sins. To give you some perspective on this crowded sea of humanity, New Year's Eve at Times Square attracts about one million and the hajj in Mecca attracts three million. Although their ultimate aim is to purify in the river, the masses also enjoy magicians, elephants, chariots, and holy men called sadhus who perform superhuman feats.

Somatheeram's clinic has 30 therapy rooms, 12 doctors, and 70 massage therapists. Many of the herbs used in the massage oils (daily two-hour massages are part of everyone's regime whether your dosha is *vata, pitta,* or *kapha*) are grown right on the resort's grounds, and the oils and medicine are prepared in its own laboratory.

You'll stay in a traditional beachside Keralan cottage thatched with coconut fronds and be treated to healthy, vegetarian meals, all prepared Ayurvedically. Two or three evenings each week, Keralan entertainers perform on an outdoor stage next to your candlelit dinner. You'll experience Bharatanatyam, an Indian temple dance, and Katha Kali, a unique dance and drama performance of Indian mythology.

The McCords also plan three excursions to temples (including a shrine to Swami Vivekananda, the first yoga master to visit the West), fishing villages (on a houseboat along Kerala's famous canals), and Kovalam Beach, where you can shop for Keralan handicrafts.

The 17-day retreat, including airfare from San Francisco, breakfast, and dinner each day, seven Ayurvedic treatments, and lodging, starts at $4,200.

HOW TO GET IN TOUCH

Expanding Light, 14618 Tyler Foote Road, Nevada City, CA 95959, 800-346-5350 or 530-478-7518, www.expandinglight.org.

embark on an odyssey

GREEK ISLANDS

Sailing puts you in a time warp where you get to know yourself again.
—Matt Barrett, occasional Greek sailor

83 The country of Greece is made up of more than 2,000 islands, only 169 of which are inhabited. Lots of big cruise lines herd tourists from one island port to another. That may not be surprising, but it does beg the question: Why?

Greece has hundreds, probably thousands, of small yachts for charter. Although there are dozens of options (you can bareboat it alone, sail in a flotilla, or hire a captain and/or a crew), chartering your own yacht gives you freedom, independence, and the luxury of visiting islands not crowded with the same few thousand passengers you just had breakfast with. And it's not as expensive as you might think.

Granted, your own yacht won't provide team beer chugging, guitar combos strumming "Feelings," or tour directors who, during your scheduled two-hour shore adventure, steer you in and out of seashell museums. In fact, should you opt to charter a yacht, you'll be called upon to make a lot of your own decisions. Like in which sun-drenched paradise should your yacht-for-the-week meet you? Do you prefer hopping among pristine, uninhabited beaches or do you relish hours-long stretches of fast, open sailing?

Charter yachts provide the same basic amenities as a cruise ship—private cabins, a skipper to work the sails, a choice of water toys, and, if you want, onboard haute cuisine. Or if you'd rather, you can sleep on the deck, man your own sails, throw the toys overboard, and eat at quaint island tavernas. The point is, where you dock, when you eat, what you wear or don't wear—it's all up to you.

But you'll probably want to consult your skipper. He or she is not only familiar with the islands, coves, winds, and currents but also knows the best cafés for espresso, which jellyfish to avoid, and the quickest place to find medicine in case you don't listen. Greek skippers, licensed by

PAN'S LABRYINTH

Hydra, a 21-square-mile Greek isle with whitewashed houses and tavernas, all topped with red terra-cotta-tiled roofs, is probably on thousands of lists of "Places to Visit before You Die." Why? Because this gorgeous island that rises steeply out of the Aegean Sea to the 2,000-foot Mount Ere forbids automobiles. The only way to get around the quaint island is by foot or by donkey. Locals fish for sponges and build boats, and an artists' colony that sprang up in the last 50 years has attracted the likes of Leonard Cohen, Mick Jagger, Keith Richards, and members of Pink Floyd. But the most famous guy on the island is Pan, a former Green Beret who once ran the most "in" bar on the island. It was called Pan's Bar, logically enough, and had everything American from T-shirts to Kansas license plates. Although Pan's Bar is now closed, Pan himself, a walking encyclopedia of all things Hydra, is still the go-to guy if you want tourist information—the best place to bunk, the best beach, the best way to get two big suitcases on the back of a donkey. You can't really miss the former bar owner—he's the short (5-foot), stocky guy with the long white beard who walks Hydra's three streets.

the Greek government, know more about the islands than any guidebook.

The best part of chartering a yacht is the flexibility. There's no such thing as a deadline or an itinerary. You can get up each morning, size up the wind conditions, and decide which island you'd like to sail toward. Your only real job is to pity the rest of the world.

Most yachts are hired through brokers, whose job it is to inspect the vessels and play matchmaker between crews and sailing wannabes. Globe Merchant, a Chapel Hill, North Carolina–based brokerage, works with dozens of captains and boats. It is run by American sailor David Econopouly, who lived in Greece for seven years, built his own 34-foot cutter, and has extensive sailing experience.

He'll start by asking which of Greece's five groups of islands you want to explore. The Saronic Islands, the closest ones to Athens, include Aegina, Poros, Spetse, and Hydra; you can also pull in anywhere on the shores of the Peloponnese. The Cyclades, to the east of Athens in the Aegean Sea (Santorini and Mykonos, to name a couple), are the most visited, and because there are so many of them, you can practically pick any direction and go. The Dodecanese Islands, located in the eastern Aegean, are close to Turkey and less touristy. The Ionian Islands, off the western coast of Greece (including Corfu and Kefalonia, where *Captain Corelli's Mandolin* was filmed), require a plane or ferry ride from Athens. The Sporades, also more distant, are north of Athens and include Skiathos, Skopelos, and Skiros.

Among the many boats and captains Econopouly represents are Billy Joel Leck, a Brit who has lived in the Greek Islands for 20 years; Stefan Ritscher, a German mechanical engineer who commandeers the *Caraya II* with his Greek archaeologist wife, Fotini; and Markos Voutsinos, who can even perform weddings on his 55-foot, Syros-based cutter.

Although prices vary depending on the size and class of the boat, here's a rough idea. A week in low season on the S/Y *Stressbuster*, a 50-foot, five-cabin boat crewed by Kostas Ghiokas, a former Greek Olympian yacht racer, and Lynda Morris Childress, former managing editor of *Cruising World* magazine, runs $6,993 ($4,843 for the yacht and $2,030 for captain, crew, cook, and VAT). Divide that between five couples (one per cabin) and the cost is a mere $1,400 per couple.

HOW TO GET IN TOUCH

Globe Merchant Yacht Charters, Box 114, Carrboro, NC 27510, 877-850-1519, www.charterayachtingreece.com.

walk patagonia

CHILE

Angels whisper to a man when he goes for a walk.
—Raymond Inmon, British author

84 Walking is a revolutionary act. Free from the confines of our 1.5-ton, 150-horsepower cages, we no longer peer at the world through a tiny frame of tinted glass. We are in the world and of it. We can hear it, smell it.

That's why Country Walkers, a Vermont-based travel company, thinks it's the only way to travel. The company believes its trips offer an intimacy with a place that you just can't get when zooming by in a bus or a car. Offering more than 60 itineraries around the world—from Sedona, Arizona, to Bhutan—these trips give you the chance to make discoveries you would never make at our normal warp speed. You'll stop in tiny cafés, meet locals, and breathe in plenty of fresh air. And do we really need to point out the health benefits? Everyone from fitness guru Kathy Smith to your doctor will tell you that walking burns calories, boosts energy, lowers blood pressure, and reduces your risk of diabetes and heart disease.

On Country Walkers' trip to Chile's Lake District and Patagonia, you'll walk between 5 and 12 miles a day, starting in the resort city of Puerto Varas, with its Middle European architecture, on the shores of Lake Llanquihue. From this gateway to the region's magnificent national parks, with views of both Osorno and Calbuco volcanoes, you'll visit a working farm, an archaeological site, two national parks, and Lake Todos Los Santos, about which Theodore Roosevelt wrote, "Surely, there can be no more beautiful lake anywhere than this." You'll ferry to Chiloe Island, just off the coast, considered to be the heart of traditional folk culture, with a rich mythology and lifestyle rooted in the misty climate.

In Patagonia, the second leg of the trip, you'll walk various routes through the Torres del Paine National Park, viewing Laguna Verde, the Paine Massif, Toro Lake, Refugio Chileno, and the glaciers of Almirante Nieto.

RAFT THE FU

In 1990, Eric Hertz, owner of Earth River Expeditions, was the first to raft the entire 31 miles of Chile's Futaleufu, a recently discovered river deep within the Andes. When he heard that Chile's hydropower company, Endesa, intended to dam the "Fu," as they had dammed the country's other great white-water river, the Bío-Bío, he quickly organized a group of rafters to bring public attention to the wilderness gem. He picked a good crew for getting attention: Robert Kennedy, Jr., Dan Aykroyd, John McEnroe, Julia Louis-Dreyfus, and a couple of Cirque de Soleil acrobats.

So far, the Fu is still undammed, and Hertz's company has gone on to offer hundreds of river trips down this ferocious river with 8-foot drops, Caribbean-blue water, and Class III, IV, and V rapids. Earth River has developed three private camps along the Fu where rafters can stay while making the voyage. One of them, Cave Camp, has 12 cave dwellings, each expertly concealed and invisible from the' river, and a network of intertwining trails with wooden bridges over huge boulders. Tree House Camp, with eight tree houses nestled in old-growth forest, has a zip line, a natural hot spring, steep waterfalls, and 10-acre Frog Lake. There's even a 300-foot granite spire that Earth River guides, all certified in mountaineering and technical climbing, use for rappelling guests.

Earth River Expeditions is part white-water outfitter and part conservation group. Hertz and his partner, Chilean Roberto Currie, have devoted their lives to saving the world's last great wilderness rivers. As Hertz says, "Rivers are the best way to experience the wilderness without destroying it. And we all need the wilderness to renew ourselves."

If you'd like to raft Earth River's Futaleufu and experience riverside hot tubs, cliff dwellings, tree houses, lakes, and granite climbing towers, they offer near-weekly trips between November and April. The cost for the ten-day trip runs $3,100. *Earth River Expeditions, 180 Towpath Road, Accord, NY 12404, 800-643-2784, www.earthriver.com.*

The price for this 11-day trip, including guides, accommodations in comfy hotels and hosterias, most meals, and park fees, is $5,298, plus the mandatory $225 flight from Puerto Montt to Punta Arenas.

HOW TO GET IN TOUCH

Country Walkers, P.O. Box 180, Waterbury, VT 05676, 800-464-9255 or 802-244-8813, www.countrywalkers.com.

soak in the african savannah

ETHIOPIA

In Ethiopia, I saw stuff that reorganized how I saw the world.
—Bono, lead singer of U2 and global activist

85 Before Addis Ababa became the world's coolest name for a capital (it means, "new flower" in Amharic, the official Ethiopian language), it was called Fil Wilha, which means "hot springs." So it's no big leap to ascertain that this is a country made for soaking.

From the sulfurous fumaroles of Ethiopia's Rift Valley to the remote lava springs bubbling out of the majestic Simien Mountains, there are hundreds of places to sit back in a warm pool of water, relax, and just breathe. Some of the springs are developed with small hotels and campgrounds nearby. Others can be hiked to or found in Ethiopia's many national parks. But all of them offer fascinating things to see during your off-hours.

Take the Wondo Genet Hot Springs, for example. This favorite of Emperor Haile Selassie's is near Shashemene's world-famous Rasta Village (Rastafarians from around the world make pilgrimages here) built on land donated by the mysterious emperor himself. The Bilen Hot Springs are near the Herto village where scientists found Lucy, the newsmaking, 3.4-million-year-old hominid. At the hot spring near the walled, mostly Muslim city of Harar, you can feed hyenas.

Here are just a few soaks to consider:

Bilen Hot Springs. Most people come to Ethiopia's Awash Valley where this hot springs is located, four hours north of Addis Ababa, to add to their bird lists (440 varieties have been recorded there) or to see the resident lions, hippos, and crocs. But while the birders are chasing down rare yellow-throated serins, buff-crested bustards, and white-crowned shrikes, you can settle into the mineral springs alongside Afar tribal nomads. The

Bilen Lodge, with 15 huts made from papyrus reeds, sits on Elalaytu, a hill overlooking the springs and the grass reeds that fringe them. The lodge can arrange camel treks guided by native Afars.

Bilen Lodge, c/o Village Ethiopia, Box 15151, Addis Ababa, 251 1 15523497, www.village-ethiopia.net/afar_region_loge.htm.

Sodere Spa Resort. One of Ethiopia's most developed hot springs, Sodere is located along the banks of the Awash River. It has an Olympic-size, thermally heated pool and is popular with weekenders from the capital. In the mid-1990s, it was the site of peace talks between several factions vying for control of Somalia. There are campgrounds and small bungalows, and also masseurs who will rub out any kinks. The only drawback is keeping the monkeys (there are hundreds of them) away from your drinks and beach towels. Located 15 miles from Adama (which is about 60 miles southeast of Addis Ababa), you can catch a ride on the blue-and-white minibuses.

Sodere Spa Resort, Box 3154, Sodere, Ethiopa, 251 1 51 7187.

FOR WHEN YOU'RE A RAISIN

As hard as it might be to pull yourself out of these refreshing hot springs, here are some don't-misses in this startlingly beautiful and historically rich country:

- **Axum.** The ancient capital of the Queen of Sheba, Axum is where some say the original Ark of the Covenant containing the Ten Commandments rests.
- **Gondar.** With more castles and churches than any other African city, this ancient city is known as Ethiopia's Camelot. The oldest and most impressive of Gondar's many imperial structures is the two-story palace of Emperor Fasiledes with a tower that has views of Lake Tana in the distance.
- **Lake Tana.** The 37 islands scattered throughout this giant lake, the source of the Blue Nile, shelter fascinating churches and monasteries, some dating back to the 13th century.
- **Lalibela.** Legend has it that Lalibela's incredible 13th-century rock-hewn churches, 11 in all, were made with the help of angels. As the country's most popular attraction, it is often called the eighth wonder of the world.

Wondo Genet Hot Springs. Surrounded by amaryllis, jacaranda, and bougainvillea, this hot springs looks more like a Costa Rican jungle than an African savannah. Monkeys swing in the fig trees overhead. Heated by volcanic activity below, the water is used by residents to cook potatoes and corn. Other locals study at the College of Forestry and research medicinal and oil-bearing plants such as castor, vernonia, and jatropha. Located about 150 miles south of Addis Ababa, this hot springs with the picturesque view of Lake Awasa has a restaurant, souvenir shop, and marked trails.

Wondo Genet Hot Springs, Box 3154, Wondo Genet Hot Springs, Ethiopa, 251 1 51 7187.

HOW TO GET IN TOUCH

Travel Ethiopia, Box 9438, Addis Ababa, Ethiopia, 251 11 5 523 165, www .travelethiopia.com.

explore the heart of the coral triangle

PALAWAN, THE PHILIPPINES

The Coral Triangle is the center of world marine diversity.
It is coral's homeland.
—Charlie Vernon, marine scientist

86 The Coral Triangle, a 2.3-million-square-mile ocean expanse surrounded by Indonesia, Malaysia, and the Philippines, is the epicenter of marine diversity. Its Sulu and Sulawesi Seas shelter 600 species of coral (the Caribbean, to give you some perspective, has just 60) and more than half of the world's species of reef fish, including pygmy seahorse (if you can see them—they're only a quarter of an inch tall), striped longfin bannerfish, and the false clown anemonefish.

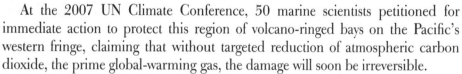

At the 2007 UN Climate Conference, 50 marine scientists petitioned for immediate action to protect this region of volcano-ringed bays on the Pacific's western fringe, claiming that without targeted reduction of atmospheric carbon dioxide, the prime global-warming gas, the damage will soon be irreversible.

So, fingers crossed, the region will be saved. Nevertheless, this is not a trip to postpone. Palawan, a 1,760-island archipelago on the western edge of the Philippines, provides the perfect hub for divers and snorkelers who want to explore this unique, threatened refuge. It has endless miles of reef, the requisite pristine beaches, caves, limestone cliffs, and one of the last clans of dugongs, large marine mammals that feed on Palawan's sea-grass beds. Because dugongs graze the beds standing upright with their fins outstretched, many scientists believe these distant relatives of the elephant are the culprits behind the mermaid myth. Palawan also has two underwater World Heritage sites—Puerto

It's called Artcafé, and, indeed, it's a beachside café with home-baked bread, yogurt, pizza, and the best coffee in Palawan. But more than food, Artcafé in El Nido is one-stop shopping for any question a tourist can think up. Owners Judith and Tani Distal (she's from Switzerland, he's Filipino) arrange all sorts of island-hopping, snorkeling, windsurfing, and walking tours. They started their establishment as a T-shirt shop and still sell T-shirts, all designed and printed by Tani, but it didn't take them too long to figure out that the people who buy the shirts also want to know the best place to ride horses and where to rent kayaks. Judith even serves as the local representative for SeAir, the local airline that flies thrice weekly to El Nido. There's live music every night, as well as colorful locals and travelers. *El Nido Boutique and Artcafé, Sirena Street, Buena Suerte, El Nido, 5313 Palawan, Philippines, 63 906 255 1020, www.elni doboutiqueandartcafe.com.*

Princessa Subterranean River Park and Tubbataha Reef National Marine Park. As remote as the region feels, it's easily accessibly by plane from Manila.

Here are three places to get your dive on:

Dive Link Resort. It's a short ten-minute *banca* (Philippine outrigger) ride from Coron town on Busuanga Island to the coconut grove on Uson Island that in 1999 became the Dive Link Resort. From the resort's colorful cottages, each named for a Filipino fruit, it's easy to reach more than 80 islands with white-sand beaches, coral beds, and lush forests. Besides the ample diversity of coral, divers come for the wrecks—37, at last count. At the end of World War II, it seems, General Yamashita docked Japanese ships here allegedly filled with looted treasures from Indochina. Even though many of them were disguised as Red Cross ships, an American general ordered them bombed and sunk, leaving a veritable treasure trove for divers. Rooms with bamboo furniture and porches start at $88.

Dive Link Resort, Manila Sales Office, Unit 15A Atherton Place, Tomas Morato corner Roces Avenue, Quezon City, Philippines, 63 2 376 2048 or 63 2 387 2019, www.divelink.com.ph.

Dolarog Beach Resort. This chic, back-to-nature resort is so laid-back it doesn't even have phone service. What it does have is lush, grassy lawns, a palm-grove-backed beach, tasteful cottages, and a superb al fresco restaurant manned by Italian Edo Flisi and his Filipina partner. Rates start at $75 and include lodging, two meals daily, snorkeling equipment, paddleboats, kayaks, and one island-hopping adventure in Bacuit Bay.

Dolarog Beach Resort, El Nido, 5313 Palawan, Philippines, Internet phone service Skype, at "dolarog," www.dolarog.com.

Lagen Island Resort. Set in a cove fringed by thick primary forest, Lagen Island Resort is a showcase of the town of El Nido's diverse variety of birds and mammals. Included on *Conde Nast Traveler*'s 2006 Green List, the resort has taken the lead in the conservation of Palawan's marine and forest resources by helping to secure governmental protection, collaborating on scientific research, and planning environmentally responsible development. The resort's entire staff, from gardener to dive guide, are all trained in ecology, geology, and history. A trail at the back of this resort winds past trees with roots taller than Shaquille O'Neal. For the romantics, Lagen Island Resort will gladly rustle up a private table for two in a garden clearing, around the bay, or perhaps on a floating raft in the middle of the lagoon. Singles start at 16,500 pesos ($400) a night.

Ten Knots Development Corp., 18th Floor 8747, Paseo de Roxas Street, Salcedo Village, 1226 Makati City, Philippines, 63 2 894 5644, www. elnidoresorts.com.

SAFARI SURF SCHOOL
catch a wave

NOSARA, COSTA RICA

The rest of the world disappears for me when I'm on a wave.
—Paul Walker, American actor and recent teenage heartthrob

87 With 621 miles of coastline, it's no big surprise that Costa Rica, with its bathwater-range ocean temperatures and surf as consistent as spring dandelions would turn into a learn-to-surf nirvana. The only downside in all this perfection is that formerly charming coastal towns like Tamarindo and Jaco have become overrun with loud-talking, sunburned Americans in tropical shirts.

Luckily, there's a quaint coastal town on the middle of Costa Rica's thumb that has managed to remain a quaint coastal town, mainly because it's 40 miles from the nearest paved road. Tucked away on the Nicoya Peninsula, Nosara—and its Playa Guiones, a 4-mile beach with one of the Caribbean's best breaks—is just right for learning to surf, taking yoga lessons, or practicing your guitar riffs.

Nosara's uncrowded surf and relaxed lifestyle were just what brothers Tim and Tyler Marsh, owners of the town's laid-back Safari Surf School, were looking for when they came to Costa Rica in the mid-1990s. Originally from Hawaii, the

---

HOMEWORK

Back when Tim and Tyler Marsh started surfing four decades ago, learn-to-surf schools were unheard of. Now, says Tim, the elder of the brothers, "Surfing is everywhere. It has even become respectable. It's a multibillion dollar industry."

The sport is so respectable that it now has its own encyclopedia, a 774-page tome with 1,489 entries from "A-frame" to "Zog, Mr. *See* Sex Wax." Compiled by Matt Warshaw, the former editor of *Surfer* magazine, *The Encyclopedia of Surfing* (Harcourt, 2003) chronicles the history, champions, and jokes of the sport and makes for fascinating bedtime reading. Yes, this comprehensive reference book is entertaining and educational, at the same time detailing everything from the best surf movies to the ongoing standoff between long and short boarders.

---

brothers grew up surfing, teaching what Tim called "tourist girls" how to ride a wave. Tim even competed for many years in the Pro Am and National Scholastic Surfing Association circuit. After college, the Marshes traveled the world, from Tahiti to Malaysia, looking for the surf and the scene of their imagination, a place where they could share their passion for the sport.

When Tim was urged by a friend to try Costa Rica and eventually found Nosara, he knew he'd come home. "It reminds me of what Hawaii must have been like a hundred years ago," Tim says. "There are no street lights, no paved roads, it's very junglesque. I mean, howler monkeys wake you up in the morning."

And it's not just Nosara they love. Playa Guiones couldn't be more perfect for a surf school. "It's almost like it was created by God for surfing," Tim says. "It has what we call a playground type of wave. It's the most ideal beach for beginning and intermediate surfers. It has a sand bottom and a gradual descent that slows the swell down. It breaks out 150 yards, so beginners can get a good 50-yard ride. They can get the feel of dropping into a wave, which is ultimately what surfing is all about. Like any sport, the faster you go, the easier it is to do."

At the Marshes' Safari Surf School, you'll take two lessons a day (in the morning when the waves are at their best and in the late afternoon, just in time to watch the sun set), taught by Tyler and a team of mostly local Ticos (a colloquial term for a native Costa Rican), and have afternoons off to explore the nearby 125-acre biological preserve, hike to waterfalls, or take a yoga class. The Nosara Yoga Institute (www.nosarayoga.com), situated in the jungle at a quiet remove from the surf scene, offers several vinyasa classes daily.

Time it right and you might be fortunate enough to encounter an olive ridley turtle laying her eggs. These giant amphibians occasionally show up year-round right on Playa Guiones, but more regularly at Ostional, a half-hour drive north.

As for the guitar riffs, Bill Macpherson, who has played guitar with everyone from Dizzy Gillespie to Hootie and the Blowfish, started Native Vibe Music camps in Nosara in 2007 (www.nativevibemusiccamps.com).

A seven-day package that includes surf lessons, daily yoga, accommodations at the Marshes' Casa Tucan, and two meals a day runs $2,070.

HOW TO GET IN TOUCH

Safari Surf School, Nosara, Costa Rica, 866-433-3355 or 506 682 0573, www
.safarisurfschool.com.

BEER CAN REGATTA AND HENLEY-ON-TODD
enter a zany boat race

NORTHERN TERRITORY, AUSTRALIA

*There is nothing—absolutely nothing—half so much worth
doing as simply messing about in boats.*
—Water Rat, *The Wind in the Willows*

88 Unless you're a top-notch yachter, one of the world's best, you probably won't be entering the America's Cup. But there's always a pair of Australian boat races that have been on the sailing calendar for more than three decades. Granted, the prizes and prestige aren't quite as lofty, but these two events, held yearly in Australia's remote and easygoing Northern Territory, are twice as much fun, raise money for a good cause, and are guaranteed to make you chuckle—something scientists have proven is good for your health.

Beer Can Regatta. On Boxing Day 1974, Hurricane Tracy practically wiped out the Northern Territory capital city of Darwin. Work crews sent in to rebuild the town, unaccustomed to the humidity, ended up consuming larger than normal quantities of beer. Since recycling hadn't come into vogue just yet, mountains of empty beer cans began piling up. Lutz Frankensfeld, one of the territory's many colorful, larger-than-life characters, hatched a scheme of holding a boat race with all the vessels fashioned out of empty beer cans. The inaugural 1975 race not only eliminated the litter problem but was so much fun that they've held it every year since on Darwin's famous Mindil Beach.

If you want to enter a boat, you're warmly welcome. Just know that your boat must be constructed entirely out of stubbies (that's Aussie for beer cans). It can be any shape and any size, and you'll get points for creativity—and lots of extra points if your vessel happens to be seaworthy. Yes, many of the beer can boats have been known to wallow, flounder, and sink. If you want pointers for building your craft, the Darwin Lions Clubs, which now sponsor the family event (kids can make their boats out of soda cans), provide a six-page Beer Can Yacht Construction Guide on their website. Unfortunately, there are no blueprints for past years' beer can canoes, beer can speedboats, beer can Viking ships, and the like, some complete with fire hoses and other secret weaponry.

The rules are listed on the website, along with this proviso: "The rules have been known to be bent by the scrutineers." The two most important rules: Be in it and have fun. If you don't like to get wet, consider entering the accompanying tug-of-war, flip-flop tossing, sand-castle building, or "hole in one," where golfers attempt to drive a ball into a bucket placed in an ocean-moored dinghy 200 feet from shore.

Unlike the America's Cup, where entrants average $100 million on their yachts, the entry fee for the Beer Can Regatta is a mere A$50 (about U.S.$43). Depending on the tide, the regatta is held on a Sunday in either July or August.

Beer Can Regatta Association, P.O. Box 1496, Darwin, NT, 0801 Australia, 61 409 823 871, www.beercanregatta.org.au.

Henley-on-Todd. In 1962, meteorologist Reg Smith proposed that the central Australian town of Alice Springs host a regatta similar to the famous Henley-on-Thames race between Cambridge and Oxford Universities. The fact that the town was more than 900 miles from the nearest significant body of water was never considered a hindrance. Rather, the bottomless yachts, tubs, kayaks, battle boats, and other vessels in this annual event are powered by their crews' leg muscles as they run up and down the dry, sandy Todd River bed, Fred Flintstone style.

In this regatta, you don't even have to supply your own boat. The sponsoring Rotary Clubs provide the vessels, unless, of course, you're feeling particularly creative and want to BYOB (bring your own boat). In that case, just make sure your vessel resembles a boat and can completely encircle your four-person crew while scrambling and stumbling to the turning buoy and back. The entry fee is a mere A$10 (U.S.$0.88). The grand finale is a race between two large boats built on tractor bodies outfitted with water cannon and fire hoses filled with water and flour. The Henley-on-Todd, or HOT as it's affectionately called, is held every August or September—except in 1993 when it was canceled due to rain!

Henley-on-Todd, P.O. Box 1385, Alice Springs, NT, 0871 Australia, 61 8 8952 6796, www.henleyontodd.com.au.

study martial arts at the temple where it all began

SONGSHAN, CHINA

The ultimate aim of karate lies not in victory nor defeat, but in the perfection of the character of its participants.
—Master Gichin Funakoshi

89

China's ancient Shaolin Temple where kung fu was allegedly born is probably the most famous Buddhist temple known in the Western world. It's where Kwai Chang Caine, or "Grasshopper," played by David Carradine in the TV series *Kung Fu*, studied the lessons taught by Master Po and Master Kan. It's also where four-time national martial arts champion Jet Li filmed mainland China's first kung fu hit. According to conspiracy theorists, martial arts icon Bruce Lee, who lived to be only 32, was murdered for revealing some of Shaolin's 1,500-year-old secrets.

You can take your pick of how the fame started. The official story places the origins of the Shaolin tradition in the sixth century, when a Buddhist monk named Bodhidharma, noticing his new charges were in ill health and unable to devote themselves to the physical rigors of contemplative practice, began offering the physical drills that are said to be the basis of kung fu. It's still actively practiced by the monks, who combine the martial art with Zen Buddhism practice.

But as to when everybody began, as the song says, "kung fu fighting," you need to look back a few thousand martial arts movies to "Shaolin Temple," featuring the Chinese kung fu star Jet Li. Li borrowed as his plot the Shaolin Temple's most famous legend, the one about 13 monks who rescued the Tang emperor from a vicious warlord.

For a while, anyone vaguely familiar with Chinese martial arts could hang up a shingle and claim to be a Shaolin kung fu school. But the monks recently persuaded

READING, WRITING, 'RITHMETIC, AND KUNG FU

Kung fu, at least in central China, is compulsory at all secondary schools. Parents like it because it's good exercise, and the kids like it because their heroes, Jet Li and Zhang Ziyi, do it in films. Some parents even go so far as to send their kids, age 4 to 10, to Dengfeng for a three-year training program in wushu. These children follow a demanding regime of fitness training, stretching, weapons, and wushu from 5:30 a.m. to 9:30 p.m., six days a week. But at the end of the course, they are almost guaranteed a job as a security guard, traveling troupe member, or maybe as an actor in an action film. Many parents believe their children have a better chance of getting a job with good kung fu skills than with a university education.

the Chinese government to declare the 170-movement practice a recognized brand, which protected it under rules of the World Trade Organization. "Shaolin wants to preserve our uniqueness, for the same reasons that developed countries value individuality," says the temple's leader, or abbot, who goes by the name Yongxin. "It's a process that the society has to go through, spreading standards. Shaolin has a lifestyle that has lasted over 1,000 years."

Today, the world's most famous Buddhist temple is home to more than four dozen *wushu* (martial arts) schools. Although the Chinese government recently razed the schools' former buildings that lined the road leading to the temple, the schools themselves were relocated to nearby Dengfeng, where monks and their apprentices still dispense daily lessons in kung fu.

Foreigners are invited to join in the fun, although calling it "fun" might be stretching it. The lessons can be rigorous, and the true life of Shaolin is simple and austere, alternating the swinging arms and breaking boards with meditation and chanting prayer.

Tagou School of Martial Arts, the largest of the 50 or so schools, trains 10,000 students, many of whom are hoping to be the next Jet Li or Jackie Chan. They gather each morning and late afternoon to practice with the famous "fighting monks."

If you study at Tagou or one of the other Dengfeng Shaolin schools, you'll get your own coach, your own room in the Dharma Hall, and the chance to watch the daily Shaolin demonstrations. Although serious students usually begin their day with a 4:30 a.m. training run (and you *are* free to join them), the wushu lessons don't officially begin until 8:30. You can choose between studying kung fu basics or more advanced weapon forms. There are also lessons in *tai ji quan, qi gong,* and other martial arts.

Although it's possible to show up at Shaolin and sign up for classes, it's probably best to book a trip before you leave. Joy Dupont, a former United Nations employee, organizes ten-day trips to Shaolin Temple to study both martial arts and tai ji quan. An upcoming trip, escorted by Dupont and George Xavier Love, a doctor of oriental medicine, acupuncture physician, and Qi Gong master, includes several days in Beijing, an excursion to the Great Wall, reflexology classes, a cruise down the Yulong River, and shopping in Yangshuo in addition to the Shaolin martial arts training.

With meals, accommodations, kung fu instruction, and other cultural activities, these trips cost $2,000 to $2,500, depending on the level of accommodation.

HOW TO GET IN TOUCH
Club Meditation, P.O. Box 3322, Palm Beach, FL 33480, 561-844-3882, www.ChinaSportsAndTravel.com.

fly-fish new zealand

NEW ZEALAND

Some go to church and think about fishing,
others go fishing and think about God.
—Tony Blake, fly fisherman

90 At one time, Western novelist Zane Grey held ten world records for large game fish. He was the first to catch a fish over 1,000 pounds, and his last world-record catch (a 618-pound silver marlin) wasn't broken until 1953, 14 years after his death.

So, when the celebrated sportsman wrote that New Zealand was a "fly fisherman's Eldorado," you can be sure it was more than a fish tale. In fact, if it's a trophy trout you're after, New Zealand and its copious rivers and streams should be at the top of your to-do list. Both the North and South Islands are crisscrossed with pristine, gin-clear, trout-growing waters. Even an average-size New Zealand trout weighs in at around 4.5 pounds.

Most New Zealand guides swear by "sight-fishing," which means carefully stalking the river and spotting your fish first before tempting to land it with a dry fly or nymph. That means you'd better be prepared to do lots of walking. Of course, the country's expert cast of eagle-eyed fishing guides are well known for spotting record-setting rainbows and lunker browns.

The North Island's Tongariro River, long considered one of the world's best trout rivers, offers fishing year-round, but during the migratory run in late autumn and winter (remember the seasons are reversed down under), the place can get mighty crowded. Here are three ideas for beating the rush:

Hire a guide. Knowing the prime fishing habitats, the structure of a streambed, and the best time for a run or a glide takes some research. That's why it's helpful to hire a guide who will not only spot trout for you but also help you set a fly, find a good vantage point for observing both your fish and your fly, and coach you on making a cast with some hope of success. Some Kiwi guides even offer a unique "no fish/no pay" policy.

ZANE GREY WAS HERE

Zane Grey wrote two books about fishing in New Zealand. *Tales of the Angler's Eldorado,* which detailed his fly-fishing pursuits at Lake Taupo, also detailed his big-game fishing on Otehei Bay off Urupukapuka Island, the biggest of the Bay of Islands' 144 islands. Located off the east coast of New Zealand's North Island, Grey's cabin (along with a few others) has been turned into a resort called the Zane Grey Resort. From there, you can fish for striped marlin, Pacific blue and black marlin, broadbill swordfish, yellowtail, and mako, hammerhead, and thresher sharks. The resort also offers kayaking trips and archaeological walks to visit Maori *pa* sites around the bay. *Zane Grey Resort, P.O. Box 99140, Newmarket, Auckland, New Zealand, 64 9 403 7009, www.zanegrey.co.nz.*

New Zealand Professional Fishing Guides Association, P.O. Box 213, 295 Gladstone Road, Gisborne, New Zealand, 64 6 867 7874, www.fishingguides.co.nz.

Book a stay at a New Zealand fishing lodge. There are many fishing lodges in New Zealand such as Lake Rotoroa Lodge, a lovingly restored lodge in Nelson Lake National Park (www.lakerotoroalodge.com, 64 3 523 9121), to the Motueka River Lodge (www.motuekalodge.co.nz, 64 3 526 8668) that the London *Sunday Times* named as one of the seven best places in the world to stay. Expert fishing guides are part of the package. A list of New Zealand fishing lodges can be located at www.nzfishing.com.

Get out in the wild. If you have plenty of money, helicopters are a great way to access New Zealand's pristine wilderness. Or if you'd rather do it on the cheap, consider raft fishing, jeeping to a private property, or hiking—all options offered by Fishing in New Zealand, a company that offers custom-designed fly-fishing trips to both islands. On the four-wheel-drive trip, you'll stay at a private 3,000-acre property owned by an indigenous Maori family. With about 4 miles of the Whanganui River to yourself, you'll be guided by Kelvin and Rocky, fed by their brother Danny, and invited to go spotlight possum hunting, eeling (Danny will fry them up for breakfast, if you're interested), horseback riding, and to participate in a traditional Maori *hangi,* a social event much like a Hawaiian luau. Rates for a four-night, three-day trip start at NZ$3,640 (U.S.$2,811).

Fishing in New Zealand, 38 Mapara Road, Acacia Bay, Taupo, New Zealand, 64 7 376 8555, www.fishinginnewzealand.com.

FLY-FISHING HEAVENS

The beauty of fly-fishing is that it typically takes place amid some of the planet's most gorgeous settings. Here's just a sampling of spots where scenery and bountiful fish converge:

- **Alaska.** One of the best places in the United States to fly fish, its countless options range from streams to lakes, from rainbows to salmons. Some of the best haunts: Chilkat River, Susitna River, Kenai River, and Kah Sheets Lake.
- **The Alta, Norway.** The great Alta River in northern Norway is considered the greatest Atlantic salmon fishing river in the world. Period. Fish the size of Vikings are regularly taken—ranging from the standard 25 pounds to monsters capping 50 pounds and more.
- **Belize.** Perhaps the world's capital of salt fly fishing, Belize promises bonefish, permit, and tarpon. Turneffe Atoll, about 30 miles off mainland Belize, with its deeper waters, tends to boast larger fish; bonefish, the most popular take (or attempt, anyway—these fish are among the most difficult to catch on a fly), prowl these waters in schools of 300 or more. Belize is also popular for its vast variety of non-fly-fishing activities, meaning everyone will be happy.
- **Kola Peninsula, Russia.** The domain of submarines, ships, and nukes during the Cold War, when the region reigned as the world's most heavily militarized place, the Kola Peninsula is now famed for its outstanding Atlantic salmon fishing. Double-digit hauls of big salmon are common.
- **Patagonia, Argentina.** In the shadows of the snow-capped Andes, this natural paradise is famous for its brown trout, brook trout, and rainbow trout. You'll stay in *estancias* (ranches) and have access to miles and miles of pristine, clear-running rivers—many say this is what Montana was 50 years ago.

---

go vegetarian on a holistic cruise

CARIBBEAN SEA

> You can be the richest or the most educated person in the world, but if
> you don't have your health, you don't have anything.
> —Sandy Pukel, co-owner of A Taste of Health

91 We know that cruising has earned the nickname "float and bloat" for a very good reason. But on this cruise, a seven-day voyage around the Caribbean, you'll eat healthy, macrobiotic food, take classes in nutrition and alternative medicine, and actually come back weighing less than when you embarked.

Every day on this unusual cruise, you'll be invited to classes in such vitalizing subjects as meditation, yoga, *tai ji quan,* cooking, nutrition, age reversal, and spiritual development. You'll learn from well-known experts like Deepak Chopra, Bernie Segal, and Lindsey Wagner, the "Bionic Woman" who went on to write vegetarian cookbooks.

A Taste of Health was started by Sandy Pukel, who owned a popular Coconut Grove, Florida, natural food store for 35 years. If you saw the classic documentary about Woodstock, he was the guy being interviewed sans clothes. Of course, that was before he had his macrobiotic transformation.

In 1971, after meeting Michio Kushi, the famous Harvard macrobiotic researcher, Pukel borrowed $4,000 from his father to open Oak Feed, a Miami store that sold bulk grains, nuts, and seeds. But more than just running a retail store, Pukel was on what you might call a macrobiotic mission. He taught cooking classes. He counseled people with breast cancer and diabetes. He started a nonprofit foundation to educate kids about the importance of what they eat.

Pukel wanted nothing less than to teach the whole world about food's healing qualities and about alternatives to conventional medicine. His store (and the workshops) became popular, and he soon became known as a sort of health guru and celebrity.

When Pukel first proposed the idea of spreading the macrobiotic gospel further with an alternative to the traditional "cruise," the cruise lines laughed him out of their offices. After all, they insisted, cruise-line customers choose them for their rich, always available food.

Finally, Pukel found a believer in an Italian cruise line, which happened to have a vegetarian captain on one of its ships and a commitment to green practices. The line was willing to give Pukel's far-out idea a shot. They even agreed to let him bring in his own food and his own gourmet chefs, as long as Pukel's group would provide the same white-jacketed service and lavish, albeit macrobiotic, five-course meals that the cruise line was known for. In 2004, the first "Holistic Holiday at Sea" launched from Fort Lauderdale to rave reviews.

The experience is repeated and grows every year. In 2008, for example, the cruise offered a hundred classes taught by such renowned experts as Dr. Neil Barnard, professor at George Washington University and founder of the Physician Committee for Responsible Medicine; Dr. Sherry Rogers, author and teacher of environmental medicine at medical schools in six countries; and Marilu Henner, who is not just an actress but also the author of several books on healthy living. Perhaps the most popular event is the recovery panel discussion that Pukel puts together every year, featuring people who healed themselves of life-threatening diseases.

Classes offered from 7 a.m. to 10 p.m. each day are optional ("People's only complaint is we offer too much to do," Pukel says) and some prefer to simply relax in the ship's Turkish baths, saunas, and three swimming pools, showing up only to indulge in the lavish feasts of mushroom risotto, seitan stroganoff, lentil pâté, and pear crisps.

The seven-day "voyage to well-being," as Pukel likes to call it, starts at $1,195 per person.

HOW TO GET IN TOUCH
A Taste of Health, 434 Aragon Avenue, Coral Gables, FL 33134, 828-749-9537, www.atasteofhealth.org.

enjoy a spa fit for a king

HUA HIN, THAILAND

That's spa as in soak-away-your cares, as in peel-away-those-wrinkles, as
in wipe-away-that-old-fashioned-stressed-out-way-of-being.
—Pam Grout, *Girlfriend Getaways*

92 Not far from the giant emerald Buddha at Wat Phra Chetuphon, a 17th-century temple in Bangkok, sit statues of yogis doing "self-massage"—which should be your first clue that this is a country that knows how to spa.

Not that anybody's going to argue. Thailand has long been known as Asia's spa capital, and its many spas offer an endless list of treatments. Since the second and third centuries when Buddhist monks brought ancient Indian healing techniques to what was then known as Siam, every village has had a traditional healer who uses herbs, spirituality, and stretching to release blocked energy. But with more than 700 registered spas (the Ministry of Health keeps track), how do you pick the right one?

A good place to start is Hua Hin, a seaside village along the Gulf of Thailand with wooden fishing piers along a sweeping 5-mile beach. Unlike many of Thailand's popular resort beaches, Hua Hin retains an authentic, provincial flavor. It's three hours south of Bangkok by car or train and has been a royal getaway since the 1920s when King Rama VII, who built a palace there for

USING YOUR NOODLE

Hua Hin, like most Thai cities, has lots of open-air stalls and mobile carts peddling Thailand's famous noodle dishes. If you're tired of spa food or just want to walk the tangle of Hua Hin's back streets, try out Jeak Peak, Hua Hin's most famous noodle shop. It has been at the same corner of Naebkehardt and Dechanuchit since 1945 and sells all sorts of noodle dishes, seafood, satays, and even *kanom jeen,* a sweet noodle usually reserved for special occasions.

Queen Rambaibarni, hired British engineers to punch a railway through deep jungle, eliminating the long, not-so-comfortable elephant rides.

When Bhumibol Adulyadej, Thailand's current, much beloved king and the world's longest reigning monarch (since 1946), is in Hua Hin, he spends most of his time at the royal Klai Kangwon Palace. Klai Kangwon (which translates to "far from worries") could be the mantra for the exotic, lush spas that have sprung up here.

Here are four of the best:

Anantara Resort and Spa. Set along Hua Hin's main beach, this 14-acre resort feels like a beautiful jungle, with rooms spaced around lagoons and sculpture-lined pools. From ancient Ayurveda to Reiki, this spa offers a wide variety of treatments, including a signature three-hour Shirodhara massage that ends with a soak in hot water. Rates start at 6,900 baht ($232)

Anantara Resort and Spa , 43/1 Phetkasem Beach Road, Hua Hin, Prachuab Khiri Khan 77110, Thailand, 66 3252 0250, www.anantara.com.

Chiva-Som. Chiva-Som means "haven of life," and this spa's 47 suites, set on seven acres of beachfront, attract such celebs as David and Victoria Beckham, Hugh Grant, Naomi Campbell, and Kylie Minogue. Beyond just soaks and facials, it offers a wide variety of treatments to cleanse, purify, and heal the body and soul. Counselors assess personal needs and design a program that's apt to include yoga or *tai ji quan,* swimming, various treatments, and daily massage. It also has an adjoining medi-spa where U.S.-trained doctors offer Botox and cosmetic laser treatments. Rates range from 51,673 baht ($1,665) for a three-day stay during low season to 1,451,197 baht ($46,760) for a 28-day stay in high season.

Chiva-Som, 73/4 Petchkasem Road, Hua Hin, Prachuab Khiri Khan 77110, Thailand, 66 3253 6536, www.chivasom.com.

Evason Six Senses Hideaway Resort and Earth Spa. The spa at this luxury resort located about 13 miles south of Hua Hin comprises nine domes and a meditation cave made entirely out of rice husks and straw. Many of the ingredients used in the treatments are grown and harvested right on the property, including rice, coconut, avocado, papaya, lime, aloe vera, cucumber, pandanus leaf, lemongrass, ginger, galangal, candlenut, and turmeric. Guests can also stay in Spa Suites—private wellness sanctuaries—where therapists make house calls. Rooms start at 4,000 baht ($134).

Evason Six Senses Hideaway Resort and Earth Spa, 9 Moo 5 Paknampran Beach, Pranburi, Prachuab Khiri Khan 77220, Thailand, 66 32 632 111, www.sixsenses.com/evason-huahin.

Sofitel Centara Grand Resort. Queen Rambaibarni originally built this hotel, Thailand's first, as a guesthouse for royal parties. Perhaps its even bigger claim to fame was its appearance in the 1984 movie *The Killing Fields*, when it was made to replicate a Phnom Penh reporter's hotel. A few years ago, it was reborn as the 207-room Sofitel. With enormous balconies, antique furnishings, and white colonial architecture, it offers a wide variety of spa services in its nine treatment rooms, each laid out in the resort's gardens. It also has a golf course, Thailand's first, built in 1924; the Museum Café, which serves afternoon tea; and a manicured topiary garden with foliage shaped like animals. Rates start at 4,281 baht ($138).

Sofitel Centara Grand Resort, 1 Damnernkasem Road, Hua Hin, Prachuab Khiri Khan 77110, Thailand, 66 32 6776240, www.sofitel.com.

take a metaphysical pilgrimage

EGYPT

You are not a realist unless you believe in miracles.
—Anwar Sadat, former president of Egypt

93 Ahmed Abdelmawgood Fayed grew up within 200 yards of the Sphinx in a palatial home that faces the Great Pyramid. For five generations, his family has been responsible for all excavations at the Giza pyramids. He has given tours of his country to Henry Kissinger, Liz Taylor, Princess Diana, the Grateful Dead, Sally Jessy Raphael, and Shirley MacLaine.

Despite his master's degree in archaeology from Cairo University, Fayed's tours, at least the ones he likes to give now, are otherworldly in nature. He calls them "metaphysical tours," and they evoke the great wisdom and spiritual energy of the ancient civilization that Fayed thinks has much to teach all mankind. He believes that the accumulated knowledge of the ancients—a sort of spiritual Library of Congress—rests in the Great Pyramid and that Egypt's great temples along the Nile correspond with chakras in the human spine.

Fayed's Guardian Travel Company—named after the Sphinx, who Fayed believes is the "guardian of knowledge"—brings in about 5,000 spiritual tourists a year. And even those who think they're coming to Egypt for, say, a nonspiritual cruise down the Nile, often get rocked to the core. He rattles off dozens of stories of everyday tourists whose lives were dramatically changed after experiencing Egypt's ancient and powerful energy sights. For one, Britain's Field Marshal Herbert Kitchener, after visiting the Aga Khan, gave up his military career to pursue humanitarian endeavors.

For those who come with spiritual enlightenment as a goal, well, Fayed knows just what to do, having lectured on Egyptology at the Edgar Cayce Foundation in Virginia Beach, Virginia, every summer since he was 15. His forte is arranging private time at, for example, the Great Pyramid or the Sphinx for special spiritual rituals.

"The ancient Egyptians left behind a legacy—artifacts that we can see and feel," Fayed says. "Also, remember that this place was a school where people went to get their

OTHER SPIRITUAL HOT SPOTS

Other "acupuncture points" around the world that are said to hold powerful energies include:

- **Medjugorje, Bosnia-Herzegovina.** On June 24, 1981, the Virgin Mary appeared to six young people, telling them to convert their hearts and lives back to God. Reportedly, she still makes appearances, and hundreds have come back minus crutches, wheelchairs, and other burdens.
- **Rosslyn Chapel.** Thanks to *The Da Vinci Code,* this 15th-century Episcopal church in Roslin, Scotland, draws seekers looking for the crypt.
- **Sedona, Arizona.** Vision quests, soul retrieval, emotional integration, shamanic healing, spiritual hiking? Sedona and its powerful vortices offers them all.
- **Stonehenge.** It has been speculated that this megalithic ruin in southern England was a temple for worshipping ancient earth deities. Others claim it's an astronomical observatory for marking significant events on the prehistoric calendar. Still others believe that it was a sacred site for the burial of high-ranking citizens from the societies of long ago.

---

education. Plato, Socrates, Moses came to the temples of Egypt to learn these secrets."

To an outsider, spiritual tourists look like any others. They take camel rides, cruise the Nile, carry cameras, and purchase cheesy souvenirs. Occasionally, though, the distinctions manifest themselves, such as in an after-hours ritual in a private burial chamber. Fayed's guests lay down in the rutted sarcophagus of an Egyptian prince, as was prescribed in the training of priests in pharaonic Egypt.

A 12-day spiritual tour with lodging, meals, airfare from JFK, and all the spiritual bells and whistles runs $3,500. And you can add on excursions to, say, the holy St. Catherine's Monastery and Mount Sinai, or the city of Alexandria.

HOW TO GET IN TOUCH
Guardian Travel, 526 Redbird Court, Virginia Beach, VA 23451, 757-422-5568, www.guardiantravel.com.

ride horses to machu picchu's sacred sister

VILCABAMBA VALLEY, PERU

That glancing-over-your-shoulder fear, the sort of adrenaline rush you hope for at ancient ruins, is still attainable at Choquequirao.
—Ethan Todras-Whitehill, travel writer

94 Last year, 800,000 people visited Machu Picchu, the far-from-lost "Lost City of the Inca." It's Peru's number-one tourist attraction, and, unless you take the 5:30 a.m. bus from Aguas Caliente or stay at the on-site hotel, you're sure to share the place with several large tourist groups and their microphone-blaring guides. But what Hiram Bingham, the Yale historian who first brought the pre-Columbian city to fame in 1911, failed to mention about his great discovery is that, two years earlier, he had investigated another lost Incan city just up the hill.

Choquequirao—which is just as big, just as much of an architectural feat, and has just as many sun-worshipping temples and terraces as its famous sister—is a bit more daunting to get to. It's perched at 10,000 feet above the Apurimac River, and, until 1995 when the Peruvian government in anticipation of added tourism revenue completed a footbridge, the only way to get there was to climb up and down a 7,000-foot canyon and swing across a single cable stretched across the rapids.

When Gary Ziegler, an American archaeologist who worked on the first excavation, began organizing exploratory expeditions to Choquequirao in 1994—"archaeotourism," he called it, in which paying tourists helped fund exploration—it took 12 support staff and 28 horses to cross the 6,000- to 15,000-foot canyons and ridges. But the trek was worth it. Choquequirao was like Machu Picchu in 1911, before it was excavated, before the Peruvian government decided to build a train and let advertising agencies film beer commercials there—a move it's regretted ever since a 1,000-pound crane being used by the J. Walter Thompson ad agency fell on a centuries-old sundial.

Make no mistake. It's still an arduous, several-day trek to reach Choquequirao, including one 8-mile day in which you climb 5,000 vertical feet up. But, unlike Machu Picchu, once you get there you're virtually guaranteed to be one of only a handful of people at the very most. Only 8,000 people make it here a year.

Manu Expeditions, owned by British ornithologist Barry Walker (who also happens to be Cusco's British consul), in conjunction with Ziegler's Adventure Specialists, offers 15-day horseback riding adventures to Choquequirao. Sure, you'll also spend a day at Machu Picchu and other shrines to Incan deities, but your ultimate destination is the remote Incan citadel that, so far, is only 30 percent excavated. Ziegler speculates that this relatively new find is where Tupac Amaru, the last Incan leader, was raised by Incan priestesses.

Manu's 19th-century-style expedition, with all supplies carried on horses and mules, starts, like most Incan tourism venues, in Cusco. You'll be led by experienced locals (Ziegler and Walker still lead some of the tours), guided by Quechua packers, and treated to traditional coca tea as you hear the legends about the lost cities of Vilcabamba.

On your horse, you'll follow a well-preserved stone Inca road, camping beside fluted glaciers and ancient Inca shrines as you climb slowly up into the cloud forest. Finally, on the 12th day, you'll arrive at Choquequirao, where,

GO TAKE A HIKE

If you opt to go to Choquequirao on your own, it's a strenuous 20-mile hike that starts in Cachora, a tiny town nestled in the Salkantay Ridge. As of yet, there's no direct bus service to the little village, but you can catch a taxi for the 100-mile trip from Cusco. Although Cachora's main road was recently paved (in anticipation of the onslaught of tourists) and an Internet café sprang up, it's still a quaint village that is keeping its fingers crossed that it can avoid the pitfalls that have befallen Aguas Caliente, the nearest town to Machu Picchu that has mushroomed—from 500 to more than 4,000—since the site made it onto every adventurer's life list. For now, Cachora still belongs to its residents, farmers whose way of life hasn't changed in centuries.

DON'T FORGET TO SPILL YOUR DRINK

After years of abiding mother's advice to hold our cups up straight, we find that in the Incan culture, it's perfectly acceptable to spill your drink. In fact, it's expected. In reverence to Pachamama, the Incan fertility goddess (only in some parts of Peru, Chile, and Bolivia she's been replaced by the Virgin Mary), imbibers of chicha, a drink originally made from the berries of the molle pepper plant, now made with corn, purposely spill the first sip on the ground. It's a toast they call *challa* and, while many people perform the toast every day, there's a special celebration each year called Martes de Challa (Challa's Tuesday), when people not only dump their drink, but they bury food, throw candy, burn incense, and, if they're a *yatiri* (a traditional priest), sacrifice guinea pigs and burn llama fetuses.

It's an apology of sorts to Pachamama (Mother Earth) for all we've done to disturb her. Yatiris, in fact, regularly create offerings for those who ask by wrapping up herbs, small tablets of sugar with symbols (houses, dollar bills, hearts, condors, etc), llama wool, and, of course, the llama fetus, which are then burnt after pouring chicha on top.

---

with a backdrop of jungle and 17,000-foot ice-sculptured mountains, you can almost imagine priests praying to the gods of the sun.

The cost for the 15-day journey—horses, food, guides, and lodging (sometimes in tents, sometimes in local inns)—is $3,745.

HOW TO GET IN TOUCH

Manu Expeditions, P.O. Box 606, Cusco, Peru, 51 84 226671 or 51 84 239974, www.manuexpeditions.com, or **Adventure Specialists,** Bear Basin Ranch, County Road 271, Westcliffe, CO 81252, 719-783-2076, www.adventurespecialists.org.

cycle through the alps

The hills are alive with the sound of music.
—Title song from *The Sound of Music*

95 Austria is not the kind of place to go if you have an inferiority complex. If you have even the slightest tendency to compare yourself to others, you'd be better off going to Haiti or maybe Bombay, India. Because in Austria, all the women have peaches-and-cream complexions and look like some variation of the St. Pauli girl. They all recycle, they all ride bikes (one mother of two-month-old twins biked 38 miles straight up a mountain), and they all smile even when it's apparent that you are a complete idiot and don't know a word of their native tongue. They, of course, speak yours fluently. Their gingerbread cottages are all spotless (I dare you to find a single withered geranium in the flowerboxes), their charming cobblestone streets don't have so much as a discarded gum wrapper on them, and their mountains are so beautiful they make you weak in the knees.

The Austrians, in fact, have everything most of us have ever aspired to. Unfortunately, we're still working on most of those qualities—especially the one where you're able to effortlessly bike up tall mountains.

A good way to overcome your insecurity is to show up at Austria's Tauernradweg, a stunning bicycle path that runs along the northern boundary of the Hohe Tauern National Park. Most of the Tauern bicycle path goes downhill. That is, if you start at the end with the Krimmler waterfall. (The other option, which we don't want to think about, is starting the 195-mile trip in Passau, Germany, and going uphill.)

If you go with a tour packager, they'll transport your gear and make all the hotel arrangements. The only thing you'll be responsible for is yourself and your water bottle, which you can refill in the dozens of little villages along the route. In one small village, you can have the pleasure of filling your bottle with ice-cold water flowing from the mouth of a wood-carved knight.

The Krimmler waterfall, which is to Europe what Niagara is to the United States, is in the middle of Hohe Tauern National Park. This is Europe's largest national park and has 236 glaciers, 304 mountains with elevations over 9,000 feet, and a souvenir stand that sells yodeling teddy bears and felt hats like the one Heidi's grandfather wore.

The Tauernradweg follows the valleys of the Salzach River. And although it winds by castles, herb gardens, charming inns, and farmers who wave—or better yet, hand you an apple—it's marked well enough that you don't have to go with a tour packager. Every 12 miles or so, there's a green sign that tells you where you've been, where you're going, and what you're likely to see there. At one point on the path, there's even a sign that asks you to kindly close the gate so the cows won't escape. If they did, though, they wouldn't be too hard to find, since they all wear cowbells that jangle as they turn their head to watch you bike by.

The charming inns serve lunches with lots of fresh salads, venison, trout, spätzle, dumpling soup, and a wonderful pancake dish made with flour, eggs, and sugar. And along the route, you can stop and take a tour of a salt mine, a fun affair that

MOZART FOR DUMMIES

Long before the von Trapps were singing about their favorite things, one of the world's great composers was writing music about his. Wolfgang Amadeus Mozart, born in Salzburg in 1756, composed 626 pieces, including 24 operas, 41 symphonies, and more than 40 concerti. By the time he was eight, he'd toured London, Paris, Rome, Geneva, Frankfurt, and The Hague. Still, he died penniless with unfulfilled dreams when he was 35, never getting the respect of the Austrian royal family.

Salzburg, the city that gave him scant encouragement when he was alive, worships him today. The city is a veritable museum to his achievements. You can visit his birthplace, his home, the grave of his father and widow, and even buy a chocolate confection known as Mozartkugeln with, of course, his picture on them. There's now a musical foundation, an airport, a public square, and more than 16 streets named either Mozart or Wolfgang.

involves dressing up in unfashionable white coveralls, sliding down wooden rails, and singing "Row, Row, Row Your Boat" as you cross the water where the salt was mined. Outside Werfen, you'll find a magnificent castle built in 1077 where more beautiful young Austrians in costumes reminiscent of King Arthur and the Round Table perform a falcon show.

Most of the Tauern bike path is located in the province of Salzburg, which—surprise, surprise—is governed by the city of Salzburg, which means "city of salt." Back in the days when the city was named, a huge dynasty was built on what they called "white gold." This was before refrigeration when salt was essential in preserving food. It might have been more correct to call gold "yellow salt," because salt was far more valuable.

The dynasty was owned by the Church, which left an incredible architectural legacy in Salzburg. Beautiful squares, cathedrals, and castles, each one prettier than the next, make up the city. Don't miss Mirabell Palace with its beautiful gardens, statues, and fountains; the marionette theater; the glockenspiel that chimes a different Mozart tune every month or so; and the ancient winding streets where you can find everything from Mozart's birthplace, complete with his first piano, to European confectioners.

One-week bike tours of the Tauern bike path, offered by Bike Direct Tours through the Austrian National Tourist Office, start at $700 and include lodging, bikes, and luggage transfer.

HOW TO GET IN TOUCH

Austrian National Tourist Office, Margaretenstrasse 1, A-1040 Vienna, Austria, 43 1 588 660 or 212-944-6880 (in New York), www.austria.info.

scout the himalaya's outer edges

TIBET

*It changes time. You can be gone for two or three days and feel
like you've been gone a year, because you see things that are all new,
and your mind just wakes up.*
—Bill Abbott, president of Wilderness Travel

96 We'd love to give you an itinerary of Wilderness Travel's upcoming exploratory treks to Tibet, but, frankly, nobody but the Tibetan monks has ever been there. C'mon, do you really think Lewis and Clark had an itinerary?

No, when Wilderness Travel offers what they call "Exploratory Expeditions," that means you and your comrades will be among the first, at least among the first Westerners, to see the place. You'll be like Marco Polo, Robert Peary, or Sir Edmund Hillary. And in this mysterious land of Buddhist temples and mist-shrouded peaks, much remains blissfully unexplored by outsiders.

Not that WT is going to send you off unprepared. Their Exploratory Expeditions are led by popular veteran tour leaders who have already cased most of the joint, but always wanted to explore, say, the source of the Tsangpo River, as in the case of a 42-day Tibetan trek that hadn't been hiked by Westerners since the early 1900s, or to scale the peaks in Pakistan's Hunza Valley, as in the case of an upcoming 23-day expedition through 2,000 miles of mountains and deserts between India and Russia.

The guide for many Tibetan treks is Gary McCue, who literally wrote the book on trekking in Tibet (called, no big surprise here, *Trekking in Tibet: A Traveler's Guide)*, speaks fluent Tibetan, and lived for many years in Kathmandu. He has pioneered many of WT's Himalayan expeditions, including "In the Footsteps of Heinrich Harrer," which retraces the final stretch of the journey of the author of *Seven Years in Tibet.*

Last time McCue set out to explore far-western Tibet, he found an unknown acre of hot springs that tumbled out the side of a mountain near Lake Manasarovar. And even though tourism to Tibet is up 30 percent (thanks largely to the controversial

SPECIALTY TRIPS

Besides the Exploratory Expeditions, Wilderness Travel offers what they call "specialty trips," built around symposia by such internationally renowned guests as Jane Goodall, the late Sir Edmund Hillary, Reinhold Messner, Will Steger, Barry Lopez, and Frans Lanting. And whenever there's a total solar eclipse—when the sun, moon, and Earth are perfectly aligned—WT sets up a special eclipse camp in some exotic locale with an esteemed astronomer. In 2008, for example, WT is setting up camp in the Altai Mountains of western Mongolia with UC Berkeley astronomy professor Alex Filippenko.

new Qinghai-Tibet Railway), McCue says, "It's hard to find wilderness this wild and remote that doesn't require Reinhold Messner–level skills to reach. It's the closest you can come to what the explorers experienced 150 years ago."

One of the upcoming Exploratory Expeditions is going to Tibet's legendary Oracle Lake. Officially called Lhamo Latsho ("life force lake"), this ethereal body of water, located at 16,000 feet, is where every Dalai Lama has had prophetic visions about the future of Tibet. Like Buddhist pilgrims who come to this holy lake, you'll hike beside Tibetan nomads and visit monasteries, hermitages, and caves.

Wilderness Travel, which offers a hundred off-the-beaten-path journeys in 60 countries, most of which *do* have itineraries, was started in 1978 by Bill Abbott, who conceived the idea after 18 months of bumming around South America. Back in Berkeley, where the company is still headquartered, he and partner Robert Wolfson set up a seat-of-the-pants desk (a door over two sawhorses) and ran a 1-inch ad in the *New Yorker* offering arduous treks into the wilds of South America. They were blown away by the response.

Wilderness Travel offers 17 Exploratory Expeditions in 2008, its 30-year anniversary. They range from kayaking and snorkeling the Philippines' Palawan Islands to camel rides across the Sahara. The price tag for a recent monthlong expedition to Tibet was between $8,695 and $9,895 (depending on the number of people who sign up).

HOW TO GET IN TOUCH

Wilderness Travel, 1102 Ninth Street, Berkeley, CA 94710, 800-368-2794 or 510-558-2488, www.wildernesstravel.com.

celebrate silence

It is in deep solitude that I find the gentleness with which I can
truly love my brothers. The more solitary I am the more affection
I have for them.
—Thomas Merton, Catholic mystic

97 Cell phones, honking cars, IM chimes, blaring TVs, 24-hour grocery stores and laundromats—the relentless march of never-ending noise, the accepted accompaniment of our anxious lives. Don't you sometimes just feel like screaming, "Stop!"?

Throughout Bali, on the one-day Hindu holiday of Nyepi, everything does stop. Stores shut down, streets are deserted, and Ngurah Rai International Airport suspends operations for the 24-hour period. The gorgeous beaches, usually packed with sun worshippers of all ages, are empty except for a squawking seagull or two wondering what happened to their lunch.

For Nyepi, every Hindu in Bali is obligated to devote himself or herself to quiet introspection and spiritual cleansing. The idea is to sweep out old thoughts and make room for the peace of God and their higher self. Even the 10 percent of Balinese who aren't Hindu observe the holiday.

Nyepi literally means "Quiet!" and if the rules of the Hindu New Year are in doubt, just check out the official circulars posted throughout villages by the governor: "No lights may be lit, no work can be done, no travel may be undertaken, no amusement can be enjoyed."

If you're a tourist, well, you have little choice but to sit quietly in your room and contemplate. While it may be a bit disconcerting at first—talk about being in foreign territory—Nyepi is a refreshing break from the normal hubbub. It's a chance to listen to the natural world (the crickets are still chirping, the waves are still crashing) and to settle back into the comfortable rocking chair of your own soul. As Thomas Merton said, "When I am silent, I hear my true self. Silence teaches us to know reality. If our life is poured out in useless words, we will never hear anything."

Don't even think about going out on Nyepi. This official government holiday is taken seriously. Traditional spiritual police (they're called *pecalangs*) dressed in black and wearing ceremonial hats patrol the street, sternly rebuking anyone daring to be out or to so much as allow noise or light to escape from their homes.

The Balinese Day of Silence falls on a different date every year, usually in late March or early April. Marking the first day of the Saka calendar, it falls on the first new moon following the spring equinox.

Even if you aren't eager for quiet self-reflection, the festivities leading up to Nyepi and following it are well worth putting it on your non-Saka calendar. For the three days before Nyepi, the Balinese observe Melasti, a time when sacred objects and effigies are brought to local rivers to be ritually cleansed. They leave gifts to nature outside their doors to make up for all that we humans have taken. The day immediately before Nyepi, known as Tawur Kesanga, is a night of wild revelry. After priests ceremoniously lure bad spirits out of the temples, homemade bamboo cannon are shot and villagers take to the streets with torches and drums. Young men parade the streets with huge papier-mâché effigies built on bamboo poles. The effigies called *ogoh-ogoh* represent evil spirits whose fangs, bulging eyes, and scary haircuts (one effigy looked an awful lot like the creature from "The Grudge") will eventually

THE KISSING FIELDS

The residents of the village of Banjar Kaja gather on the day after Nyepi for a unique ritual called *med-medan*. Young boys and girls congregate on the local green—boys to the left, girls to the right—and gradually move closer until they're close enough to kiss, which they proceed to do with wild abandon. And since one "charge of the lips brigade" is never enough, the ritual usually culminates with some of the kissing couples being moved to designated "kissing fields," although concerned parents bring buckets of water to cool off romantic ardor that gets out of hand.

Some couples credit med-medan for the beginning of their relationship. And as for shy boy and girls who try to beg off, the ritual is mandatory, and any reticence disappears anyway after villagers repeat well-known legends of natural and personal disasters that befell nonkissers of the past.

CAN'T KEEP QUIET?

Bali tourists without the wherewithal for inner reflection can easily catch a boat (or fly the day before) to Lombok, an island just 60 miles east of Bali that has a different language, different customs, and a religion that doesn't require vocal celibacy. Lombok, often described as Bali's "country cousin" or "Bali in the 1960s," has the second highest mountain in Indonesia (Mount Rinjani), miles of pristine beaches, waterfalls, a beautiful crater lake, and lots of little craft villages set amid rice terraces. In Lombok's Gili islands, transport is limited to horse-drawn carts. Refreshingly, Lombok has no official tourism department, but you can find out more at www.lombok-network.com.

be burned or unceremoniously ditched on street corners as the young men scurry home to beat the 6 a.m. curfew.

On the day after Nyepi, the Balinese celebrate Ngembak Geni, a holiday we could all benefit from. Fresh from their day of quiet contemplation, they extend forgiveness to all, asking anyone with whom they had unresolved issues for a new start. As the Goo Goo Dolls said in their song "Better Days": "Everyone is forgiven now, 'cause tonight's the night the world begins again."

HOW TO GET IN TOUCH

Bali Tourism Board, Jl. Raya Puputan 41, Renon, Denpasar, Bali 80235, Indonesia, 62 361 235600, www.bali-tourism-board.com.

NORTHWINDS POLAR EXPEDITIONS

kite the arctic circle

GREENLAND

*The endless light and space on the Greenland ice cap is like travel on
another planet. The 24 hours of light is spiritually lifting.*
—Matty McNair, owner of NorthWinds Polar Expeditions

98 In 1888, after making the world's first schlep across the Greenland ice cap, Norwegian Fridtjof Nansen was greeted by artillery salutes and a cheering crowd of 50,000. We can't promise the artillery salutes or the cheerleaders, but it is quite possible to follow the Nobel Prize winner's tracks along the Arctic Circle using kites to pull you on skis.

Once you get the hang of it (it's called kite skiing and it's the fastest-growing winter sport on the planet), you'll travel between 10 and 30 miles per hour. If you already know how to ski moguls, you're halfway home. Matty McNair (yes, that Matty McNair—the one with all the records, the one who finally proved Robert Peary could have made it to the North Pole in 37 days) will provide instruction, the gear, and even the champagne once you reach your final destination.

Her company, NorthWinds Polar Expeditions, offers trips across the Greenland ice cap and to the North and South Poles. And when she's not speaking to groups about her amazing accomplishments, she works with explorers-in-training, those folks hankering to set their own world records. She coaches them on everything from how to raise funds (these record-setting trips don't come cheap: a McNair family jaunt to the South Pole rang in at roughly $250,000) to how to pack a 150-pound *pulk* (sled) with tents, stove, and beef jerky to how to cope with temperatures that sometimes plummet to 40 below.

The Greenland trips, led by either McNair, her husband Paul Landry, or one or both of her two kids, usually go out in May when the sun shines 24/7. Before letting you loose on the world's second largest ice cap, they'll get all the necessary permits, round up the equipment, and give you thorough instructions in coping with polar conditions and the rigors of kite skiing, which, on a windless day, means tromping through snow, not zipping across ice. You'll train in Frobisher Bay, on the southeast coast of Canada's Baffin Island, where you'll learn how to get in and out of your ski kite harness, how to launch your kite, and how to catch the wind's power zone.

Depending on your skill and the wind, the 345-mile journey can take between seven days (Matty's kids, Sarah and Eric, hold that record) and a full month, starting on the west coast of Greenland and finishing near the small Inuit settlement of Isortoq.

Outdoor adventures like this are McNair's passion. Before starting NorthWinds in 1990, she worked for Outward Bound for 23 years. She knows how to "take people to the edge without letting them fall." She has dogsledded around the 2,400-mile perimeter of Baffin Island, led the first all-women's expedition to the North Pole (1997), completed three expeditions to the South Pole, canoed around New Zealand, climbed South America's highest mountains, and written two books on white-water canoeing.

And in her spare time, she plays a mean fiddle, throws pottery, and paints.

Most of McNair's trips are custom designed, requiring a year or longer to put together. A monthlong "Greenland Kiting Expedition" runs about $15,000. Weeklong spring polar training with a focus on kite skiing on Frobisher Bay costs about $3,000.

HOW TO GET IN TOUCH

NorthWinds Polar Expeditions, House #727, P.O. Box # 820, Iqaluit, NU X0A 0H0 Canada, 867-979-0551, www.northwinds-arctic.com.

GOLF GREENLAND

There aren't a lot of sand traps on the golf course in Uummannaq, Greenland. In fact, the greens should probably be called "whites," because the entire golf course, laid out on a fjord, is built on three feet of solid ice. Every year, the World Ice Golf Championship, attracting golfers from around the globe, is held on this small island off Greenland's northwest coast. Using brightly colored balls that are easier to spot on the white, barren landscape, golfers compete in two 36-hole games: first, a Ryder Cup–style tournament called the Niemann Cup (after Arne Niemann, a local hotelier who came up with the crazy idea), and then the world championship itself. And since most of the locals, 80 percent of whom are Inuit, had never played golf before Niemann's 1997 brainchild, the World Ice Golf Committee also offers an ice golf school. Now sponsored by Drambuie, the World Ice Golf Championship has been televised by BBC, ESPN, CNN, and the Golf Channel.

raft, kayak, and snorkel in paradise

FIJI

> If you're going to fly halfway around the globe to a tropical wonderland like Fiji, you better be certain to go to places you could never go, do the things you could never do, and leave with the feeling that there's nothing better you could have ever done anywhere else.
> —Tim Neville, travel writer

99 Fiji is made up of 300 islands. So we'll forgive you if your stereotype has to do with beaches and bikini-clad 18-year-olds with blistering sunburns.

But remember how mom advised judging on outer appearance alone? If you look deeper into Fiji's native heart, you'll find wild, inner beauty: towering mountains, roaring rivers, and villagers who have never heard of the United States or television, let alone Britney Spears.

If you look hard enough, Viti Levu, the largest island in Fiji's archipelago, is hiding the Upper Navua River, which rages through a narrow gorge with steep, 165-foot walls. This majestic ravine that few human eyes have ever beheld holds a coveted spot on O.A.R.S.'s storied list of seven white-water wonders, right next to the Grand Canyon, Chile's Futaleufu (see sidebar p. 241), and British Columbia's Klinaklini. In fact, George Wendt, the founder of Outdoor Adventure River Specialists, better known as O.A.R.S., a guy who was rafting before most people even knew what rafting was, claims the Upper Navua is his all-time favorite river.

And he should know. Closing in on four decades and more than 400,000 guests since it first dropped rafts on the Colorado River, O.A.R.S. puts in on every major river in western North America, plus a few in Ecuador, Mexico, Peru, and the Galápagos Islands.

On O.A.R.S.'s Upper Navua trip, you'll see some of Mother Nature's greatest handiwork, including a natural cathedral with emerald archways and the

MORE THAN A PRETTY FACE

When O.A.R.S. (along with a few other rafters) first navigated the Upper Navua in 1996, they were awestruck by the pristine beauty that, at that point, had no protection. Sure, not many people had seen it, but if they ever did—watch out. Logging companies would be drooling over its towering rain forests, resorts developers would be hatching schemes right and left for capitalizing on its scenery.

That's when O.A.R.S. and a consortium called Rivers Fiji decided they needed to make sure this paradise stayed the way it was. Together with a couple of other outfitters, they launched the Upper Navua Conservation Area (UNCA). For starters, they had to convince the nine indigenous clans along the river, known as *matagali*, that conserving the river was a better use for the land than extracting gravel. They next had to seek permission from the Native Land Trust Board and then pitch it to the Great Council of Chiefs.

The result of their negotiations, a 25-year lease to 650 feet on either side of the Upper Navua River, is the world's first freshwater resource being protected and conserved solely by white-water tourism. And needless to say, Rivers Fiji's pact with the matagali, the Great Council of Chiefs, and the Native Land Trust Board may be one of the most unique cooperatives on the planet.

Since it was established in 2000, UNCA's conservators have discovered two new freshwater fish, sighted the globally endangered pink-billed parrot finch, and found a healthy new population of sego palm.

---

reverberating hymn of cascading waterfalls, 75 in all. And that's just one day of the eight-day "Highlands to Islands Multi-Sport Adventure."

In addition, you'll sea kayak through tunnels in mangrove forests brimming with mud lobsters and kingfishers. You'll river kayak through the rain forest, camping one night in the Nakavika Village, where you'll share a kava ceremony with the tribal chief and his minions, some of Fiji's last headhunters (no worries—the last reported beheading was decades ago). Your only real challenge will be the Class III and IV rapids.

The "Highlands to Islands Multi-Sport Adventure" costs $2,375, including meals and lodging at the Pearl South Pacific Resort, a boutique resort between Nadi and Suva, and all rafting, kayaking, and snorkeling.

HOW TO GET IN TOUCH

O.A.R.S., P.O. Box 67, Angels Camp, CA 95222, 800-346-6277 or 209-736-4677, www.oars.com.

bike across cuba

SANTIAGO TO HAVANA, CUBA

100 WoW Cuba, with offices in both Prince Edward Island (PEI), Canada, and Havana, has been hosting cycle tours to Cuba since 1994. It all started in 1992 when Gordon MacQueen, an American expat who ran an adventure travel company in PEI, read an article about Cuba bartering sugar for a million Chinese bicycles. Since Cuba's prime riding season happened to coincide with Canada's off-season, he contacted the Canadian embassy in Cuba, which soon invited him for a visit and a discussion about forming a bicycle tour company.

"Everyone in Cuba rides a bike, and there were special bike lanes all through Havana designated for bikes only. Hardly any traffic on the road, it was a paradise," says MacQueen's daughter, Kristen, one of his four kids, now married to a Cuban and living in Havana. "Of course, after riding to work and school every day, the Cubans thought we were crazy. Who would want to ride bikes on a holiday?"

But the crazy Canadians made it work. Kristen's brothers Danny and Darryl, despite getting waylaid by a hurricane, took bikes down on a commercial ship, and the first tour from Santiago to Havana went out in January 1994.

Today, from November through April, WoW Canada offers a variety of one-week bike tours, as well as the annual Vuelta Cuba, a popular two-week cycling tour from Santiago to Havana, led by Danny and his wife Mirley, a former member of Cuba's national cycling team.

On the Vuelta Cuba, you'll average between 30 and 40 miles a day and visit such spots as a lake in Baconao Park, a World Heritage biosphere, an artists' colony, the colonial city of Trinidad, a natural hot springs, the Bay of Pigs, and Bodequita del Medio, Ernest Hemingway's favorite Havana haunt.

WOULD YOU LIKE A BOOK WITH THAT CIGAR?

A landmark study by the National Endowment for the Arts reported that Americans of all ages are reading dramatically less than they did ten years ago. But in Cuba, at the famous cigar factories, reading is alive and well. Every day, while cigarmakers cut leaves and roll cigars, a designated reader (*el lector*) entertains them with selections from the morning newspaper, classic literature, and the latest novels.

Workers vote for their top reading choices, which traditionally came from the likes of Zola, Balzac, Hugo, or Cervantes, but recently included potboilers like *The Da Vinci Code*, football scores, and the weekly output records of the workers themselves.

A tradition that began at Havana's El Figaro cigar factory in the late 1800s and has spread to cigar factories the world over, listening to the lector is anything but a passive undertaking. Cigarmakers often engage in heated group discussions after the reading, even going so far as to take encyclopedias and other reference material to their desks to clarify their arguments.

The two-week Vuelta trip, with all the trimmings (top-notch bike equipment, two sag vehicles, a bike mechanic for those occasional mishaps), lodging, and most meals is about $2,700.

HOW TO GET IN TOUCH

WoWCuba, 430 Queen Street, Charlottetown, PEI C1A 4E8, Canada, 800-969-2822, www.wowcuba.com.

index

Index | **285**

Index | **287**

acknowledgments

Thanks to my daughter, Tasman, who loves to travel and explore every bit as much as I do. Thanks to Barbara Noe who, even though I was a bit of a problem child last book, let me go out in the playground and do it again. And thanks to all you creative guides, tour operators, artists, and world-changers who keep coming up with adventures that rock all of our lives.